THE NON-ORDINARY RESIDENTS

Voices from Migrant Domestic Workers amid COVID-19

NOVIA BIN

ISBN: 9798584775780

Cover photo by: Sring

Illustrations by: Liza

Printed in the United States of America

To migrants and global citizens

Contents

PART FOUR: THROUGH THE LENS OF THE DOMINANT GROUP 209

Acknowledgements

I am deepest indebted to those migrant domestic workers who were willing to share their stories with me and befriend me. Without the information provided by them, my understanding of domestic workers' life would be only remaining at a stage of imagination, which, I'm afraid, is limited by my experience. Among them, I would like to give special thanks to Liza, the illustrator of this book. As a domestic worker and a union leader at the same time, I could imagine how hard it was for her to spare some time to draw illustrations. Also, a very special thanks to Sring, the photographer for the book cover. She is brilliant!

Then I would like to thank all my proof-readers: Laura, Sim, Greg, Sean, and Kate. Four of them are my former colleagues. They are all incredibly wonderful human beings. Kate, a friend of Gary and me, is a marvellous cosmopolitan single mother who is nearing the end of degree in French and Linguistics (she has received a grade of A). Congratulations, Kate! Ronnie, you didn't proofread any part of this book because you were too busy with teaching and writing your own book. But I still thank you for encouraging me to write a book after I failed to change my PhD research topic. Brian, it is such a pity that you were not included in the team. I blamed your email, as it somehow spammed me. Nonetheless, I want to thank you for all the jolly good time when I worked with you.

Thank you, coffee, for accompanying me every morning. Thank you, the Internet, for providing free resources and knowledge that allow me to explore the world during the coronavirus pandemic. Thank you, my study room, for allowing me to focus on writing even when my partner was working from home in our tiny apartment. Thank you, IPA, APA (I mean beer) and wine, for staying with me when I was haunted by nostalgia. Thank you, ZHANG Zanbo (a good friend, a down-to-earth Chinese documentary director and a writer), for inspiring and encouraging me. Thank you, Gary, for making me smile a lot via emails. I miss you and Cassie the most, you know it.

Alan (my partner), you said that you didn't want to be thanked on this page. Okay, as you wish.

Preface

Since the late 70s, Hong Kong has developed a tradition of importing foreign labour for the management of household chores for local families. According to official data in 2019, there were 399,320 foreign domestic workers in Hong Kong.[1] Most of them are women from the Philippines and Indonesia, and a small number of them come from other places of Southeast Asia and South Asia. Usually, their job duties include care giving, cooking, washing dishes and cleaning. But sometimes non-domestic work like car washing is also included. I saw them sitting over and under footbridges when I travelled to Hong Kong with my partner. It was in summer, and the oppressive heat made us sweat while walking outdoors. Both of us felt sorry for them at that moment, but I also felt sorry that little by little we forgot about them.

In 2019, my partner Alan got an ideal job offer from Hong Kong. In his own words, the job is to use high technology for good purposes: it benefits our environment. He couldn't think of any reason to say no to it, so he accepted the offer, and I resigned my lovely job and said goodbye to my wonderful friends (including my cat Cassie too) in New Zealand. We then moved to Hong Kong together last December.

On 25 December 2019, a public holiday in Hong Kong, I saw many Southeast Asian women sitting in a car park just opposite a railway station. I felt overwhelmed about this, though I had seen them sitting on the road like this before. It was windy out there. Hong Kong's winter may be far from "intolerable" for many visitors or travellers, but for those who are from tropical regions, it is a totally different story. Many of the women sitting on the concrete floor were using umbrellas to shield themselves from the wind. I took a photo of them from the other side of the street and shared it with some of my friends, discussing with them how people are marginalised in different societies.

Since that day, I've had a strong desire to talk to these women and get to know them. I want to know how they feel; I want to know how they work and live in Hong Kong; and I want to know their other identities beyond just being "a maid". Unfortunately, my partner and I got a fever and a sore throat just a few days later. At that point, some media in Hong Kong had already begun to warn local residents about "the unknown pneumonia" (which was later known as coronavirus or COVID-19 after it had become a global pandemic), suggesting that it may be linked to SARS. To make sure that we didn't get "the unknown pneumonia" and we were not a threat of the lives of others, we went to a clinic to get checked. I remember the doctor got a bit nervous after he knew that I got a fever and a sore throat. He asked me quietly and cautiously, "Have you been to Wuhan recently?"

It turned out that we had influenza A and not "the unknown pneumonia". Nevertheless, we had fought for the fever for more than two weeks, and then I began coughing violently for another six weeks (my partner recovered earlier than me). Some people in Hong Kong have become more sensitive about coughing since the first case was confirmed on 23 January 2020. I still remember a young woman was scared away while I was coughing in an open space with a face mask. After SARS, many Hong Kong people have formed the habit of wearing a face mask if they get sick. I followed this same habit, but I didn't expect that for the following months, face masks would become such an important part in all residents' everyday lives. To make them less worried, I tried to keep myself indoors. I have also practised social distancing the entire time since January because of my influenza. Fieldwork or informal interviews with the migrant domestic workers were unlikely to be completed in that time, and the unlikelihood had lasted for another few months because of the coronavirus pandemic.

On 5 February, the Hong Kong government temporarily closed many border-control points as well as some public facilities. Travel restrictions and a 14-day compulsory quarantine for inbound residents or travellers have taken effect since then. Universities and schools in Hong Kong all announced that they would postpone the start of the spring semester. Students later had online learning, and staff in various companies were encouraged to work from home. Different degrees of social distancing had been practised for the next few months. The HK government tightened restrictions on 27 March because of the second wave of COVID-19 infections. Public gatherings of more than four people (both indoors and outdoors) were banned. There were mandatory closures of entertainment sites, and social distancing in restaurants was applied as well. These series of social distancing measures had been only loosened a bit till 8 May when the ban of public gatherings of no more than four people was turned into no more than eight people; and in the meantime, many entertainment venues were allowed to resume business again. On 16 June, the HK government announced that the maximum number of people at public gatherings would be extended from eight to fifty. This period of time in Hong Kong will appear as the "semi-lockdown" in my book (To some domestic helpers, the semi-lockdown ended in May because their employers began to allow them to meet their friends as usual on their rest days).

The COVID-19 pandemic has stricken both global health and the global economy, and it has put marginalised people into further isolation. Millions of people have been infected by the virus;

thousands of people have died from it; and millions of people have lost their jobs due to the pandemic. Additionally, based on reports worldwide, domestic violence had soared because of the lockdown. The coronavirus pandemic is like a cursed mirror that reflects all global issues particularly concerning inequality and injustice. And Hong Kong can't get out of it.

During the semi-lockdown in Hong Kong, many businesses had been severely hit by the outbreak of COVID-19, and many staff had no income by the time their workplaces were temporarily closed. The unemployment rate in Hong Kong broke the highest record in 15 years, rising to 6.2% in June.[2] Educational inequality was more noticeable when every student had to receive online education, as it is difficult for some to gain the access to technological devices and enough space for learning. Face masks became rip-offs overnight in February due to the demand. I remember a box of 50 surgical face masks imported from Indonesia was once sold for HK$290. I wonder how many Indonesians could afford face masks in their home country. And how about those Hong Kong people who share the narrow space with their families and who must rely on meagre relief provided by the government? Could they afford these face masks? Local domestic violence has been reported more frequently since the coronavirus outbreak, and the average Hong Kong women's workload at home increased considerably amid the semi-lockdown. As for the women who hired maids, the increasing workload had been naturally transferred to their maids. COVID-19 has influenced this society in different dimensions. And the social movement which has continued for more than six months in Hong Kong since June 2019 also halted because of the social distancing restrictions.

The domestic workers' routine gatherings on Sunday and in public holidays had been cancelled. Thousands of them were forced to work during their rest days, and many of them were in more debt because their family members back home became jobless and those working in Hong Kong needed to send more money back. It is fair to say that the powerless and marginalised people in Hong Kong became even more vulnerable due to the financial crisis and health crisis. And my idea to write a book about the marginalised migrant domestic workers budded under this circumstance.

Technically, I haven't lost a job in Hong Kong as I hadn't got one from the beginning. I started to look for a job after I completely recovered from coughing, and it was already at the end of February. My choices are very limited as my Cantonese is not proficient. At first, I got some interview invitations from different departments at a local university for the position of "senior research assistant", but after April, a job interview invitation became a luxury. I failed to get a job because of this and that. One typical reason was some interviewers were worried that I was unlikely to complete an 18-month contract, for they somehow believed that I wouldn't stay in Hong Kong for that long. In fact, they later proved that they had the foresight. With political tensions climbing and freedoms declining in Hong Kong, my partner and I did have a plan to leave Hong Kong when we could.

This is the first time in my life I have ever experienced unemployment. As an independent woman, I had to spend so much time to get used to this. But the bright side of my jobless situation is that I have more time to get along with myself and explore this world for my own because I want to understand. The photo I took appeared in my mind every now and then, and I started to do some online research about what a migrant domestic worker's life is in Hong Kong.

Thanks to Global Voices (a non-profit international media organisation aiming to provide "citizen media stories around the world"), I gained so much inspiration, and from its articles it helped me generate some questions before my first informal interview with a Filipino domestic worker. My plan to write a book about migrant domestic workers was first supported by my partner Alan, and fortunately, his salary can afford to cover our expenses. So, he encouraged me to forget about the hopeless job hunting and do something I really want to do regardless of money and gains. With both financial and emotional support, I then spent more time to dedicate myself to my preliminary research about domestic helpers in Hong Kong and wait for the day that I can talk to them face-to-face.

I began my first informal interview on 21 June. I call it "informal interview" because I didn't record any conversations between me and the interviewee, nor did I list the interview questions on a notebook which is what I previously did when I worked as a research assistant in NZ. Using a recording device may liberate my brain as I wouldn't have to remember so many things at once, but I decided not to do it after careful consideration. I was afraid that the domestic workers may feel unconfident expressing themselves when seeing a recording device in the first place. Likewise, they might be too cautious to tell me the whole story if I used a recording device after I just met them (my consideration was proved to be very reasonable later). I thus decided to use a more anthropological method—fieldwork—to join their gatherings to do informal interviews as well as observation and to spend more time with them. To ensure the reliability of my reflections based on the informal interviews, I took notes about the key words and key numbers during the interview process. And if there was anything that I wasn't sure, I would text my new friends to double check or join their gatherings again to gain relevant information. Yet, when I interviewed the staff of the unions, they were happy to let our conversations be recorded, as one chairperson from a union put it, *"I think you'd better record it because I'm going to be very talkative. And I don't want you to be too busy with taking notes."* Aside from interviews and observation, I also used some official documents, media reports, and some relevant academic articles to get additional information.

Due to my previous academic training, I had followed the ethical guidelines during the interviewing process to ensure the interviewees' rights. I managed to get ethical approval before my PhD confirmation (though I didn't complete my study after the confirmation), and I can say that it is far more difficult than writing a term paper. The good thing is; however, it prevents me from becoming a reckless and presumptuous interviewer when I am eager to feed my curiosity. To ensure the interviewees' well-being, ethical guidance had always been considered during all interviews. There were no information sheets or consent forms, but I can guarantee that every domestic worker was fully informed about my aims and that they voluntarily participated in my informal interviews. To protect their privacy, the helpers who accepted my informal interviews were free to choose a preferable pseudonym.

Before conducting my first informal interview, I thought about what I should do if any domestic workers I talk with have an emotional breakdown. I came up with different plans to deal with it. But in fact, I barely used the plans. To my surprise, I was the person who was usually more emotional than them. I felt a bit ashamed that they sometimes needed to comfort me while they were sharing their sad stories or feelings, as we all know that it should be the other way around.

In this book, the people I care about have different names, different characters, different experiences, and different identities. They are formally identified as "migrant domestic workers" or "foreign domestic workers", and they are also known as "helpers", "maids", and "jeh jeh" (it means "older sister" in Cantonese) in Hong Kong. Their identity is mainly constructed through their job or their national identity. But they have other identities that are usually invisible in mainstream society. Through reading their true stories and knowing more about their situations, I hope that more people will care about them, treating and respecting them as equal human beings.

Noam Chomsky said that humans are facing the crises even more severe than COVID-19, as we can recover from COVID-19, but we can't recover from something else such as nuclear war and global warming.[3] He mentioned that we are facing a neoliberal plague, and I agree with him about this. On top of that, I believe that we are also facing a plague of indifference, which will lead human beings to many disasters in the future. A great number of people in this world still care about others on the basis of nationality, race, social status, etc. And they tend to be indifferent to the out-group members who do not share the same citizenship or social status. Caring about migrant domestic workers doesn't require a person to be a Filipino or an Indonesian in advance. I want to care about them because I believe I am a member of this human society, and so are they (I would be happy to be included as a member of animal society as well).

Before expecting a global community where human rights and human dignity are entitled to all, let us start to see and care for others and unite to act for a better world.

PART ONE: POVERTY AND MARGINALISATION

Anyone who has ever struggled with poverty knows how extremely expensive it is to be poor.

James Baldwin

1. **Lucky Lucille**

Sunday, 21 June 2020   Temperature: 32°C   Humidity: 65%

Sunday is a special day for migrant domestic workers in Hong Kong and the only day in a week when they are not supposed to work. For those who have ever been to Hong Kong, they may have seen such a scene: on Sunday, many Southeast Asian women sit in various corners of this city to chat and relax with friends. Their relaxation contrasts sharply with that of the local people, as if they live in two different worlds.

I have wanted to gain an understanding of the migrant domestic workers for a long time and began some informal interviews as well as observation in June 2020. People still went out with a face mask because of the lingering pandemic, and the weather started to get hot. I met Lucille on a Sunday afternoon when she and other domestic workers were relaxing and socialising. The weather app told me the feel-like temperature was 39°C, which is not the most horrible heat index for Hong Kong's summer, but staying outside at more than 30°C coupled with high humidity for the whole day is not that hard to imagine. I went to an area near my apartment where the domestic helpers usually congregate. There were several dozen women sitting in an open space in separate groups. Shade, a public toilet and nearby convenience stores suggest that they have seriously considered the location for what looked like a big picnic party albeit on a concrete floor.

(That's the open space near my apartment)

(That's where I talked with my first interviewee. I took this picture on a weekday afternoon)

I approached a group of young women who were sitting near a flowerbed by asking if anyone of them could speak English. One woman answered in fluent Cantonese that they do not and enquired of me whether I needed to find a helper in my apartment. I then used Cantonese to ask her if she knows anyone around who could speak English. She pointed at a woman who was chatting with her friends in a nearby group.

The woman preferred to be called Lucille, to reminisce about her grandma Lucia. After giving a short self-introduction and telling her my purpose to talk with her, Lucille said that she would be happy to answer my questions so as to let me know people like her better.

Lucille has been working in Hong Kong for 14 years, with 12 years working for her current employer. She has got a bachelor's degree in education and a teaching certificate in the Philippines. In fact, Lucille isn't the only one from the Philippines who is over-qualified to be a domestic helper in Hong Kong. A number of females who are professional and well-educated in the Philippines came to Hong Kong to work as maids, because it is very difficult for them to find well-paid jobs in their home country, and female domestic workers have been sought by many families in fast-paced Hong Kong to help with housework or liberate independent Hong Kong women from trivial household chores. For migrant domestic workers like Lucille, Hong Kong is not only the place to provide relatively decent salary for them compared to their home countries but is also regarded as a springboard to get possible job opportunities in other countries. Canada had been Lucille's ideal destination since she started to work in Hong Kong. She had worked hard on her English and saved money for this. However, she said she's a bit too old to go to Canada (the real reason is that she doesn't want to leave Snow, her employer's dog).

Through the conversation with Lucille, I was amazed by her English proficiency. When I asked Lucille how she learned English, she said she was so lucky to have some very good teachers who could speak excellent English at university, and she likes learning English as well. In fact, Lucille didn't realise how good her English was till her employer suggested one of her job duties would be communicating in English with the child of the employer, and the employer was willing to pay her more because of this.

The monthly salary of migrant domestic workers ranges from 4,630 to 6,000+ HKD (594 to 774+USD), and Lucille gets comparatively higher salary than her peers. Also, based on her words, she is lucky enough to have a good employer and good accommodation. According to Hong Kong law, migrant domestic workers have to live with their employers, and the employers are required to provide accommodation for their helpers.[4] As one of the most densely populated cities in the world, Hong Kong's flats are always linked with ridiculously high prices and small sizes. Whether the migrant domestic workers can live in a comfortable room or not depends on their luck, and whether they can be fairly treated also depends heavily on their luck. Lucille can be considered as one of the lucky stars among all Southeast Asian helpers in Hong Kong because she lives in a relatively spacious room of the 1,000-square-foot flat which cannot be afforded by most Hong Kong people. On top of that, her employer has always been nice to her.

Lucille works from 8.30-9.00 in the morning to 8.30-9.00 at night with lots of break time. Before COVID-19, she only needed to prepare dinner on weekdays as her employer usually had a breakfast and lunch near the workplace. And unlike most maids here, Lucille can dine with her employer at the same table and express her opinions freely. The daughter of the employer, who is studying overseas, is already a grown-up now. Another family member is an adorable female dog named Snow. Lucille showed me some pictures of the dog. *"Taking care of her is one of my major responsibilities now. And I enjoy the time with her,"* told Lucille. *"Ah she prefers to share my bed with me, you know, my single bed! Sometimes she occupies my space, and I must put a soft mattress on the floor just in case anyone of us falls off from the bed,"* continued Lucille in her pleasant voice.

I asked Lucille to use three words to describe herself. She chose "independent", "strong", and "happy". During the conversation with Lucille, I did feel that she is such a marvellous woman who can think independently and has a positive attitude toward life. Her favourite thing to do in her spare time is to go hiking or cycling with her friends when the weather is fair. As for her future, it seems Lucille has no plan to get married or have children whatsoever as she feels so happy and free to be single. Her dream is to become a nurse. She planned to save money and go back to school one day to get relevant qualifications about nursing. Lucille said, *"Being a teacher is never my dream but my parents'. I want to pursue mine."*

Before this informal interview, I made a guess for the possible reasons why the migrant domestic workers choose to sit on the concrete floor with some cloth or mats rather than the places such as their rooms or shopping malls or restaurants or anywhere to let them feel more comfortable. I worried that they may not be able to afford drinks and meals in fancy cafes and restaurants, because they have to save money and send it back to their families in their home countries. Or maybe they have to suffer from the temptation of consumerism in those high-end malls when they go there to enjoy air conditioning and relaxation, so they try to avoid it? Or if they stay at "home", they are very likely to be made to work on their rest days? Some guesses may be true, but at least, for lucky Lucille, her reason is not like any of the guesses mentioned above. She can stay at home on Sunday without worrying that her employer would ask her to work, and she is even allowed to invite her friends to relax in her employer's flat on her rest days. Yet she still prefers to have some fresh air outdoors. If she does not go hiking or cycling, she will find some open spaces to stay with her friends even on summer days.

"Friend" is such a beautiful word. As an outlander in a city where their identities are mainly constructed as a maid or helper by mainstream society, even thinking about the word "friends" makes an individual associate with equality and fraternity. Lucille has lived in Hong Kong for 14 years. The same amount of time for people to receive an education from kindergarten to high school in Hong Kong, and they are expected to make some friends in such a long time. However, Lucille has made no local friends during her 14 years; nevertheless, she has a friend-like employer here. The beautiful word connoting equality and fraternity is disconnected with local people for her. She said, *"Many Chinese people here think we are inferior, so there're not many opportunities for us to make friends.*

But I'm glad my employer is a very different Chinese. She isn't like them." Lucille doesn't think she has ever experienced direct discrimination in Hong Kong. Again, she used the word "lucky". Even so, this lucky star still finds she and her peers are marginalised by the dominant group while sitting in different places on Sundays. *"We feel like we do not exist in this city when they pass by. They don't care about us...and I don't want to care about them,"* said Lucille disappointedly, *"occasionally, there are a few people coming to ask whether we are OK or need any help, but it doesn't happen a lot."*

According to 2019 service report published by Mission for Migrant Workers (a non-governmental organisation based in Hong Kong), the working and living conditions of migrant domestic workers worsened in 2019 and continue to worsen in the shadow of COVID-19. Among approximately 400,000 migrant domestic workers in Hong Kong, more than 96% of the migrant domestic workers experience overwork and insufficient rest; 44% of them work over 16 hours a day; 45% of them are forced to work for a few hours on their only rest day in a week; one out of five do not have regular rest days at all; over half of them do not have a private room; 29% of them are not provided with sufficient food; 15% of them reported physical abuse; 10% of them reported that their salary was illegally deducted; and 2% of them reported sexual harassment and forced sexual intercourse. In addition, based on "Online Survey on the Situation of Migrant Domestic Workers during COVID-19" in March 2020, 40% of the informants had not been allowed to go out during their regular rest days from early February to early March, and approximately 20% of them had been asked to work during their regular rest days.[5]

Luckily, Lucille was not abused or forced to work on her rest days during the coronavirus pandemic. Her workload did not increase too much compared to her friends. Even though she needed to cook more because her employer had been working at home for several months, she still didn't find it exhausting. *"My employer isn't fussy. She's really considerate and kind to me. I don't have to cook for three meals a day, she sometimes asks me to buy takeaway,"* said Lucille. However, many helpers that Lucille knows are not as lucky as her.

They not only bear more domestic duties but also need to bear more pressure from both their employers and their families. Overwork for household chores and holiday deprivation were not rare for foreign domestic helpers during the semi-lockdown in Hong Kong. Apart from that, many of them were in debt because they needed to send more money to support their family members who lost their jobs in their home countries. *"So many people in the Philippines lost their jobs and needed money to cure diseases because of the COVID-19. I'm just lucky that my family isn't in that situation,"* said Lucille.

The Anti-extradition Bill Movement in Hong Kong which started in June 2019 has impacted domestic workers as well, yet the protests halted due to COVID-19. The social movement aims to protest the proposal which allows fugitive offenders extradited to mainland China. The proposed bill was widely criticised because it was deemed as a looming danger to Hong Kong's judicial independence and local activism. Arising from the Hong Kong government's indifference and repeatedly reported police brutality, this social movement has lasted for more than 6 months with five demands: 1. full withdrawal of the extradition bill; 2. a commission of inquiry into alleged police brutality; 3. retracting the classification of protesters as "rioters"; 4. amnesty for arrested protesters; 5. dual universal suffrage (for both the Legislative Council and the Chief Executive). For Lucille and many other migrant domestic workers in Hong Kong, the social movement in 2019 means something different. When tear gas was found in many streets of this city and when the conflicts between protesters and police became aggravated, some open spaces for helpers to use in the past were not safe for them anymore. On their rest days, many of them had to reduce the time spent outdoors when tensions between the police and activists were flared. But if they chose to stay at the residence provided by their employers on Sunday, some of them would be asked to work. During the 2019 anti-extradition bill movement, our lucky Lucille wasn't forced to work on those Sundays when she kept herself indoors, but she just missed the days when she could hang out with her friends to breathe fresh air in the places where they used to go.

The Other Side of Luck

"Lucky" is the most frequently used word in Lucille's narrative. When I reviewed all the data and information documented by different organisations, I did realise how lucky Lucille is. But even for our lucky Lucille, she still has a miserable history which is unknown to her parents. It was her first employer that created her miserable experience.

When Lucille resigned her teaching job in the Philippines and moved to Hong Kong to explore her new life, she did not expect it would turn out to be some experience that she'd rather forget. The first two years in Hong Kong were a painful ordeal for her. Her first job in Hong Kong was to serve a young couple (her female employer and the husband), a child and an elderly person. She was asked to get up at 5 o'clock every morning and then prepare three breakfasts for different people as her female employer said that *their biological clock and daily timetable are different*. After preparing for breakfasts, it was *"endless work"* quoted from Lucille. A sound sleep was a luxury for her back then, as she was made to work till 11.30 to 12.00 every night, which meant her sleep was less than 6 hours. Even on the only rest day of a week, she had to prepare breakfasts for everyone she served and arrive at her employer's flat before 7.00 pm to cook a dinner for the family. Worse than that, the only food provided by her employers was leftovers and instant noodles, and she had to dine separately from her "masters". She told me that in that time, her body weight dropped dramatically and she looked terrible. Her parents worried about her so much when they had a video chat with Lucille. *"At that time, because I didn't have enough rest, my skin condition was also very bad, you know, many pimples. My parents always asked me why I looked so miserable and thin,"* continued Lucille with self-mockery, *"I didn't want to make them worry. So, I had to lie to them. I told them it's because I couldn't get used to the weather here. What a funny excuse!"*

Doing laundry could be tricky too. Lucille's first employer only allowed her to use the washing machine for herself once a week, which could be understandable in winter. But in summer, Lucille needed to change her clothes every day. Though the indoor air conditioner worked effectively, domestic work is essentially physical, and physical work makes people sweaty sometimes. She didn't want to pile up her clothes for seven days, nor did she have enough space in her room for doing that. So, Lucille hand washed all her clothes. Yet her female employer was still not pleased, as she didn't like the idea that Lucille, as a maid, changed her clothes each day. *"My first female boss kept asking me why I needed to change clothes every day as if I am a bad woman to do so,"* said Lucille.

Lucille, like many other new domestic workers in Hong Kong, did not know what her rights were at that time. She didn't dare to resign her job because she was in considerable debt for the first year, and she was so scared that she may have a worse employer if she complained to the Labour Department and tried to terminate the contract. Lucille described the scraps she had as the cat food and dog food in the countryside of the Philippines. *"I don't know how I survived from the fatigue, hunger and anxiety every single day for the first two years. I felt I was like a slave,"* said Lucille with bitterness. *"Even though we're from a poor country or a poor family, it doesn't mean that we should be treated without human dignity. We're humans too."*

"Slave" may sound distant to some people, and they would argue that slavery does not exist today, as it had been abolished centuries ago. Admittedly, chattel slavery, in which the slave status was inherited and the enslaved people can be wilfully disposed as the property of the owners, is internationally illegal in this day and age. The truth is, however, traditional slavery hasn't left us for good. It has evolved into new forms, like some new viruses. According to Anti-Slavery International (an international NGO based in UK), any form of forced labour against the workers' will is seen as modern slavery. Other common forms of modern slavery/neo-slavery include debt bondage, descent-based slavery (yes, it still exists in some corners of this planet), human trafficking, forced/early marriage and sexual exploitation, and slavery of children.[6] Professor Ronald Weitzer from Gorge Washington University further defines modern slavery occurring in the workplace: "slavery is now considered a regime of maximum economic exploitation, social isolation, and total coercion control over the workers".[7]

Take Lucille's experience for example, forced labour and maximum economic exploitation are both obvious. I don't think that Lucille would be volunteering to work for 17-18 hours per day and use only 5-6 hours to sleep, nobody would. Beyond that, she was certainly underpaid if the ridiculously long working hours were considered. I have so many questions to ask: Did her first employer have the sense of ownership over her? Did any of the employers' neighbours know how the family treated their maid behind the closed door? Why did her employer have decent food while she had only leftovers and instant noodles? Isn't it a kind of exploitation when she could have got food allowance from her first employers, but instead, she got leftovers? How many cases like this remain ignored or unknown? How much does the Hong Kong government care about these domestic workers who are regarded as outsiders in any sense? I think I will explore the answers with Lucille and other domestic workers in the future.

At the very moment, with all these questions in mind, I thought of "the right to have rights"[8] mentioned by Hannah Arendt. As stated by Arendt, "the right to have rights" should be guaranteed by humanity that ought to transcend borders and existing ideologies. It has been more than 60 years since Arendt made her point about a basic condition of a human society, and yet our modern human community hasn't guaranteed it till now. Ironically, on the contrary, borders and ideologies along with the greed for tangible benefits often transcend humanity.

Arendt believes that human rights should exist as a universal and inalienable characteristic of the human condition, and no authority has the power to take it away. Once a human being's basic rights coupled with human dignity are denied through force or coercion, it is the time when that human being is in danger of encountering modern slavery. In one of Arendt's books The Origins of Totalitarianism (first published in 1951), her criticism on slavery is still relevant today. She writes:

Slavery's fundamental offense against human rights was not that it took liberty away (which can happen in many other situations), but that it excluded a certain category of people even from the possibility of fighting for freedom—a fight possible under tyranny, and even under the desperate conditions of modern terror (but not under any conditions of concentration-camp life).[9]

We may not want to recognise it, but there are some certain types of people who are more subjected to modern slavery. Those who are destitute, powerless, marginalised, and helpless are most likely to be the victims. They are so vulnerable because they are excluded from the possibility to fight "under the desperate conditions of modern terror". Their rights to defend themselves against the increasing power of the regime or individuals are deprived, and to make me more disheartened, the power of many individuals who are enslaving or exploiting others is explicitly or implicitly entitled by authorities.

Lucille's true story sometimes makes me confuse the meaning of "marginalised" and "invisible". Would the life of individuals like Lucille become better if more people can truly see them and care about them and if their "right to have rights" can be well guaranteed? I hope they are luckier.

2. Singapore or Hong Kong?

Sunday, 28 June 2020   Temperature: 32°C   Humidity: 67%

I went to the same place to find helpers who would love to talk with me and share their stories this afternoon. Just near the open space, there were more domestic helpers found along the riverside. Groups of them were sitting on a narrow passage with a wall and a fence. Some were leaning against the wall, and the fence facing the river helps ventilate so that they can feel the warm breeze which is, after all, better than nothing.

It was already very hot when I arrived there. The first person I talked with was Emma. She was delighted that I wanted to join their "party". Susie sitting next to her was making a video call with her family members in Indonesia. She welcomed me with a smile and a wave. Another nearby helper whose name I didn't know was sleeping. She looked exhausted. They were all sitting or sleeping on a piece of cloth beneath which was the hard concrete floor. After joining them for a few minutes, I managed to draw attention from other helpers. They appeared to be overwhelmingly curious about my presence. Emma told them something with excitement in Indonesian. Then they smiled and waved at me enthusiastically. Their facial expressions brought me back to my childhood as if I were the popular child moving to a new place and everyone wanted to make friends with me. "Hi", I waved back to them and told them I'd talk to them later. They nodded with satisfaction.

Before my two informal group interviews, I asked each of them to think about a name they feel happy to be addressed. Some of them were excited about this and told me their English names. When I asked what their employers usually call them, four out of five told me they are called "jeh jeh", meaning "older sister" in Cantonese, which the Hong Kong employers commonly call their helpers. It seems most employers try to sound more respectful to their helpers, but in terms of practice, it is a different story. Once I was searching some information about the attitudes of Hong Kong people towards foreign helpers. I found a discussion regarding how helpers should address their female employers. An employer complained that her helper called her "jeh jeh". She believes that she should be addressed as "madam", because "jeh jeh" is somewhat confusing and that may make other people mistake her for a helper. This employer received sympathy from so many other female employers online and she got some suggestions on how to correct the way the helper calls her. Only Siti, who came from another group but eagerly to join my conversation with Emma and Susie, is called by her name. *"My employer now is really good. The past no good,"* she said.

Emma has been working in Hong Kong for more than 6 years. She pointed at a big area and told me the helpers sitting or sleeping there are all from Indonesia, and the Filipino helpers were relaxing in another area. Currently, Filipino helpers still outnumber Indonesian helpers as the most dominant community of migrant domestic workers in Hong Kong. According to HK Immigration Department in 2019, there are almost 220,000 domestic helpers (55%) from the Philippines, and over 170,000 domestic helpers (43%) from Indonesia.[10] Local people believe there are different advantages in hiring Filipino helpers and Indonesian helpers. Taking language as an example, it is reckoned that Filipino helpers usually speak better English, whereas Indonesian helpers speak much better Cantonese. Emma told me it's kind of true. She said she would not know how to speak English if she had not worked in Singapore for ten years. Susie at that time had already finished her video chat with her family and told me she had worked in Singapore as well. That was the time when Siti joined us. I guess it was the keyword "Singapore" that took her notice. The three women all learned English in Singapore by chatting with their employers. Before that, they barely spoke any English. Emma said with admiration, *"We don't have chance to learn English when we're in Indonesia, not like the Filipinos, they have better chance."*

"Since you have worked in different places, which one do you prefer, Singapore or Hong Kong?" I asked all of them. Almost simultaneously, they said "Hong Kong". Their shared reasons are about salary and holidays. They are all paid at more than 4,600 HKD per month in Hong Kong, but if they now work in Singapore, their monthly salary would be much lower. Apart from this, they have a regular rest day each week and "annul leave" biennially in Hong Kong, but when they worked in Singapore, they had rather fewer holidays. Emma only had one rest day a month in the first two years in Singapore, and she demanded a regular day-off every week after her employer expressed the preference to continue hiring her. Susie had been working in Singapore for seven years. She had similar situation with Emma for the first two years, but after that, she was only allowed to have one more rest day per month. Siti, even worse, had neither regular rest days nor annual leave when working in Singapore for two years.

I can't imagine working continuously for two years without having any days off. And I don't think anyone on this planet should live or work like that. But I have to face the truth—the cold and cruel truth in our modern world—that some people were or are living like that. I did some research about the situation of the helpers in Singapore after coming back to my apartment, forced labour is still very common there even though my new friends from Indonesia told me it's getting better now because many helpers started to have a few more holidays in Singapore just a few years ago.

Singapore sounds like a nightmare according to Siti. Except for the part about learning English from her employers, it seemed she did not want to recall her life in Singapore that much. Siti repeated "no holiday" as it's the only thing she was thinking of. Susie has a great sense of humour, and she played the role of bantering with her friends and cheering them up. She could tell if her friends were thinking of some sad things and she was always ready to distract their attention from the past misery. When the right timing came, Susie made fun of Siti's English accent by saying *"You have some flowers in your mouth"*, and she had a dig at herself for being less hard-working because she doesn't live in an apartment as big as Emma and Siti do. Susie didn't talk about herself too much except on one occasion when she mentioned her family. I asked her whether she missed her family much since she can only go back home every other year. She then told me something about her child and how she misses her ten-year-old son and husband every single day. She tried to hold back her tears when she said, *"All I do is for my family"*.

With regard to their living condition, Siti was very satisfied with her current room. She said it's bigger than many other helpers' rooms here because her employer lives in a spacious apartment with more than 1,000 square feet, which, on the other hand, suggests her workload is heavier when she cleans it. Susie's room is fine. She said it's just a normal room for a helper to live in. However, Emma lives in a very small room in a 700-square-foot flat. There are five people living in that flat including herself. Her employers are a couple who live in a relatively big room, their two children share one room, and she has the helper's room. Emma described her room was as narrow as the passage we were sitting on. I estimated her room is around 1.5 metres wide. Nonetheless, they all feel lucky because they do have a private room, whilst many others don't.

As housing prices are extortionate in Hong Kong, dwellers have to be very good at making use of space. It is therefore very common to find three bedrooms in a 700-square-foot flat which is relatively spacious for a family in Hong Kong. The price of such a flat varies from district to district. Based on my search results, a second-hand flat measuring 700 square feet costs at least 7 million HKD (approximately 900,000 USD) in a less developed district. A standard double bed in Hong Kong (it's sometimes called small double) is generally 1.22 metres wide and 1.83 metres long so as to suit the standard size of a small double room here. My flat is in Tai Po, the New Territories, a region that is less expensive as far as living costs are concerned. I live with my partner in a two-room flat of around 300 square feet, and its monthly rent is about 11,000 HKD (≈1,394 USD). It is said that it can be sold at the price of over 5.5 million HKD (≈almost 710,000 USD), if it isn't influenced by COVID-19. A bigger room (the standard size of a double room in HK) can only accommodate a standard Hong Kong double bed and a bedside table. And if I wilfully put a queen bed (152*190 cm) in this room, its door would fail to close. The smaller room is used as my study room in which there is a wardrobe, a desk with a mini bookshelf and a comfortable chair. Yet when I'm there with books and music, my study room becomes the cosiest space for me, hidden away from the hustle and bustle of this busy city.

Based on a report published by the Census and Statistics Department in 2017, 82.2% of the domestic households in Hong Kong live in a flat measuring 215 to 753 square feet, and approximately 8% of the domestic households live in places which are even less than 215 square feet.[11] For some underprivileged residents whose salary cannot afford a relatively comfortable flat, they may have to rent a shelter of only 70 square feet shared by two adults and a child. The data may explain why many migrant domestic workers in Hong Kong have very small rooms to live in, but it does not justify other aspects of their poor life.

Paid annual leave is written in Hong Kong government's guide concerning the employment of domestic helpers from abroad,[12] but it seems that so many employers in Hong Kong have a different understanding of annual leave. Though one rest day in a week is regulated, daily working hours are not clarified by the Hong Kong government, which makes domestic workers very vulnerable to forced labour and overwork.[13] In addition, the official guide for migrant domestic workers uses some vague language requiring employers to provide helpers "with suitable living accommodation with reasonable privacy".[14] However, suitable accommodation and reasonable privacy are hard to guarantee with the compulsory live-in rule, let alone the comprehension of "suitable" and "reasonable" may be entirely different to different people in such a crowded city. It again depends on the luck of the helpers, like gambling.

Apart from the factors mentioned above, the two-week rule, which discourages domestic workers to change employment freely, puts the unlucky helpers in an even more passive and risky situation. The Immigration Department of the Hong Kong Special Administrative Region (HKSAR) stipulates that foreign domestic helpers must leave Hong Kong within two weeks if their contracts are prematurely terminated unless they find a new employer and get an updated visa within two weeks.[15] For those helpers who have completed a two-year contract but want to find a new employer, this rule applies to them as well. Nonetheless, Susie and Emma told me that a domestic worker could look for a new employer two to three months in advance of the termination date. In Hong Kong, domestic helpers' work permits are sponsorship-based (their employers are the sponsors). If helpers change their employment, both they and their employers shall give the notice to the Immigration Department. Finding a new employer within two weeks might be not that difficult in normal situations in Hong Kong, but obtaining an approved new visa by the immigration department within two weeks is mission impossible (the normal time frame for the Immigration Department in Hong Kong to process the application and issue a new visa is about 4-6 weeks). For most domestic workers, returning their home countries to look for a new employer and wait for a new visa only means uncertainties, and uncertainties are undesirable. As a result of the two-week rule, domestic workers who have encountered ill-treatment or forced labour may choose to continue tolerating their abusive employers.

For many helpers, even making formal complaints to the labour department is not optional because they have rational reasons to dread being fired if they do that. Leaving Hong Kong without enough savings would be the least favourable thing for most domestic helpers, because a great number of them have to support their families in their home countries where job opportunities are very limited and the salary is far less well-paid. Systemic exploitation of foreign domestic helpers, I regret to say, is therefore a result connived by the Hong Kong government along with employers who neglect helpers' basic human rights.

Emma, Susie and Siti all have to wake up at around 6.30 and start to work after that. The time they finish their work is somewhat different. Emma and Susie usually work till 9-9.30 pm, whilst Siti has to work till 10.00 pm; nevertheless, they all have one hour for lunch break. "Why do you have to work so long every day?" I asked Siti with shock.

"Because my boss's house is very big to clean. I have to clean it every morning and do many other things," Siti replied first, "I need to go to the market to buy meat and vegetable to prepare for cooking. Oh, I have to take care of the elderly people in the house too. My boss is very kind, he say I can sleep for a while in the afternoon, but I have no time."

"Any children in that house you need to take care of?" I asked.

"One study in Australia and the other is a middle school student. Not hard to take care of the middle school student," answered Siti. Siti's current employer is her third one during her 12 years in Hong Kong. She told me that she is the most satisfied with her current employer.

Emma and Susie share similar schedule every day, but some duties are different due to the people they need to take care of. Susie's employer has only one child who is a middle school student. In contrast, Emma's employer has two children who are all primary students, which increases her workload in taking care of them compared to Susie and Siti. *"I need to send the kids to school every day and pick them up. No bus to go to the school. I must walk for 20 minutes to get there. In summer, I take an umbrella. The sun is too strong outside,"* said Emma. Susie told me that it takes much more time to take care of children or elderly people compared to kitchen work.

Regarding the influences of COVID-19 on them, the Sunday gatherings had been suspended for a few months due to a ban on public gatherings, and they were all made to work more. Emma and Susie were allowed to go out for a couple of hours on their rest days from February to May, and luckily, they were not forced to work too much on those Sundays when they were at their employers' residence. Siti, however, was somewhat emotional talking about this, because she had been working for 3 continuous months without any day-off despite extra pay for working every Sunday.

Anna and Indah

Anna and Indah were from the group that gave me an enthusiastic welcome. The pity is that only two of them speak English, whilst others in that group preferred to speak Cantonese—the language I am not proficient enough in to have a long conversation. Like Susie, Siti and Emma, Anna and Indah had also worked as helpers in Singapore where they learned English but had no holidays. Anna had worked in Singapore for four years, and now has been working in Hong Kong for six years. She has a family with two children in her hometown. Anna told me that her current employer is satisfied with her work performance and is very nice to her. She got this job opportunity because her employer prefers to hire an Indonesian helper who can speak English rather than a Filipino helper. Then Anna said something that impressed me, *"My employer doesn't have good impression on Filipino helpers because her last helper is a Filipino and my madam isn't happy about her. I am not saying it's right or wrong. I just think every society has good people and bad people. One bad Filipino helper doesn't mean they are all bad. Indonesian helpers are not always good. I hope people won't say we're all bad if they hire not good Indonesian helpers."*

Anna is so empathetic and considerate that I was touched by her words. I guess she hasn't received a series of training on critical thinking like many people who have received university education do, yet she appears to be a natural thinker. Many would crow about their own group and accept this kind of social recognition without thinking, albeit at the cost of denying another whole group of people. Thankfully, Anna is not one of them. The great thing about Anna is that she didn't want to take credit for her community due to this kind of irrational generalisation, nor did she want to take this chance to feel better than her counterparts. In many cases, one may take that conclusion for granted and feel superior to another group of people, but Anna didn't. She is not under the spell of feeling superior. I think there are two ways to get out of a superiority complex. The first one sounds rather impossible: it requires us to have no concept or awareness of "superiority" and "inferiority"; however, we'll be exposed to these concepts sooner or later in our society. The second one is more practical, but it requires us to be vigilant all the time and use our rationality and morality to resist the temptation of superiority. I believe Anna uses the latter.

I could not help asking myself: would Anna have a passion for philosophy or sociology if she had gained better access to all sorts of resources since she was born? I bet she would.

Indah, the youngest woman in that group, had worked for two years in Singapore before working in Hong Kong. She has a boyfriend in Indonesia, but she hasn't seen him in person for one and half years, because this is her second year of working in Hong Kong and her biennial leave isn't ready yet. Indah told me she likes shopping sometimes, but she can't spend much on it as she needs to transfer money to her parents every month. Both Anna and Indah need to work from around 7.00 in the morning to 9.00-9.30 in the evening. *"Sometimes, I work till 10.00 (p.m.),"* said Anna. She seems a bit busier than Indah because she has to look after two children for her employer, whilst Indah's employer has only one child.

Unlike Anna or any other helpers that I talked with, Indah does not have a private room. She told me she shares a room with her employer's child, and her bed is above the child's. There are only two rooms in that tiny apartment, and it seems there is no other way. Despite this, Indah enjoys her time with the child as she frequently said "my child" to refer to her. *"I want to have a private room of course. But my child is too little, and it has no other room. It's good for me to look after her if I live with her in the same room,"* said Indah with a big smile, *"I don't mind lah."* ("lah" is a modal particle in both Singaporean English and Hong Kong English).

Anna and Indah, like many other domestic helpers from Indonesia, believe in Islam. Luckily, they both are allowed to pray at their employers' residence. They told me that, however, some Muslim helpers are not allowed to pray because their employers are scared. "Scared, why?" I asked.

"I don't know," replied Anna, *"perhaps some people are scared of our religion, and think we may do some bad things if we pray."* I began to wonder whether some of their unfair treatment is related to Islamophobia. I asked them whether they must cook pork for their employers. Anna and Indah told me some of the helpers do not have to cook pork at all, whereas they need to cook pork a few times a month, which is nonetheless acceptable for them. *"I think God will understand us. We have to survive. I say sorry to God every time I cook pork,"* added Anna.

Interestingly, when they mentioned the local people in Hong Kong, they used "Chinese" to refer to them instead of "Hongkongers" which is a preference for numerous young people in Hong Kong. Indah said, *"People from Hong Kong, mainland China, Taiwan and Singapore, we all call them Chinese".* Anna nodded her head to show her agreement with Indah. It made me recall my conversation with Lucille last weekend. Lucille also used "Chinese" instead of "Hongkongers" or "Hong Kong people" to refer to the local people here. "Hongkongers", a word suggesting a new identity constructed by the younger generation in Hong Kong, is widely seen on mainstream media but is not used much by these migrant domestic workers. To outsiders like them, "Chinese" is more like a simplified concept in the sense of ethnicity rather than national identification. Apparently, foreign domestic workers in Hong Kong don't seem to notice the local people's struggle with their identity. Ironically, on the other hand, mainstream society may not find out the multiple identities within these helpers either. I wonder if these two communities tend to give up knowing each other. If people must be so obsessed with identities, I'd prefer a world where the first and foremost identity is "human".

The five helpers I talked with were not eager to comment on the Hong Kong social movement in 2019. It seems they thought it is a very controversial topic and they didn't want to trigger an argument before knowing my political opinions. Anna told me her employer who is in favour of protesters advised her to be very careful when police violence escalated. I asked Anna and Indah whether they felt scared last year. Anna said she was a bit scared sometimes. *"I am not saying it is good or bad,"* said Anna with careful words, *"policemen are more scary actually. But sometimes when their fights with protesters are violent, we are also scared if we are outside".* Indah thinks the helpers who live in the New Territories should be affected less than those who live in Kowloon or Hong Kong Island where protests happened more frequently and so did police brutality. Both Anna and Indah believe that COVID-19 has had a greater impact on their life.

The semi-lockdown brought about by COVID-19, which had lasted for a couple of few months in Hong Kong, was a tough time to Anna and Indah. They were not asked to work for the whole day on Sundays when their gatherings were banned, but their workload had increased a lot from February to June because of the spread of the virus. Due to health reasons, many companies had applied a home office policy from February to June, and all the local schools' on-campus classes had been replaced by online education. For the five helpers I talked with, it was an affliction that they had gone through. With their employers and the children spending more time at home, the helpers' housework such as caregiving, cleaning and cooking became heavier, and the relationship between some employers and helpers soured. Besides their routine work, sterilising and sanitising almost everything that was touched had also become a major part of their daily housework. Anna and Indah had been asked to take a shower before changing and hand washing their clothes once they returned to their residence. *"Sometimes my boss ask me to take two showers a day,"* said Anna.

Anna and Indah's regular rest days were strictly controlled by their employers who were afraid that their helpers would get infected if they went out to see friends on Sundays. They were only allowed to leave their residence for a few hours with a precondition that they would not have a small gathering with friends. Even though they were lucky to be permitted to breathe fresh air outdoors on Sundays, it didn't seem to be that pleasant for them anymore due to the nit-picking and troublesome sterilisation process after returning to their residence. In addition, the mass panic over the coronavirus had led to some panic buying for weeks. Face masks, disinfectants, toilet paper, and rice had become the scarce resources that people rushed to buy for a long while in Hong Kong. For many Hong Kong residents as well as domestic helpers, going out back then was something they had to think twice about for they had a limited number of face masks to reuse and a limited number of disinfectants to sanitise themselves with. As a result, Anna and Indah had to stay at their employers' flats on many rest days during the semi-lockdown and did some work without extra pay when it was necessary.

The experience of these five migrant domestic workers resonate with the result of the aforementioned online survey investigated in March 2020, and their growing amount of housework amid the semi-lockdown in Hong Kong invites us to envision the domestic workload of women who have not employed a domestic worker but who had been working from home while in the meantime bear most household duties under the coronavirus pandemic. Hong Kong is a city in which western and Chinese values coexist. One of its identities is seen as an international financial centre, while the other is identified as a society influenced by traditional Chinese culture. Yet it seems that Hong Kong people's attitudes towards housework and caregiving tend to be more affected by a bad part of the tradition, as household chores are still largely believed to be women's work. According to Hong Kong Federation of Women's Centres, a great many females' housework doubled due to the Coronavirus outbreak.[16] If female citizens from Hong Kong's mainstream society needed to shoulder more domestic responsibilities during the pandemic resulting from gender stereotyping or gender discrimination, then I'm afraid that the discrimination against foreign domestic workers in Hong Kong may be more concerning not only because of their gender but because of their race and identity. It is fair to say that the pandemic has further marginalised the migrant domestic helpers in Hong Kong.

Indah said she wanted to ask me some questions about my life in New Zealand before I left. I accepted her informal interview and introduced the lifestyle in New Zealand by showing some pictures to her. She was so excited, and her excitement about New Zealand attracted other domestic helpers' attention. I then told her how migrant workers are treated and what basic rights they have in New Zealand. Anna sitting next to me was translating our conversation in bahasa Indonesia (the official language and lingua franca in Indonesia) to those who do not speak English. They admired most when I mentioned migrant workers in New Zealand can choose employers and their minimum wage should be no different compared to New Zealand citizens. Some of them started to imagine another kind of lifestyle with dreams written on their faces. I somehow associated this scene with Of Mice and Men.[17] I bet when

George and Lennie, the two migrant field workers, retell their dream—which is to settle down and have their own farm—their yearning for a better life must be the same with the domestic helpers sitting beside me.

It was a delightful afternoon chatting with them except the weather was muggy. I had stayed with them for around three hours, and when I was ready to leave, the five domestic helpers I informally interviewed all expressed gratitude for coming to talk with them. The other helpers sitting in the vicinity all said goodbye to me. I called Siti's name and told her I would visit her next time when she's free. She was so surprised that I still remember her name. *"Next time, I may not be here. My boss may ask me to work, I don't know I can see you or not,"* said Siti with a pity.

At the end of the day, I felt a bit pain in my buttocks. When I woke up the other day, my butt still hurt because the concrete floor was indeed not so friendly to sit on for hours. Ouch!

3. Parallel Universe

Wednesday, 1 July 2020   Temperature: 32°C   Humidity: 68%

Today is a public holiday in Hong Kong. Based on the regulations of the Hong Kong government, domestic helpers should have a rest on public holidays as well. I decided to visit the domestic helpers whom I talked with last Sunday afternoon. Emma and Susie were sitting in the same place. Yet I didn't see Siti, Anna, and Indah. I bought some Indonesian snacks and desserts to share with these Indonesian helpers. They all felt excited. Since it was my second time to meet them, some of them already felt close to me. An Indonesian helper that I didn't talk to much before suggested taking a photo for some helpers and me. I suppose this photo can help people know more about where and how they relax on their holidays.

Susie saw me first. She waved at me and invited me to sit with her. Emma was sleeping beside Susie. To wake her up, Susie yelled at her, *"Emma, your friend is here!"* Then Emma saw me, and quickly made room for me to sit (I felt so guilty about this). Emma and Susie asked me not to worry about Siti, Indah and Anna for working on a public holiday. *"Their employers will pay them. It's OK lah,"* they said.

Siti, Anna and Indah were not the only helpers who were not here today. It seems almost half of the helpers were absent today. I hoped many of them were exploring this city instead of working. Before 5 pm, the helper who took a photo for me left us to go to her employer's place. She came to say goodbye to me and explained that it was because she had to go back earlier today to cook. After she left, I asked Emma and Susie whether they needed to work on public holidays or Sundays. Susie answered for Emma, *"She's so lucky! She doesn't need to do anything after she's back. She just take a shower and then go to sleep. But I need to wash dishes for my Mam and Sir. It's OK lah. Some helpers have two big sinks of dishes wait for them to wash,"* Susie gesticulated at me and laughed. I asked Susie whether she feels buttock pain after sitting on the concrete floor for a whole day. Susie said she does but she kind of gets used to it.

Emma and Susie looked more relaxed today. They showed me some pictures of their houses and family members in Indonesia. They all have a big and beautiful house back home. Susie has a nice and well-designed house. To buy that house, she had saved her salary for working for seven years in Hong Kong; otherwise it would nearly be impossible to buy such a house if she had been working in Indonesia. Emma also told me that she could afford a house in Indonesia because of her savings from working as a helper in Hong Kong. They both felt gratified about this. When Emma showed me a picture of her well-furnished bedroom in which there is technically a real queen bed, I was utterly surprised by how big it was, and my reaction surprised myself as well. I guess I sometimes forget how big and comfortable my room was while living in New Zealand. Humans' memories are easily blurred by reality.

When they showed me the pictures of their life in Indonesia, it naturally evoked happy memories from their past when they were with their families or it may have evoked imagination for their beautiful future where the big house and their family members and friends are all there. Nostalgia, however, is intertwined with both sweet and bitter parts. The sweet parts are too mesmerizing but, in the meantime, too remote, and hence it makes the bitter parts even more overwhelming. *"Sometimes, I don't know when it's going to end,"* said Susie. This time, Susie didn't hold her tears back, she cried. I gave Susie a piece of tissue paper and she continued, *"I repeat my work every day. On Sunday, I just stay here. No surprise! And I count the days until I can go back. I miss them (her family members). I miss them so much, but I can't go back now. I have to feed my family."*

Emma has divorced like some other female helpers working in Hong Kong. Being a married migrant helper means that they have to deal with distant relationships with their husbands, which is tough and cruel for them. These helpers choose to work overseas to improve the life of their families, but they often end up with broken marriages. Emma laughed at herself for the money she made but lost her husband. She hasn't had a new family yet, and she has no children or husband to miss. Nostalgia haunts her in a different way. Intimate relationships are not something that Emma misses but something that she longs for. Emma said that she wants to learn Mandarin and go to Taiwan to work one day, because there are more Indonesian men working there and she hopes to find a partner there.

Susie has an older sister called Daisy who has been working as a domestic helper since 1999 in Hong Kong. Daisy did lots of favours for Susie and gave her plenty of advice about her job. Daisy is now working in a big apartment with a great employer in Causeway Bay. *"My sister's employer is so good, you know! Just like us, she is free on Sunday and public holidays, but she also has two-week holiday every year, with salary!"* Susie's admiration oozed.

Daisy suggested that Susie should demand for a private room during job interviews before coming to Hong Kong, but Susie was too unconfident and scared to do so for her first job in Hong Kong. Nonetheless, she did ask her potential second employer whether she would have a private room during the job interview. *"The employer asked me if it's OK to live in the kitchen. In the kitchen! I know some helpers are living in the kitchen, but I don't want that. So, I refused that,"* added Susie, *"I become brave after that."*

One of the troubling things for Susie and Emma is to vary the food they cook. Repeated exposure to food is acceptable, but they still need to avoid cooking the same dishes in a week. The mental work to plan for serving their employers with different food is not as exhausting as their physical work, but it can be stressful nonetheless. Susie said she must take notes about the dishes she had already cooked in case she forgets. If she cooks the same food within just a few days, she is afraid that her employer will complain. Emma said that her employer is not that fussy about the food, but she still pressurises herself. I thought about my own situation. I am responsible for cooking in most cases, while my partner washes dishes. Usually, I only need to cook dinner. However, just like Emma and Susie, I have the same kind of trouble avoiding cooking the same dishes each day. Of course, my partner is not my employer and I do not have to please him in that way because of our belief in equality, but I am still bothered by the pressure from myself. Having inspiration for what to eat every night is not easy for me, while many helpers have to rack their brains to plan different dishes for three meals every day. Luckily, neither Emma nor Susie is provided with leftovers. They can have their meals with their employers at the same time though they dine in the kitchen.

A cloudy day makes sitting outdoors easier but not to a large extent. Some of the helpers were fanning themselves with local newspapers. They have no idea what's written on the newspapers because they cannot read Chinese. I noticed that the headlines of the newspapers were all about endorsing the Hong Kong national security law which was approved by the Central government of China on 30 June and would come into force on 1 July. Compared with the anti-extradition bill in 2019, this new law has received more criticism since it was proposed, and its enactment is believed to symbolise the end of Hong Kong's autonomy. In the narrative of the Chinese central government, national security law aims to ensure "one country, two systems" and let Hong Kong to remain as peaceful and stable as in the past. However, a large number of people in Hong Kong society and the international community have shown concern that this law will turn Hong Kong into a police state and the government may make use of it to jeopardise Hong Kong' freedom of speech and rule of law. In particular, they worry that the criminal acts stipulated by the national security law are more likely to be used for targeting dissidents in the name of "secession", "subversion', "terrorism" and "collusion with foreign forces".

On the same day in Victoria Park—a place that entails political implications in Hong Kong—thousands of activists marched there against the national security law despite a police ban. By contrast, in another corner of the city, or in many other corners of this city, the marginalised domestic helpers sitting on the concrete floor did not know what's happening there, nor do many of them even know what the national security law is. When I sat with them, they barely talked about the issues that Hong Kong mainstream society pays attention to. By the same token, people in mainstream society seldom talk about the issues the domestic helpers are facing. I read some news about the protest later that day and thought of the time I spent with those helpers. I had an illusion that we all may live in a parallel universe. The dominant group and the migrant domestic workers may have lived in the same city for years, but I wonder how much they know of each other.

On Marginalisation

Migrant domestic workers have long been marginalised in Hong Kong. They do not have the same eligibility for the right of abode as other visa holders do. According to the Immigration Department of HKSAR, valid visa holders can apply for a permanent residence after having "ordinarily resided in Hong Kong for continuous period of no less than seven years",[18] but the migrant domestic helpers can't because they are excluded from the list of "ordinary residents" under the Immigration Ordinance in Hong Kong.[19] Nor can they share the same statutory minimum wage with members in mainstream society. The minimum wage of "ordinary residents" or non-domestic workers in Hong Kong is HK$37.5 per hour in 2019,[20] whereas the minimum wage of migrant domestic helpers is HK$4,630 per month albeit with accommodation and food which mostly depends on good fortune.[21] Some may argue that if counting accommodation and food provided by the employers, migrant domestic workers' disposable income is actually not bad, or even better than some local residents. But let's also count in this way: for those domestic workers who are forced to work 16 hours a day (44% of them work 16 hours a day according to MFMW's report in 2019), their hourly salary could be less than HK$11. If domestic workers could choose, I suppose most of them would choose getting the same minimum hourly wage as Hong Kong ordinary residents and then usetheir salary to rent a room and buy food for themselves.

The tragedy of marginalisation is not that it excludes a certain group of people from fully participating in economic, political and social life of mainstream society (though it is terrible enough), but that the marginalised group needs to take the blame and consequences for being excluded. The commonly seen or heard reasons to justify marginalising other groups are: "They do not fit in our society". Or "they do not care what we care". However, all sorts of pretexts like these are part of the effects of marginalisation not the causes—even though there are any arguable causes—nothing in the world should be a reason to deprive people of equal rights and dignity. The marginalised groups are stereotyped and labelled as the ignorant "others" for not knowing about local issues, the ungrateful "others" for not even trying to engage with mainstream society, and the privileged "others" for having some "rights" that the dominant groups do not necessarily have. Their failure to blend into mainstream society becomes thus uncivilised and uncooperative; not being well-informed about political, economic and social issues of the larger community entails arrogance; and being treated differently may be seen as taking advantage of their inferior status.

However, many may ignore the fact that the helpers who were using the newspapers to fan themselves are too isolated to be informed with local issues or integrate into mainstream society. The failure to blend in Hong Kong society is not a failure of the marginalised helpers but a shared failure for both the non-marginalised group and marginalised group to achieve mutual understanding and social justice. At least, for the helpers I have known and talked to, it would be ideal if they could and if they were allowed to fit in the host society. They have tried or did try hard to blend in, and it would be thus unfair to deny their efforts or suspect their motivation in the first stance. The entrance tickets to mainstream society are the social resources that those foreign domestic helpers have lacked—which I hope it is not something difficult for us to realise or comprehend—if we have ever noticed where they relax and how they relax on their rest days. Insufficient access to mainstream society implies insufficient access to equal rights and opportunities, and the lack thereof which leads to inferior status of the marginalised. As a saddening result, the inferior status of the helpers further deepens the prejudice from the non-marginalised group and is usually used as an excuse to justify the unfair treatment the domestic workers have received—that less social respect and fewer economic benefits merely fit into the origins and abilities of the group.

Ideally, the marginalised groups should be sympathised. In reality, however, those people are more likely to be stigmatised rather than sympathised because of their inferior status. "Inferiority", as we all may know, just like its counterpart "superiority", is a word denoting inequality. And the fatal passion for superiority contributes largely to discrimination. In many cases, I regret to say, one tends to feel not that guilty for discriminating the people who are de facto marginalised and helpless. The non-marginalised group's compassion to those underprivileged individuals vanishes once they find there is a link between the marginalised and the inferior, as compassion for the marginalised or underprivileged groups only exists when the giver believes the receiver shares the equal status. In this context, prejudice is not prejudice but a convenient "fact", and discrimination not discrimination but a reasonable practice. This theory can be applied to our attitudes towards animal welfare as well. Many of us feel compassionate about animals that are brutally treated as we think they are equal with us and should be free of suffering. However, if we think animals are naturally inferior to us, our compassion for animals will be shown rather less.

Discrimination occurs when it involves individuals who think they are superior while others inferior, and the justification of discrimination always sounds like a circular argument. Affirmative Action in the United States was just initiated several decades ago to dismantle discrimination on the basis of race, gender, etc. And though we are still marching towards an era of equality, we are not there yet. Discrimination will be always there as long as some still think they are superior and should thereby have more rights and resources than the inferior. If we watch movies or TV series whose story setting is before the Millennium, then we can find loads of scenes revealing explicit discrimination (I am not suggesting we can't find these discriminatory scenes on TV or in reality now). In hindsight, the justification of discrimination is full of irony. In an episode of the third season of Yes Minister (a British political satire sitcom), the two screenwriters were apparently not happy about the discrimination against women in the early 80s. Many dialogues show how women in that time were prejudiced and discriminated against in the workplace. Particularly, a dialogue between the minister Jim Hacker and his permanent secretary Humphrey is very impressive. When the minister Hacker tries to create more job opportunities for women in the government, Humphrey is reluctant to agree. To defend his own standpoint, Humphrey provides a very typical circular argument: *women are intellectually inferior; otherwise, there should be more female leaders and influential women. And because there are fewer women leaders—which proves that women are not equally intelligent and competent as men—they are less eligible to enjoy the same opportunities and rights as men.* This sort of logic can be drawn on to so many forms of discrimination, and what people need to do is just to change the keywords of the sentences. Here are some examples (irony alert): 1. Black people are intellectually inferior, otherwise, there would be more successful people of them; 2. Domestic helpers in Hong Kong are intellectually inferior, otherwise, they would get higher salary or they would have other sorts of jobs. These presuppositions all bring about the same conclusion for the people who discriminate others: the discriminated individuals are not as good enough as their counterparts, so it would be unfair for the "inferior" others to have the same social resources and it would be acceptable to treat them differently.

However, the cause-effect relationship is upside-down. As I argued before, it is excluding the certain group of people that results in their lack of access to social resources and rights and then a disadvantageous position, not the other way around. The migrant domestic helpers in Hong Kong are not inferior to anyone. They are just unlucky to be born in less-developed societies where many of them are stricken by poverty, and where they have fewer opportunities to gain access to better education, better jobs, and a better life. Their bad luck doesn't mean that they cannot be decent humans, nor does their bad luck deny the fact that many of them are clever, knowledgeable (like Lucille), competent, and respectable. They just don't have enough opportunities and choices.

As a result of marginalisation/social exclusion, mutual indifference is almost inevitable. On the one hand, Hong Kong mainstream society's neglect of domestic helpers has been ever-present, while on the other, the helpers' willingness to get connected with mainstream society may have reduced due to long-standing marginalisation and discrimination. And it is not a mental protest for helpers themselves against the majority in mainstream society but a natural reaction of an ordinary human being when it comes to marginalisation. I believe, under normal circumstances, care tends to be mutual and becomes long-lasting as well as reciprocal if the care is benign. When we care about someone, we may not get the equal care back, but if our care has been constantly denied and excluded, our intention to care is more likely to be rejected by our inner voice from time to time. Lucille's words popped up in my mind, and the sentence *"They don't care about us, and I don't want to care about them"* began to linger in my ears. Those domestic workers have tried and tried but still fail to be "ordinary residents" in Hong Kong, what should they care? People like Lucille have media and political literacy allowing them to have the same sort of compassion as mainstream society does, but I wonder how many of them are highly motivated to do so after trying years to get fairer treatment and respect in Hong Kong. Let's face it: marginalisation is doomed to damage social cohesion.

The most absurd allegation against domestic helpers is that they have privileges in Hong Kong. On a Hong Kong English website called geoexpat, a topic on whether Sunday helpers are a nuisance was discussed in 2011, which managed to catch my eye.[22] Fortunately, most discussions were sarcastic about this topic and most people there felt sympathetic with domestic helpers. The initiator of this topic copied and pasted a letter of complaint posted by South China Morning Post (a Hong Kong-English language newspaper) to invite other expats to discuss. Since the original link from SCMP is not available anymore and I don't know exactly what people's reactions towards this letter were back then, I have to rely on the discussions and quotes from this website. Bonnie, the complainant of the letter believed that the helpers blocked the road and created noise on Sunday. She pointed out, here I quote: *"If these helpers want the same rights as Hong Kong citizens, shouldn't the government treat them equally when it comes to following the law?...Youngsters would be charged for loitering if they sat on the streets as a group, yet these helpers sit freely all over our footbridges, parks and roads."*

It seems there were some other responses that echoed with Bonnie, but they were not the expats' "favourite". Another letter of complaint sent to SCMP that fully agreed with Bonnie drew the most attention from the users of this website. Its title is "Residency right cannot be free". The complainant Prakash directly used the word "privilege" to describe the helpers' gatherings on a concrete floor on Sunday, and urged the Hong Kong government to charge the helpers a HK$400 levy (introduced in 2003 but abolished in 2007) to let them contribute to local economy. Beyond that, Prakash also thought that helpers in Hong Kong complained too much and ignore the facts that lots of employers in Hong Kong are equally hard-working but need to bear more pressure than them. The details of both letters, along with some responses like *"put them in the underground car parks and charge them an entrance fee"*, were largely mocked by members of that website, though there were some racist comments against both the helpers and Hong Kong people.

If sitting on concrete floor for the whole day is a privilege, then those who have condemned the helpers for having no choices but loitering outdoors can enjoy this kind of privilege for sure. I have personally experienced this "privilege", but I can tell you that I don't enjoy it that much, nor do those domestic helpers really. I am not quite sure how many people in mainstream society still hold the opinion like this, but the two who wrote the letters of complaint definitely stand for a certain type of a voice in mainstream society. And I'm afraid discrimination and loathing directed against domestic helpers still largely exist.

4. Alice in Victoria Park

Sunday, 05 July 2020   Temperature: 33°C   Humidity: 66%

To reduce the bias of my sampling, I decided to go to different areas where I could find migrant domestic helpers to talk to. I went to Victoria Park today, a place that is particularly chosen by Indonesian helpers to gather together on their rest days if they work in Hong Kong Island or Kowloon.

The picture above was taken at the time I was near the entrance of Victoria Park. It was around 2 o'clock in the afternoon. The sun was dazzling, and the feel-like temperature was 42°C. There were not so many local people wandering around.

(I took a photo from a far distance to make myself not look like an intruder.)

Later on, I found more helpers sitting on the grass. The picture may look nice because of the trees, grass, tents, etc. But compared to sitting on a concrete floor, it doesn't make it more comfortable to sit there baking in the heat. In a nearby area, a group of helpers who were in black got my attention. I approached them and asked them in English what they were doing. One of them pointed at a woman to answer my question for she was better at speaking English than the others. The woman preferred to be called Alice. She told me they were performing a kind of Indonesian martial art. I asked Alice whether I could take a photo for them, and that was the time when she started to get nervous. She said she needed to ask the permission from the leader of this community. She felt relieved when I told her that I just wanted to take a photo from the back of those helpers who were performing martial arts. "No one is going to be identified," I said.

Alice's reaction made me curious, and I figured out the reason why she was anxious about the photo thing later. According to Alice, there were a few people approaching them before: one was from a local newspaper, and the other was unknown to Alice (maybe the person was from independent media). The former took some photos of them before the semi-lockdown. Their faces were exposed, and Alice had an intuition that something was wrong. She wanted to make sure that she and her community did not cause any trouble; otherwise, it may affect their current or future employment in Hong Kong. Because she cannot read Chinese, she had to ask her employer to translate for her when she recognised their picture on a local newspaper. Her employer told her that the coverage was about helpers' awareness of wearing masks on Sunday. *"Not a big deal,"* her employer said. But I suppose the panic had still been lingering for a while in the community of helpers. Alice pointed at those helpers in black and explained to me worryingly as if I was a journalist who aimed to criticise them for not wearing a face mask. *"We are doing exercise, you know. And we can't wear a mask while doing exercise. We don't want to make any trouble,"* said she.

Alice became relaxed when I agreed with her. To make her more relaxed, I gave her more information about myself and she knew that I was just personally interested in their life in Hong Kong and I did not work for any local media. She then continued to mention another person who approached them to ask their opinions about Hong Kong people and mainland Chinese. *"It looked like an interview. But the questions are a bit misleading. It's like he's waiting for some answers, and when we didn't answer his questions as he expected, he became...what should I say...moody,"* Alice told me. *"We don't want to talk about politics here, because people are too moody sometimes. We don't want to join the battle between Hong Kong people and mainlanders, and we don't want to lose jobs because of this."* For the majority of the helpers here, losing jobs is their ultimate fear, and I can imagine sometimes how this fear makes them even more marginalised and unfairly treated.

Alice's reluctance to express her political leaning is rooted in her mind, though she's actually kind of politically literate about Hong Kong. She knows what happened in the 2019 Anti-extradition Bill Movement, and she knows the meaning of "yellow ribbon" and "blue ribbon" in Hong Kong's political context ("yellow ribbon" symbolises pro-democracy camp in Hong Kong, whereas "blue ribbons" stands for pro-government camp). Alice doesn't really like the mounting social divide due to the social movement. She described some scenes about how people with different political camps turn families/friends/strangers into enemies. After witnessing how her "grandma" (she calls the elderly woman in her current employer's family as "grandma") quarrelled with a taxi driver on their way and how they were made to leave the taxi, she has had no intention of expressing her political opinions in public anymore. *"Both of them attack each other's opinions and both of them are irritated. But my grandma is old, she shouldn't be driven away like that just because of her political opinions,"* Alice said bitterly.

Like Lucille, Alice's English is also very good (and she likes hiking too). The difference is that she didn't receive higher education in her home country before working in Hong Kong. Alice learned English while working in Singapore just like some other Indonesian helpers did. Ironically, her two employers in Singapore didn't allow her to have any holidays for 4 years, but her second employer, sent her to attend English courses and paid tuition fees for her. Alice was so appreciative about this. She said, *"I only went out on Sunday for English classes. But my second boss in Singapore let my friends visit me at home, and they (the couple she was working for) allowed me to use computer or phone at home. They're much better to me than my first employer there. Not like my first employer, they never deduct my salary. I got $300 Singaporean dollars a month when I was working for them. I still contact with them. I don't blame them for giving me no holiday, because at that time Singapore government didn't say we should have holidays. My second boss just followed the rule."* Those English courses help Alice a lot in so many ways. Not only does she find the current job satisfying because of her fluent English and working experience, she can also use English to help her community members communicate with some Hong Kong-based NGOs when they need help.

FDW Employment Regulations in Singapore

I read some news from SCMP about the situation of some desperate domestic workers in Singapore before. Forced labour is not something new there, and worse than that, appalling stories about abusing helpers can be heard from time to time. A domestic helper called Hayma went to Humanitarian Organisation for Migration Economics (an NGO to provide aid for abused domestic workers in Singapore) for help last year.[23] Apart from overwork and having no rest days, Hayma was deprived of the rights to keep her own passport, working visa and mobile phone. And the police refused to offer her any help for *"she was not physically abused"*. When I read this article, I thought my probability of encountering extreme cases like this would be low, but I was proved wrong again and again.

Maybe my sampling is a bit biased for the simple reason that the helpers would have continued working in Singapore if they had been fairly treated and paid, and in this case, I would not meet them in

Hong Kong. However, institutional discrimination and exclusion against domestic workers in Singapore should not be ignored in any sense. If we want to know more about the helpers' situation in Singapore, the easiest way would be read the employment rules for foreign domestic workers regulated by the Ministry of Manpower (MOM) in Singapore. Singapore's guide for the employment of foreign domestic workers has some similarities with Hong Kong: 1. working hours are not stipulated; 2. live-in rule is mandatory; 3. foreign domestic workers are not covered by local employment law; 4. foreign domestic workers are disqualified from being permanent residents; 5. one rest day is entitled per week; 6. doing a part-time job is not allowed.[24] In contrast, the Singaporean version is more detailed and less vague than Hong Kong's in terms of accommodation and food. Here, I do not mean that "more detailed and less vague" is necessarily "better". MOM defines what "adequate food" is and specifies what domestic workers' accommodation should be like, which is good, however, I also found something disturbing when reading the guidelines about helpers' accommodation. A guideline for employers called "modesty" suggests how employers should install surveillance cameras at home. I quote from MOM:

> If you install video recording devices at home, you must inform your FDWs (foreign domestic workers) of the devices and where they are placed. You must not install them in areas that will compromise her privacy or modesty, e.g. where she sleeps, change clothes, or the bathroom area.[25]

I believe, with all due respect, MOM in Singapore may not intend to encourage employers to monitor domestic workers by installing surveillance cameras at home, but the rule-makers did realise how common it would be and thus they thought it necessary to set standards for installing video recording devices. Practically speaking, it looks likely that MOM acquiesces in using surveillance cameras to monitor domestic workers, and as a result, it inspires the employers to do so.

Similarities and Differences between Singapore and Hong Kong on FDW employment regulations

	Singapore	Hong Kong
Similarities	1. Working hours are not stipulated; 2. Live-in rule is mandatory; 3. FDWs are not covered by local employment law; 4. FDWs are disqualified from being permanent residents. 5. A rest day is entitled each week. 6. Doing a part-time job is not allowed	
Differences	✓ Defining "enough food"	✗ Defining "enough food"
	✓ Specifying accommodation	✗ Specifying accommodation
	✗ Annual leave	✓ Annual leave
	✗ Public holidays	✓ Public holidays
	✓ Security bond	✗ Security bond
	✓ Marriage restrictions	✗ Marriage restriction
	✓ Pregnancy restrictions	✗ Pregnancy restriction
	✗ Minimum wage for FDWs	✓ Minimum wage for FDWs

Note: In Singapore, annual leave is not covered in FDWs' employment regulations, but FDWs can apply for home leave that is not compulsory and does not have to be paid by employers. Compared to Indonesian FDWs, the procedure for Filipino FDWs to apply for home leave is far more complicated as they "are required to register with the Philippine Embassy and then apply for a temporary exit document"; and they cannot apply for home leave directly but rely on their agency if they haven't completed their first 2-year-contract for the same employer.[26] With regard to minimum wage for FDWs in Singapore, MOM does not prescribe it, but the governments of Indonesia and the Philippines did require FDWs from these two countries to be paid with SGD$550 and SGD$570 respectively in 2019.[27]

Aside from home surveillance, state surveillance is also applied to those foreign domestic workers in Singapore. According to MOM, approval will be needed if an FDW wants to marry a Singaporean citizen or permanent resident.[28] It might be wise from the perspective of the Singaporean government to discourage and guard against the intermarriage between Singaporeans and the domestic workers from abroad; however, from my perspective, it does seem like an alternative form of caste system in a developed and modernised society. Beyond that, getting pregnant in Singapore is restricted for FDWs, and if they do, they will be deported to their home countries as getting pregnant does not comply with their work permit conditions (MOM requires FDWs to have medical screening every six months).[29] Prior to January 2010, employers would be financially punished if their domestic helpers got pregnant, [30] which is very puzzling to me. As stated in MOM, a security bond of SGD$5,000 will be charged by the government when an employer is about to hire an FDW, and it will be forfeited if either the employer or employee violates the work permit conditions.[31] Blatantly, getting pregnant or giving birth in Singapore violates the conditions, and if employers must act responsibly, I could imagine how many helpers in Singapore would be affected in terms of their holidays and privacy. For Alice, the reason why some employers in Singapore are stricter to their helpers is that they're afraid they may lose their security bond.

Speaking of holidays, MOM updated its policy regarding FDWs' rest days in 2013. From what I heard from the Indonesian helpers I talked with last Sunday, helpers were entitled to have a few more holidays in Singapore not long ago. As MOM states, "FDW is entitled to a weekly rest day if her Work Permit was issued or renewed after 1 January 2013".[32] However, I doubt its practicality when thinking about the security bond and its concomitant issues. After all, to some employers in Singapore, entitling helpers to a weekly rest day could mean risking them disobeying their work permit conditions, and the loss, if any, would be unfavourable to these employers.

Alice's experience of the first two years in Singapore is similar to Hayma but on a worse level. It was 2003 when Alice began working as a domestic worker in Singapore. Her first employer only gave her $20 Singaporean dollars per month while her monthly salary on her contract was $220. I was utterly shocked when I heard this, so I asked Alice whether she asked for help or sought legal aid in that time. Alice looked at me and shook her head, *"I can't. My contract was taken away by my employer, and my passport and my visa too. I was treated like a slave, but I can't do anything really, and I didn't have enough money to send to my family."* She tried to comfort me after she saw a worried look on my face, *"Don't worry about me, it's already the past. Remember? I had a better employer after that. Now, I have many friends here and I have a really nice employer."*

Belated Luck

After working in Singapore, Alice went back to Indonesia to be reunited with her family for a few years. She showed me some pictures of her two children and told me that she got married when she was 19. *"It is common for women to get married very early in Indonesia. Some women even get married earlier than me. Many women's husbands are not really good to them, but not my husband. My husband is good to me,"* said Alice with a blush on her cheeks.

However, happiness is transient, especially for those who have limited choices in their life. Alice had spent several wonderful years with her family even though their life didn't improve on a large scale because of her salary deduction. With their children growing up, both Alice and her husband realised that their family income couldn't support the two children to have further education if the couple both worked in the countryside in Indonesia. After a discussion with her husband, Alice decided to leave her home again. This time, she chose to work in Hong Kong where helpers' salaries are higher and more holidays are provided. Yet, before she began working overseas again, Alice had already taken out loans from an agency in Indonesia which has partnership with an agency in Hong Kong (she had to, otherwise she wouldn't get a job opportunity). For the first six months working in Hong Kong, she needed to spend a major part of her salary to pay back loans. What a life!

Alice has been working in Hong Kong for six years till now. Her first employer was not good to her. She had been asked to work till late every night and had been sleeping on the sofa in the living room for five years. But compared to her early experience in Singapore, she thinks it's already a blessing. She described her current female employer as "very nice" and "not fussy". Alice now has a more relaxing job than before, and even a relatively spacious helper's room. She lives with her employer in a 1,000-square-foot flat. Besides her, there are four people living in that flat: a woman who hired her, her employer's husband, the couple's child who is already an adult, and an elderly woman who is the female employer's mother. Alice's major responsibility is to take care of the "grandma". Aside from that, she cooks and cleans like other helpers do. Alice's daily routine is to work from 7.00 in the morning till around 8.30 in the evening, and she can take a break if she feels tired. Alice believes her actual working hours per day were usually no more than 10 hours before COVID-19. *"After ten years, I finally become lucky,"* said Alice with a wry smile.

Having worked in Hong Kong for more than five years, Alice finally discovered that there are some free Sunday workshops for Indonesian helpers to learn different skills. The themes of the workshops are various, including sewing, hairdressing, massaging, and dancing, and the instructors do not aim to make money by this but to share skills and enrich the helpers' life in Hong Kong. Those free workshops are thought of as a kind of informal education promoting sisterhood among Indonesian women. Alice told me with some excitement that she is learning Zumba. *"I don't know why I have to use so many years to know this. I wish I could know this much earlier,"* said Alice with regret. Then it seems she remembered something and continued, *"Oh perhaps no. I didn't have much time when I worked for my former employer. Even though I knew, so what? I wouldn't have time to practice."*

Unlike Emma, Susie, Siti, Anna and Indah, Alice's workload wasn't increased dramatically during the semi-lockdown in Hong Kong. She wasn't asked to take an alcohol bath after returning home or sterilise everything in that apartment every now and then. For Alice, the obvious change is about cooking. Before the coronavirus pandemic, she didn't need to prepare breakfast and lunch for her employer and her employer's husband on weekdays as they had the meals near their workplace. She only needed to prepare breakfast and lunch for the "grandma", and then dinner for the whole family. From February to June, the semi-lockdown had meant that she had to cook more because the whole family had been home all day. Fortunately, Alice doesn't have to try her best to vary the food while working for this employer, though she had experienced this before.

Preparing three meals a day for the whole family doesn't really worry Alice. She has something else to worry about. The COVID-19 pandemic has impacted the global economy and many people in most countries have lost their jobs. Alice's home has been severely hit by the coronavirus outbreak. According to an article published by The Jakarta Post in April, "with almost 3 million people having lost their jobs and 70 million at risk of losing income because of physical distancing, many people, especially amongst the poor and informal workers, are worried about escaping not only from the disease but also from starvation."[33] Some of Alice's family members had been jobless for months, and Alice is so worried about them. She looked anxious when talking about this as she was so concerned that she may lose her job next year. She told me:

> Now it's even more impossible for me to go back to Indonesia to find a job. But my employers here are going to move to a smaller house next year. I'm not quite sure if they still need me when the house is smaller. I hope I can stay. They're really good employers and I like my job very much. I think I'll work in Hong Kong longer than I planned if I can. Indonesia's economy won't recover soon, that's why I need this job more than ever. I have to send money back, or I don't know what will happen to my family.

The recent official data indicate that Hong Kong's unemployment rate climbed to 6.2% in June, reaching a peak in the last 15 years.[34] Society here has become a little spiritless because so many industries have ground to a halt and people's lives have been affected. Among the thousands of jobless people and those who receive less income, many of them may have hired domestic workers before. To relieve financial burden, they had to dismiss their helpers. The exact figures of unemployed helpers in Hong Kong still remain unknown, but we can be sure about one thing: domestic workers have to bear the same (or even more) financial pressure as their employers during the pandemic.

On Alice's rest days during the semi-lockdown, she was free to choose whether to relax or work. If she chose to work on Sunday, she would get HK$200 that day; and if she chose to relax on Sunday, her employer said that she didn't need to do any housework at home. However, even though Alice's employer is considerate to her, she still voluntarily does some housework on her rest days. Alice told me: *"I always think I have to do something, because this family is very kind to me. In the beginning, I still prepared breakfast for grandma on Sunday. I worried that my boss will get up late, then the grandma will be hungry. She told me I don't have to do that, but you know, she is an elderly woman. In my culture, elderly people should be cared for and respected. And then I always helped my boss to wash dishes after dinner on Sunday. My boss also said I don't have to, but I still did. Now, I think they get used to it. I don't blame them, they're good people, and I still have lots of break. I just think I'm weak, and Indonesian helpers here are weak. Filipino helpers won't do this."*

After finishing that sentence, Alice pointed to an area where more Indonesian helpers were sitting and said, "Some of them don't have enough food; some of them work for more than 16 hours a day; some of them live in the kitchen or living room. I don't think they will complain. We are too weak. We're the weakest group in anywhere." Alice's has worked for two employers in Singapore. One is a Chinese Singaporean, and the other is a Singaporean from Jordan. Rest days for migrant domestic workers were not compulsory in Singapore prior to 2013, and Alice was not lucky enough to meet an employer that allowed her to have any holidays. She spent some time working in Saudi Arabia as her second employer went back to his hometown and preferred to bring a maid back so as to live there more comfortably for several months. To our optimistic Alice, travelling is a form of relaxation. She regarded the journey from Singapore to Saudi Arabia as a holiday. "At least, I went to a new place, and my boss bought the flight tickets for me. I had different experience and I didn't spend money for that," said Alice.

I noticed that Alice was wearing a turban when I saw her, and I confirmed her religion through an earlier conversation. I asked Alice whether she felt close to Saudi Arabia since there is a large Muslim community. The answer I received was negative. Alice doesn't think a Muslim identity will make a maid's life easier in Saudi Arabia. She told me:

> Helpers' salary in Saudi Arabia is lower than Singapore, and we have no holidays. We have lower status there. Yes, I am a Muslim, but it doesn't help. I think we are still the weakest group no matter where we are.

"Some employers ask their helpers to look after the kids on Sunday," she pointed to a child and a helper near a tent and continued, "the kid over there feels closer to the helper, not his mum. He wants to spend more time with the helper on Sunday, so his mum asked the helper to take him to this park and have fun with us. The good thing is, the kid is lovely and he can have fun by himself. But even so, Filipino helpers will say no to this."

The Little Boy

The lovely child came to join us later. He is an outgoing ten-year old boy. By the level of the closeness between the boy and some helpers here, I could deduce that it wasn't the first time he's been here. The boy chose a place near us to sit, and then I heard Alice speaking some Cantonese to talk to him (Alice must be talented in languages). The boy didn't want to speak English with us, but he didn't want to be silent either. What he did was to start another conversation in Cantonese. *"Are you Chinese?"* he asked me. I answered "yes" and continued our conversation. For me, he is more than lovely.

The little boy K is very talkative. He calls his helper "jeh jeh" ("older sister" in Cantonese) amiably. For many employers who hired helpers here, when "jeh jeh" is used to address their helpers, it may connote something related to a job position and its accompanying social status. But to K, "jeh jeh" only means "older sister". He told me why he enjoys his time with his jeh jeh rather than his mum in Cantonese: *"My mum is so strict to me and she always asks me to study not to play. She doesn't allow me to play games, but when I stay with jeh jeh on Sunday, I can play games by using her smart phone. Jeh jeh is so nice to me! But this jeh jeh's cooking skills are not as good as the first jeh jeh. Wow, my first jeh jeh is pretty, kind, and good at cooking. This jeh jeh is great except cooking. You know what? She once cooked beef for us, but I think it tasted like a rock."* He laughed while mentioning the beef. Strangely enough, I do not think it is a real complaint, and if it is, the "complaint" from K is full of love.

K told me a secret that his parents aren't aware of yet: he wants to become a bus driver in the future. He has an intuition that his parents will not be happy to hear this, but he can't tell why. When I asked K why his dream is to be a bus driver, he answered me with pride: *"I like it, so I want to do it."* In K's mind, driving a bus is the coolest thing in the world. The way K talked to me made me think of one of my favourite cartoon characters McDull (created in Hong Kong), a male pig who is portrayed to be very ordinary but has so many dreams, and who has failed so many times but has never given up. McDull is widely believed to embody Hong Kong spirit: "perseverant", "hard-working", and "daring to dream".

McDull and his friends (source: Google Images)

McDull and his mum (source: Google Images)

I am not suggesting that K is like McDull, after all, K is smart and comes from a relatively wealthy and loving family; whereas McDull is not that smart, and is from a struggling single-parent family. Instead, I'm suggesting how both K and McDull are alike when they think about dreams, happiness, and success, and how they express their ideas in a similar way. A child's world is indeed simpler than adults. Many like to use the metaphor "plain paper" to refer to children, and the positive feature of the plain paper is its possibilities. Surely, we all hope that our children in human society can only exhibit good possibilities, but we may also have realised that their family, schools, and society will work together to influence their possibilities, which sometimes, can be negative.

I think K is more than lovely because he hasn't been moulded by this meritocratic society. He is so natural that he doesn't hide anything he likes and pines for. His idea of success hasn't been impacted by others, and he hasn't learned to compromise between dreams and reality. He was proud to tell me that he dreams to become a blue-collar worker in the future, while for adults in Hong Kong society wherein success is particularly defined by the masses, it doesn't happen very much. He is content to be grouped in class B (the second-best class in his grade) for he thinks the students in class

A have fewer choices: they have to become a certain type of successful people according to their parent's definition or preferences if they constantly maintain a great academic performance. And the most important thing is, he hasn't learned to divide people into different categories by race, gender, salary, degrees, or social status; nor has he learned to discriminate others yet.

Then, some past memories came to the surface. Four years ago, I met some children in an indoor inflatable playground in Christchurch, New Zealand. A kiwi girl saw me having fun alone (I had friends with me, but they were playing in another area), so she kindly invited me to join her and her friends. I was so grateful that she didn't exclude me because I am much older than her. On top of that, my skin colour is evidently different from her and her friends (they are white), but I don't think it is so evident for her or her friends. If it were, she wouldn't have pointed at a white boy and asked me whether I was his cousin after a short discussion with her friends. For her, inviting a person alone to play together is very natural, and welcoming that person is just because of a shared interest. At that moment, I was not an immigrant or an outsider in her world. She thought I was just like those who were born in New Zealand. The little kiwi girl, who was only seven years old in that time, was good at taking care of her new friends regardless of race, age, gender, nationality or anything else (I believe she hasn't changed this). I still remember how she encouraged me not to be afraid to jump from the top of the inflatable castle, and how many times she said goodbye to me when we were apart.

I am lucky enough not to have encountered discrimination in New Zealand (maybe I have, but I haven't realised it), but it doesn't mean that discrimination doesn't exist in that beautiful and peaceful society which is more equal than many other societies in this world. The human world is still full of inequality and all sorts of discrimination. We have a long way to go. I'm not here to demand a utopia wherein society is perfect and everyone is happy. I simply believe that we can do so much better. The examples of the little kiwi girl and the little boy K again prove to us that discrimination is not natural or inherited but implanted and nurtured.

Just like K, he finds staying with his jeh jeh and other helpers so much fun, so he pestered his mum to let him join the gathering of these helpers. He doesn't mind whether there is air conditioning or how many mosquitoes are going to target at him. To the little boy K, the Sunday helpers aren't a nuisance but a group of nice people who can bring him freedom to play in his own way. I don't think he has a superiority complex over them or knows how to patronise others.

Lily's Happiness

The sunlight became harsh around 3.00 pm. Although we were sitting under the shade of trees, the sun's rays still penetrated through the trees. Alice was very cool about it. She said she has already got used to this kind of weather. But I made fuss about it and used an umbrella to shield Alice and me from the sun's rays, because the place we were sitting became glaring. Some of Alice's friends bought Indonesian-style juice at the entrance of the Victoria Park to beat the summer heat. One of them came to ask me if I would like to try the juice with a bit of ice, and this young woman is Lily.

I rejected Lily's kind invitation. The reason is not that I didn't want to try Indonesian juice, but I knew she had just spent her own money on it. And I didn't want to take advantage of that. Alice asked me if I would like to have some free coffee as there would be someone to deliver it later. I said yes, and Alice left me to find the person. However, she came back to me disappointedly, because there was no free coffee left. Poor Alice then wanted to share some chocolate bars with us, but they were all melted (no surprise). *"My boss bought these to me, she's so kind,"* said Alice. Meanwhile, I noticed that Alice's water bottle was almost out of water, and the juice bought by her friends was already warm. So, I decided to go to a nearby shop to buy some iced coffee for them. Alice attempted to persuade me not to do that, but she failed.

After 10 minutes, I carried eight cans of iced coffee back and shared with the people sitting near me, including Alice, Lily and the little boy (but he doesn't like coffee, so I asked Alice to keep it for the next day). To express her gratitude, Lily brought a plate of sliced cantaloupe to share with me and sat next to me with a smile. Then I started to talk with Lily, and Alice could finally spare some time to take photos for her friends who were performing Indonesian martial arts (Alice thought it was impolite to leave me there alone).

Lily was in a long-sleeved red T-shirt and blue jeans. She looks like she's in her early 20s. With a little bit of shyness, she didn't talk as much as Alice, and she wasn't confident enough to use English either. Yet her eyes could speak a thousand words. Lily comes from a small village in Indonesia in which job opportunities are scarce for women like her. Her family is so poverty-stricken that no one could afford an air conditioner to keep cool in the scorching hot summer. Lily said that she doesn't find it very hot in summer here, as the temperature in Hong Kong is similar to her hometown and she's used to the days without air conditioning in summer. Yet she did think that winters are tough here, especially when she sits outdoors like this. She used body language to describe how she and her friends feel when sitting in Victoria Park in winter, and I think that gesture means: shivering. Usually, winter temperatures in Hong Kong are between 15 °C and 20 °C, but to be fair, the apparent temperature can be colder when it is windy. By contrast, winter in Indonesia is much warmer (23°C-32°C). No wonder it is hard for them to get used to it.

Similar to many other Indonesian helpers, Lily hasn't completed upper secondary education because her family can't afford to pay for it. To Lily, access to higher education as well as good job opportunities is apparently associated with wealth (I'm afraid it's true in many societies). *"You can't go to university if you have no money. Same for high school in Indonesia. Even for good job, you better have some money and know someone,"* said Lily seriously. She told me that if she had been better educated, she would have had more choices concerning employment. I asked Lily what her dream job was, she hesitated at first because she didn't know how to say that job position in English. So, she behaved like a studious student and ran over to ask Alice. She learned it quickly, coming back to tell me that her dream is to be an air stewardess. Then Lily laughed and said: *"It's just a dream lah. I can't be air stewardess lah. I'm not pretty. And I don't go to university."* She tried to sound as if she didn't care about it, but I still saw a tinge of sadness in her eyes, and eyes don't lie.

To alleviate her family's financial burden, Lily left her home to find overseas job opportunities four years ago. She chose Singapore as her first destination because it is far easier for Indonesians to apply for a visa if they want to work as a domestic worker there. She had worked two years in Singapore, and as we might expect, she learned some English there. When she first arrived in Singapore, it was already after 2013 when MOM revised the FDW employment regulations. "FDW is entitled to a weekly rest day," the Singaporean authority announced. However, the truth is: Lily hadn't been entitled to any rest days during her two years of working in Singapore. Nonetheless, she was much luckier than Alice because her salary hadn't been deducted and her passport as well as work permit hadn't been taken away by her employer. She got exactly the same amount of salary as her contract stated: SGD$500 per month.

Lily's eyes told me that she didn't want to talk too much about her life in Singapore, so I didn't ask her too many details about how she worked there. What I know is that she came to Hong Kong after she completed her first contract of 2 years in Singapore.

It is now the second year for Lily to work in Hong Kong. She seems to be happier here. Lily is content with the regular rest days here, and she enjoys public holidays like the Hong Kong people do. Yet her work schedule is tight. Lily is still working for her first employer. And in light of the true stories mentioned before, we all know that a helper is more likely to be unlucky when they are newcomers and know nothing about their rights. It is "yes and no" for Lily's case.

Lily doesn't have a private room like many other newcomers. She shares her room with the child whom she needs to take care of. But it's alright for her because she likes the child a lot. Lily grinned at me and said: *"I'm happy I have a real bed. I don't have to sleep in sofa or kitchen. And my salary in Hong Kong is higher than Singapore* *(she's got HK$4,630 per month here, which is equivalent to SGD$810)."*

Working from 6.00 am to 10-10.30 pm each day is exhausting for many, but for Lily, it's still better than her job in Singapore. Like most of the helpers here, Lily also needs to have her meals separately in the kitchen albeit with the same food rather than the leftovers or instant noodles. During the semi-lockdown, Lily's workload had been increased as well. Sterilisation was required to be combined with all her job duties including taking care of the child, serving, cooking, cleaning, doing laundry and buying daily necessities, and the working hours certainly became longer. Because children are believed to be a more vulnerable group to the virus and Lily's employers were very nervous about their child, Lily hadn't been allowed to go out on Sundays when the confirmed cases of COVID-19 kept rising. Instead, she was asked to work on her rest days. But then, Lily told me joyfully, *"You know, the best thing about Hong Kong is your boss will give you extra money if you work on Sunday!"*

I can't find the precise words to describe my feelings when I knew Lily's story and her attitude towards it, but I'm sure I can't think of any person I've known who finds happiness as easily as Lily.

I left Victoria Park at around 5.00 pm. At that time, Alice had already finished taking photos for her friends. When I stood up and was ready to leave, however, Alice discovered that there was a little steamed rice sticking on my dress (it was probably from the cloth I was sitting on). She then hurriedly asked all her nearby friends whether they had wipes. I saw a helper quickly brought a new pack of wipes to Alice, and Alice said to me: *"Let me help you"*. I could feel that she almost put the word "Madam" after that sentence as it is customary for her. Then my guiltiest moment came—Alice walked behind me and kneeled to wipe the rice off my dress. And it was too late when I realised it.

Alice and Lily said "thank you" to me again, and so did other helpers who were sitting near me. The little boy felt a bit disappointed to see me leaving, so he pretended that he didn't see me at all. His jeh jeh pointed at an empty coffee can and said,

"Thanks for your coffee". I said "goodbye" and waved to everyone who was around. That's how my four-hour field trip ended.

After more than one hour, I finally arrived at home with severe headache, and it didn't get better when I had a rest. Then I realised that, as a person who hasn't been accustomed to sun glare with high humidity like this kind, I may have got heat stroke. Ow!

PART TWO: THE POWERFUL AND THE POWERLESS

Domination in modern society is enacted through the widely dispersed powers of many agents mediating the decisions of others. To that extent many people have some power in relation to others, even though they lack the power to decide policies or results. The powerless are those who lack authority or power even in this mediated sense, those over whom power is exercised without their exercising it; the powerless are situated so that they must take orders and rarely have the right to give them.

Iris Young

5. Dried mangoes, David Bowie and Sixto Rodriguez

Wednesday, 8 July 2020

I met Lucille again on a weekday afternoon, as her kind employer allowed her to do so. Food became our conversation starter because of the gifts I received from Lucille. They included two packs of dried mangoes and a pack of Spanish-style shortbread called polvoron (I tried it at night, it's tasty!), all from the Philippines. Lucille pointed at the gifts, introducing them to me, *"Novia, the dried mango is very famous in the Philippines. Please try this. The sweets are not that sweet, don't worry. If you try them and find that you don't like them, you can throw them away, but I just want you to try."* Throw away? No way! As a big fan of the Filipino dried mangoes, I can't describe how excited I was to receive them as a gift.

Lucille was so pleased to hear that dried mangoes are one of my favourite snacks. I think she began to like me more because I love the food that she loves. More than that, I love the music that she loves. David Bowie is like a magical spell bringing us to another space. By mentioning his name, we can both get the pass to walk through the wall of King's Cross Station Platform 9¾, catching the train of friendship to explore our unseen spiritual world.

Lucille is an old soul. She loves the music of David Bowie and Queen (well, you know, the band not Queen Elizabeth II). Her favourite song is Under Pressure sung by David Bowie and Queen. She believes their live performance is one of the greatest performances of all time. I thought of the people I met in New Zealand who love David Bowie as well. My best friend Gary (my flatmate in NZ), some of my previous colleagues, and a lovely stranger who sells handmade cards and notebooks designed by herself. They are all genuine and wonderful people, like Lucille. I still remember several years ago, how I rejoiced in finding a handmade notebook with an embroidery of David Bowie's iconic look (hint: the cover of Aladdin Sane) in a Sunday market, and how delighted the artistic stranger was because of meeting another Bowie fan. I bought that notebook, and the nice stranger gave me another one with different patterns as a gift. She said, "Thank you for appreciating my work." Then we hugged each other, for Bowie. That was a beautiful day.

To my surprise, like Gary and me, Lucille also loves Sixto Rodrigues, the musician who was so influential and so inspiring during the anti-apartheid movement in South Africa but who wasn't aware of his popularity for 25 years. *"I knew Rodriguez when I was at university. My aunt used to listen to it,"* said Lucille. *"He's so awesome, so admirable, and so down to earth."* Talking about music with Lucille made me wallow in nostalgia. She relates to the golden days when I was living in an old house with my partner, Gary, and Cassie (my cat). I love every creature in that house, I love those records and old books there, and I love the smiley faces drawn by Gary on the eggs. Speakers can be found in every room, and there are even two in the kitchen. Gary made them. He is talented at making speakers, and he is probably the only person alive in Christchurch who can fix speakers made in the 40s. I also love Gary's taste in music. I used to feel like the best DJ in New Zealand was playing songs for me. He never raised my rent (he's the head tenant, and somehow, he insisted that he should pay more rent than us), so I raised it by myself. As a return, I got a music room decorated by Gary. He said, *"Hey, just in case you have a "cold war" with Alan or need another room to stay, that's your music room or study room now."* Gary himself, is somewhat like Rodriguez. He's down to earth, he likes helping people, and he's admirable.

Lucille didn't tell me of her love of music the first time we conversed. But I know more about her today, and I believe there's so much more to know as her friend. Now, Lucille is more multidimensional to me. She's more than a helper, she's more than a woman who likes hiking, and she's more than a person who's from the Philippines. Apart from music, Lucille is also a booklover and dog person. She told me that she always reads some English books in her spare time. And her current employer, Ms. Peggy, lets this happen. Peggy is like Lucille's friend now, but because of the employment relationship, Lucille prefers to refer to Peggy as her boss. Peggy is the best employer I've ever heard of till now. She allows her helper to enjoy doing this job; she gives Lucille enough time to relax; she trusts Lucille in many aspects; she celebrates Lucille's birthday every year; and she's very nice to Lucille's friends as well. She invites Lucille's friends to dine in restaurants; she hangs out with them, treating them as equal human beings. During the semi-lockdown, Peggy provided face masks to Lucille's friends when masks were hard to get, and she also provides food to them when they don't have enough food to eat. She's such a sympathetic, caring person.

"My boss used to listen to Chinese songs only, but now she listens to lots of English songs because of my recommendation. She said she loves the songs I shared with her, including Bowie's songs. And I'm happy about this," said Lucille. *"My boss said she's changed a lot since she met me. She likes sports more, and she's more confident than before. Also, she thinks her English has improved."*

However, this kind of employer-employee relationship isn't approved of by many of Peggy's friends. Lucille added, *"A few of them didn't say too much, but more people think my boss shouldn't be that kind to me,"* Lucille stopped for a while to think about the right word, and she continued with a bit of indignation, *"They think my boss is manipulated by me. They said if my boss is too good to me, she'll find it difficult to control me, and I'll become lazier and less obedient. Also, they said I have too much break time. But hello?! That's not fair to say that to me. I work more than 8 hours every day. I don't want more rights. I just want to be treated as a human. Yes, I'm a helper, but I am a human too!"*

Lucille's repeated mention of her identity as a human made me curious about her other forms of self-identities. I told her how I identify myself before asking her: "I think my first identity is a human, my second identity is a woman, and my third identity...well, it's always changing. I haven't decided it yet. How about you, Lucille?"

"Hmm, we're all humans. So, I won't go on emphasising it. I would say, first of all, I'm an Asian. Then...I'm an independent woman. Third, I'm a good friend," Lucille said with a big smile.

I smiled too. Lucille didn't mention her identity as a Filipino. I thought about my answer and I noticed that I didn't mention my ethnic identity or national identity either. It is not that I wanted to deny any, but that my ethnic identity just didn't come first as my identities as "a human" and "a woman" did. Maybe my ethnic identity as a Chinese comes after the first two identities. But it didn't occur to me at that very moment. It is a fact that I'm a Chinese, and it is also a fact that I'm a human and a woman simultaneously. I can't deny facts. I can be who I am with all the contextual and fluid self-identities, but above all, I want to perceive myself as a human first—an identity that includes other people rather than excludes others.

With no mention about her national identity, Lucille's answer may offend some chauvinists for they may think that Lucille tried to deny her national identity on purpose (they may be offended by my answer as well). I suppose Lucille's reason is pretty much the same—she wasn't thinking about her national identity, or it's just not as important as her other identities at that moment. Yes, she's a Filipino, and to be more specific, she's a Filipino working as a domestic helper in Hong Kong. No one is going to deny it. But she would be more than happy to be seen as a human, an Asian, an independent woman, and a good friend before she's identified as a Filipino or a Filipino helper.

Then Virginia Woolf, the great independent female writer came to my mind. She was invited, though no one could see her presence. She smiled at us and said, *"As a woman I have no country. As a woman I want no country. As a woman my country is the whole world."*[35] Virginia Woolf was a genius! I guess women's self-perceptions must have developed in a very different way from men. For centuries, women have belonged to a disadvantaged group (it is still a fact in many societies nowadays), and had been not allowed or encouraged to do anything serious in their countries. Contributing to a country had been the responsibility of only men and many rights had been particularly men's privileges. Our female ancestors couldn't have been as patriotic as our male ancestors, because their countries told them, "It's none of your business. Go home and take care of your husbands and children. That's all you need to!" Thus, downplaying our national identity and highlighting other identities are just inherited from our female ancestors, aren't they?

For Lucille, the pity is that very few people from mainstream society view her in a way as she expected. *"I hope they can see that I'm more than a Filipino helper,"* she said with some expectation.

"What will happen if more Hong Kong people can see your other identities?" I asked.

"If that happens, that will be great! Understanding and respect are mutual. I think I'll be more willing to understand their identities and their struggles if they respect me. It's the same for other helpers. We'll be their friends if they try to understand us. I mean, they just need to try…they don't even need to really understand… But it seems most Chinese people here don't care about it," she replied, pointing at her T-shit and skirt, *"even I wear like this, when I walk on the street, I can feel some people don't like it. I know what they're thinking about me, but I don't care. My boss's friends sometimes look at me in a weird way if I dress up. But you see, it's hard, Novia. It's hard for them to view us like equal human beings. Those people don't look at Chinese women in that way, only me and my friends."*

Having exchanged ideas with Lucille in different topics, I found that she's an independent woman with global knowledge and global civil spirit. However, to my surprise, she showed less political knowledge about Hong Kong, the place she has lived for more than ten years. Unlike Alice who knows the difference between "yellow ribbon" (pro-democracy camp in Hong Kong), and "blue ribbon" (pro-government camp), Lucille said that she hadn't heard of these concepts. I presume she did in some occasions. She just didn't want to dig into the details. So, I explained these concepts to her. *"Ah! I see! But I'm still confused about the recent protest. I saw it on TV, it's in Chinese. And I still don't understand what those young people were fighting for,"* said Lucille. Her English level and general curiosity definitely allow her to search relevant information if she wants, but she's demotivated. Then I explained to her what the national security law is. To let her understand better, I mentioned the Anti-terrorism Act 2020 in the Philippines—some of the terms are very concerning because they can be used to limit Philippine citizens' freedom of speech and intimidate dissidents—which is as controversial as the national security law (I did some research about the Philippines before meeting her this time). Lucille soon got it, a simple task! Her attitudes had some subtle changes, and I could feel them. They're a mixture of understanding, connection, but some hesitations due to her past unpleasant experiences in this familiar and alien city. I suppose her rationality and emotions were fighting to take the wheel. Let's hope our rationality always wins.

Ms. Peggy should be a rational person. I'm glad to know that she hasn't changed her attitudes towards Lucille even under peer pressure. Ms. Peggy is still doing what she thinks it's right: a domestic helper should be fairly treated and respected with dignity. Some of Peggy's friends have also hired helpers. I suppose one of the reasons they want to persuade Ms. Peggy to be stricter with Lucille is that they probably do not want to face the darker side of their personalities; or in other words, they do not want to admit that they're wrong and they should've been better to their helpers. Ms. Peggy reminds them of unwanted morality, and their theories about how to treat helpers are on shaky ground. For these people, assimilating Peggy by changing her attitudes towards her helper perhaps is the easiest way to let them feel better about themselves. So, they don't have to inspect themselves at midnight and ask, "Am I really right?"

Those people who disregard Lucille's identity as a human probably like dried mangoes as well, but I bet they don't listen to the songs of David Bowie or Sixto Rodriguez.

Debt and Tyrants

Through having a conversation with Lucille for the second time, more details about her early experience in Hong Kong began to surface. Lucille mentioned that she was so in debt in the first year when I first met her. I thought it was only because she needed to pay to her agency. But I didn't know how much the agency fee was, nor did I know other information about this. When Lucille told me the amount of her agency fee, I was stunned. That was in 2006, before getting her first job in Hong Kong, Lucille paid a Filipino agency 150,000 pesos, which is equivalent to HK$24,000 today. She borrowed money from her parents and one of her cousins, and paid the ridiculously extortionate agency fee by cash in her home country. Back then, domestic workers' monthly minimum wage was HK$3,400.[36] The agency fee was like Lucille's seven-month salary. Based on Lucille's words, at that time, the errant and illegal helper agencies in both the Philippines and Hong Kong were more rampant than now due to lax regulation. Some agencies charged more fees, some less. *"It depends upon the agencies and the helper's luck. We wouldn't know. Even the agency fee is not much, some agencies would charge us lots of training fees or some other types of fees that we can't predict,"* Lucille sighed.

However, the agency fee is only part of the story, and it's not the debt that Lucille especially referred to. As I described in the first chapter, Lucille was abused and treated like a slave. And when it rains, it pours.

On a Sunday of the first year, Lucille met a Filipino helper in a church. They speak the same language, come from the same place, and had similar type of employers. Soon, they became friends. One day, this new friend was crying and told Lucille that she needed help because her grandma was in hospital and needed money paying for a surgery. Lucille was so worried about her friend and wanted to help her. *"She asked me if I could help her borrow some money because she already borrowed lots of money by herself and she needed to use another name to borrow more money. She said what I only needed to do is to accompany her to go to a bank and sign my name,"* continued Lucille, *"you know, it's about her family. And it's about elderly people. Every time I heard something happening on elderly people, my heart breaks. But I was too young. I didn't know humanity a lot. So, I agreed and went to a bank with her and used my name as a borrower."*

"What happened then?"

"She paid the loan for the first month only, and then she went back to the Philippines without telling me. I only knew this from other

people. I couldn't find her. And I used my name to take out loans from the bank. It was HK$30,000. I had to pay the loan off by myself because it's under my name." It was a long silence after this. I looked into Lucille's eyes, making sure that she's OK.

She then added, *"I had no way but to tell my parents and my cousin that I had to pay back their money much later. I'm lucky I have a good family. They didn't blame me that I didn't send any money to them in the first year. At that time, I only got several hundreds of Hong Kong dollars after paying back to the bank. You know how my first boss treated me. I didn't have enough sleep. I didn't have enough food. But I can't resign. If I terminated my contract at that time, I'd have to pay to the agency the re-placement fee, which is at least HK$6,000. I can't put myself in more debt. And I can't go back to the Philippines like the person who made me get into such a difficult situation. I have pride, Novia. I can't go back like that."*

"That's really hard, Lucille… How did you get through this?"

"I have another cousin who's working in Hong Kong also. And I have a very good friend. They helped me a lot. They always comforted me and encouraged me. Every Sunday, they bought me lots of food. They knew that I didn't have enough food at my employer's place, and they knew that I didn't have enough money to buy food. I'm lucky to have them. Otherwise, I'm not sure how I could survive. That was the most difficult time in my life."

Living with fear, pressure, exhaustion, and despair, Lucille's first year in Hong Kong was more than a painful ordeal. The second year was still an ordeal, but with the loan paid off, at least Lucille could see a little light at the end of the tunnel. She could think about the possibilities to terminate the contract. Only imagining the scene to break the contract with her abusive employer could she feel joy. Nonetheless, she was only at the stage of thinking. She didn't do it.

It's been more than ten years till now. Lucille's misery is still repeated by many unlucky helpers in this international modern city. I don't know how many people are still scammed by their unethical agencies or so-called friends. I wonder if destiny is too harsh to these domestic workers. They have to be lucky to have a supportive family first; then they need to be lucky enough to find a good agency; after that, they need to be luckier to work for a good employer; and they also need the best of luck not to become the target of financial frauds or loan sharks. Luck may be randomly distributed among people. Apparently, however, the chance for marginalised people to get good luck is much lower than the non-marginalised group.

Lucille also told me some stories about her friends. A friend of Lucille is actually not a newcomer in Hong Kong. Yet bad luck has made her still live like many of the newcomers who often don't have enough sleep or enough food. Lucille's friend sometimes must eat the leftovers in the fridge that have been there 5 days, and sometimes the leftovers are from unknown places. Another friend of Lucille, who is not a newcomer either, is facing the problems like overwork and verbal abuse every day. *"If the law allowed her, she would move out immediately and rent a room by her own, even though she may need to spend most of her salary. I told these two friends not to put up with it. I also told them how to defend their rights. Sometimes my friends are at my boss's apartment, and my boss's friends are there too. I still say what I want to say to my friends. Or I deliberately say something in front of them because I hope they can realise that they are not good employers and then treat their helpers better. I know they'd overhear my conversation between me and my friends, and I know what they'd think about me. Sometimes, they told my boss that I was teaching other helpers to be less good. Even if my boss didn't tell me this, I could know it from observing their facial expressions. You know, full of disdain."*

For a certain type of employers (just like those mentioned in last paragraph), a helper knowing how to defend her legal rights is not welcomed. And it will become even more offensive if this helper suggests that other helpers safeguard their rights or is able to impart some liberal ideas. It just doesn't look right to them, as they see it as an attempt to weaken their power or turn against them. They're like tyrants in their own little tiny kingdoms, using every single way to protect their authority and precluding every possible fight against the ruling class. If we read John Locke's definition of tyranny, we'll find that it is very reasonable to associate one with another:

...tyranny is the exercise of power beyond right, which nobody can have a right to; and this is making use of the power any one has in his hands, not for the good of those who are under it, but for his own private, separate advantage.[37]

Surely, I do not intend to talk about the literal tyrants here, as it is not the focus of this book. But we can see that there is a similar pattern between the real tyrants and the tyrannical employers of the domestic helpers—they all want those who are under their power to only remember duties not rights. And if they can, they would love to wipe the word "rights" from the memory of the powerless people.

Tyrannical employers of the helpers share the similar fear with those tyrants who fear that the ruled may awaken someday realising they are exploited and abused by power, and that they might be overthrown by angry people. Unsurprisingly, both of them share similar attitudes towards the people who are supposed to be controlled. They perceive awareness of human rights as dangerous, spreading the awareness among people as subversive, and knowing how to unite other people to defend their rights as absolutely sinful. To prevent something unwanted happening, tyrannical employers and tyrants themselves all take some common measures to stabilise their power: monopolising truth and facts, stifling the spread of critical thoughts and information, and attacking potential opponents. Nothing is new. In a nutshell, they all repel people who demand rights or challenge their authority.

I suddenly recalled something I saw from a website (Helperchoice), an online platform for employers and domestic workers to match one another. On the page of "domestic helper contract termination", there are invalid reasons listed for employers to read. It says, "It is strictly illegal to terminate your foreign domestic workers in the following cases: 1. she is on sick leave; 2. she is injured; 3. she is pregnant; 4. she belongs to or has joined a trade union."[38] The fourth one is overwhelming to me. I must admit that I'm more familiar with the first three excuses. But if it's listed as one of the invalid reasons for employers to dismiss their foreign helpers, it usually suggests that the phenomenon has existed for some time and thus it needs a legally binding document to deter some potential irresponsible employers. This online platform doesn't exaggerate, I then found these items from a government document—Practical Guide for Employment of Foreign Domestic Helpers.[39] Nonetheless, I wonder how many employers and newly-arrived employees have read this official guide.

Dismissing a helper for joining a union sounds very tyrannical itself, as only tyrants are afraid of the organisations helping people to defend their rights. It is worth nothing that becoming a member of a union just means the possibilities to be more aware of what their labour rights are and how to guard their labour rights, yet as mentioned earlier, these kinds of possibilities are deemed as unwanted by some employers. Even though tyrannical employers may realise that their helpers joining a union doesn't necessarily lead to a confrontation between them and their helpers, they would rather not take any risks to weaken their power.

Generally speaking, the aim of a union is to improve the working conditions and securing the fair pay of workers. Ideally, if employers who treat their domestic helpers unfairly are willing to respect their helpers' rights, the union won't need to bother them. It will be a win-win situation. However, the paradox is that those employers with the characteristics of tyrants usually refuse to make a change. In this case, unions or other forms of legal organisations have no way but to interfere in unlawful or unfair treatment in the workplace. In societies where the employer-employee relationship is more equal, some may say that any group could be the "tyrant". But I'm afraid that it is not the case for migrant domestic workers in Hong Kong.

Through the same online platform Helperchoice, I found some advice for both employers and helpers in terms of "legal placement fee charged by domestic helper agencies". It informs domestic helpers how much of the placement fee is lawful and in what kind of situations helpers need to pay the placement fee. And it kindly reminds helpers that they will put themselves in more debt if they are overcharged by unethical agencies. In fact, choosing an unethical agency will do harm to both employers and employees. But local employers are less likely to take out loans because of this. I mean, logically speaking, employers don't have to borrow money from loan sharks or agencies to hire a domestic helper working for them. By contrast, helpers' situation is very different from the start. Most helpers have been dealing with poverty for years and are desperately in need of a job which can feed their family. Aside from this, unlike their counterparts having impacted by what they see and hear in this international financial hub, multitudes of migrant domestic workers don't have financial literacy and therefore they're more vulnerable to unlawful lending companies.

On the web page suggesting how employers should help their domestic workers, two sentences drew my attention: "Some employers think that an indebted helper is good because debts prevent her from running away. This is a very harmful misconception."[40] The second sentence is highlighted in bold (thanks to it), which shows the attitude of this online platform towards indebted helpers. Yet the first sentence entails a kind of appalling thought amongst some certain employers who are indifferent, unscrupulous, and tyrannical. They may happen to be the same group of employers who tend to abuse their helpers. "Run away" is an interesting phrase. It usually collocates with something unpleasant. If a helper is happy, she doesn't need to run away; if she is satisfied with her job, she doesn't need to run away; and if she is treated humanely, she doesn't need to run away! The helper and her employer may not get along well, or they may not like each other. Yet the helper doesn't have to run away if her working hours are tolerable, if she can sleep on a real bed, if she has enough food to eat, if she isn't beaten or insulted, and if she is allowed to enjoy holidays. Letting a domestic worker want to run away signifies a failure to be a good employer, whilst the intention to stop the helper from "running away" by making use of her indebtedness is completely ruthless.

Tyrannical employers may have a delusion that they own their domestic helpers, just like how tyrants mistake that the people ruled by them are their property. Watching their belongings run away is definitely not what they want, so they try to use every tool to prevent it from happening. Helpers' debt then becomes something positive and pleasant to those tyrannical employers, for the debt facilitates their control over their desperate helpers. The thing is, in many cases, tyrannical employers are probably conscious of what they are doing to their domestic workers, but they prefer not to care. Otherwise, the online platform for both helpers and employers would not have to highlight the misconception that "an indebted helper is good because debts prevent her from running away".

It should be acknowledged that the nature of migrant domestic workers' job is de facto unequal, as the live-in rule without limiting their maximum working hours is most likely to let the helpers be exploited by their employers. Likewise, helpers' relationship with their employers is also based on inequality: one has more power and dominance over the other. The live-in rule and two-week rule are the power bestowed by the government of Hong Kong upon employers. And the state of being in debt only worsens the difficult situation of the helpers. When debt teams with tyrant-like employers, it will only make domestic workers more disadvantaged and more powerless. I do hope that unions will be helpful under this circumstance and that a decent domestic worker will not be dismissed for being a member of a union.

6. The Boundary of Being OK

Sunday, 12 July 2020   Temperature: 33°C   Humidity: 67%

Last Sunday, Alice mentioned a union that helps Indonesian helpers who are abused or unfairly treated in Hong Kong. I am very interested in how it works. And Alice said she would love to introduce someone from the union to me. So, I went to Victoria Park again today. Having learned a lesson from last Sunday, I managed to avoid the hottest time of the day to join the helpers' gathering. It was earlier than 10.30 in the morning when I arrived there, and I bought more iced coffee this time. However, Alice, Lily, the little boy, and some other familiar faces were not there.

I didn't tell Alice I would be there today even though I have her contact information which allows me to do that. Then I realised Alice had sent me a text message saying she was doing Zumba in Wan Chai, and that she wouldn't arrive at Victoria Park until 2.00 pm. After mentally punching myself for being too silly and arrogant for a while, I decided to rely on myself to find the hidden union. And as you may have expected, I failed.

I asked different helpers whether they knew any people from the union there. Two young women pointed at a group of people and suggested that I approach them and ask. But language was a big barrier between me and that group. Nobody understood what I was talking about at first, especially when I mentioned "union". And after I changed my wording and asked them whether they knew any domestic workers who helped others to get better treatment. They thought I was there to hire a helper. Through the use of a mix of gestures and language, I finally made my point relatively clearly (I think), and the group of helpers told me that they did not know anyone like that. So, I gave them some coffee and left. Later, I passed by the two young women who had offered me advice before. They looked a bit sorry because they couldn't help me. To make them feel better, I gave them two cans of iced coffee, and naturally we started to chat.

These two young women sitting together have the same names, but to protect their privacy and make it easier for readers, let's call them Eva and Evelyn. Eva and Evelyn are all sorts of "newcomers" in Hong Kong (helpers are thought to be "newcomers" in the first two years working in HK). Eva had been working in Singapore for 3 years before coming to Hong Kong, but similar to Siti and Alice, she wasn't entitled to have any holidays while working there. Like many others who have learned English while working in Singapore, Eva also had learned some English on her first overseas experience so I did not need to use too much body language when I talked with her. However, I do not plan to go into much detail of her life in Singapore this time. Instead, I intend to explore more Eva's current experience in Hong Kong as she's still working for her first employer. I have been curious about a newcomers' probability of meeting a good employer in their first two years in Hong Kong, and whether luck plays a part.

Eva works from 6.15 to 22.00 every day, which, I'm afraid, is not the most shocking timetable among newcomers (if you still remember Lucille's experience). I asked Eva whether she has one hour for lunch break or dinner break. She looked at me as if I were a naive little girl who knows nothing about the cruel world. *"One hour? No way! 15 minutes only for a lunch break. The same with dinner break!"* exclaimed Eva. To double check I didn't misunderstand the information, I asked Eva, "You mean fifteen minutes not fifty, right?" Eva nodded, and so did Evelyn. Even though I had already heard about Lucille's misfortune, I still find it jaw-dropping that a person needs to work for such long hours a day with such short breaks. Worse than that, the timetable has to be repeated six days a week.

"But why? Why there's so much work to keep you busy? Why?" I tried to control my emotions.

"I don't know," said Eva with a shrug. *"They pay me. They don't want to waste money. So, I work, work and work…"*

"Do you have the same food as your employer at the same time?" I asked.

"No" answered Eva.

I began to worry that Eva may be provided with only leftovers and instant noodles. To make sure my concern wasn't true, I asked Eva: "Do they give you leftovers or instant noodles as food?" But Eva didn't understand the word "leftovers", nor did Evelyn. Having failed to guess the meaning, Eva suggested that I write the word down so that she could Google it. Both of these two young women knew the meaning of "leftovers" very soon. Then Eva looked at me and said: *"No, they don't give me leftovers or instant noodles."* So, what is the mysterious food that Eva has?

The truth is Eva's employer doesn't provide her with any food most of the time. As stated by the Hong Kong government, apart from the monthly minimum allowable wage of HK$4,630 (announced after 27 September 2019), employers are required to provide free food to foreign domestic helpers (FWHs). If they don't, they should pay them a food allowance of HK$1,121 per month in lieu. In practice, like what the Hong Kong government indicates: "the vast majority of employers provide free food to FDHs."[41] I also believe it is more common for employers to provide free food rather than a food allowance, though we all know that the HK government doesn't specify what kind of free food should be given or how much food is deemed to be called enough. As a result of this vague official language (even though the language is not vague, it may still be hard to fully guarantee or implement such a policy in a private dwelling), some unfortunate helpers only have leftovers and instant noodles as free and "enough" food. Eva, however, has no free food or a food allowance, which she should have in this case.

"I buy food for myself every month," said Eva.

When I asked her whether she would seek help or justice about this, Eva told me: *"It's OK for me lah. I don't eat a lot."*

"But you work a lot, and you need more energy from food. You may need to have four meals to work for so long time," I said emotionally.

"It's OK lah. I don't have time to have four meals. Sometimes I'm hungry, but I forget to eat things because I'm too busy. Sir say he can

give me some food if I want. But I don't like the food he give me. So, I buy food for myself every month," said Eva calmly.

"Do you know anyone who gets food allowance?" I asked.

"No. My friends have free food. Some get enough food, some get one meal or two meals a day, and some get leftovers and instant noodles. I hope they can get food allowance so they can buy the food they like," replied Eva.

"Do you hope you can get food allowance?" I continued to ask.

"I hope lah. But it's OK. After a few months, my two-year contract will end. I want to go back to Indonesia to see my family first, and then I want to find another employer in Hong Kong. I hope my next employer will be better," said Eva wishfully.

Eva's current situation is definitely not OK. Some must wonder why Eva didn't resign her job and change to another employer. It is a reasonable assumption that in an ideal society all employees, no matter where they come from, are well protected by employment law and free to choose their employers. Yet it is not the case for migrant domestic workers here. The job market for helpers is always one-directional. They cannot be as picky as their employers because in most cases, they are not in a position to be able to select the people they want to work for. Once they terminate their contracts prematurely (to complete their contract, they usually need to work for two years), they may need to pay their agencies up to HK$6,000 to find another employer—or to be more precise, a new employer needs to find them—except if they can provide solid evidence to prove that they have been abused. Some types of abuse, however, including working unreasonably long hours, not having enough food, and verbal abuse are hard to be proved, especially in a private home. Even if a helper can provide solid evidence of abuse, whether they need to pay a re-placement fee will largely depend on how moral their agency is. On top of that, let's not forget about the two-week rule made by the Immigration Department of HKSAR: migrant domestic workers must leave Hong Kong if they cannot find a new employer and get an updated visa within two weeks. Going back to their home countries to find the new employer and wait for the new visa means that a great amount of money is going to be spent, which poses a difficult dilemma for helpers: to tolerate unscrupulous employers or unscrupulous agencies? Therefore, as it stands, there are not so many abused helpers who are willing to terminate their contracts if they think they still can tolerate their situation and their employers.

I don't know how many helpers are tolerating abuse, but I'm pretty sure that Eva is not the only one. Having recalled Alice's comments about Indonesian helpers, I began to wonder about what Alice had implied when she mentioned "we are too weak". Did she mean that Indonesian helpers are not strong-willed enough to fight for what they deserve? Or did she mean that Indonesian helpers do not have the power or influence, and that weakness is just a result of powerlessness?

Erwiana's Abuse Case

Before jumping to conclusions, let's review Erwiana's case. In 2014, an Indonesian woman named Erwiana Sulistyaningsih grabbed the headlines worldwide for being severely abused by her female employer, Law Wan-tung, for eight months in Hong Kong. Erwiana was forced to sleep on the floor, frequently humiliated and beaten for making a mistake or responding too slowly, deprived of all holidays and rest days, coerced into giving up contact with her family and friends, and allowed to sleep for only three hours a day. Beyond that, she suffered from hunger all the time as her employer only gave her little food. Regarding how outrageous the physical abuse was, here is a quote from The Guardian:

> Court heard that Sulistyaningsih suffered broken teeth, scratches all over body and blows to her head at the hands of Law, who also jammed a metal vacuum cleaner tube into her mouth, causing her lip to bleed. On one occasion, Law also forced Sulistyaningsih to stand naked in the bathroom during winter while she splashed water on her and pointed a fan at her.[42]

Erwiana wasn't allowed to see a doctor when her injuries became too severe to work. She barely could walk at that point. So, her employer had no way but to send Erwiana back to Indonesia by giving her a flight ticket and HK$70 (I've no idea what this HK$70 is for). At the airport, the abandoned poor young woman with battered body and bruised face was noticed by another Indonesian helper.[42] This was when the ill-treatment of Erwiana was finally brought into the spotlight.

The abuse case was revealed. However, Erwiana wasn't taken seriously at first after being encouraged and escorted by her friend to seek help from Hong Kong police. The HK government and the police didn't take actions immediately and their pretext was that Erwiana hadn't called the police before so her case couldn't be that serious. Was Erwiana too weak-minded to rescue herself as someone perhaps is imaging? In fact, Erwiana realised how bad her situation was within the first five weeks. She didn't want to put up with it at all. She tried to ask for help by telling her agency what she had been through. In Erwiana's interview, she said:

> Within the first five weeks I escaped to the lobby downstairs and used the security guard's phone. I called the agency in Hong Kong asking to change employer. They told me it was too hard to do.[43]

Under this circumstance, I do not intend to use "weak" to describe Erwiana or anyone like her, because "weak" as referring to her like that sounds callous and brutal. Imagine if we ourselves had been in her shoes. Logically speaking, how can a migrant domestic worker convince herself/himself that the local police will help them when they are excluded from local employment law and not even on the waiting list to become "ordinary residents" in Hong Kong? If we had been in the same situation as Erwiana was, what would we have done? The truth is there wouldn't have been much we could have done. Erwiana was in so much debt and was told that leaving her abusive employer was nearly impossible. Since neither her government nor the Hong Kong government cared about her, I think I would use "hopeless" instead of "weak" to describe Erwiana's situation.

Erwiana came to Hong Kong with so much hope, but evidently her hope let her down. Her own government, her agency and the HK government all let her down. In her interview, Erwiana expressed her dissatisfaction with Indonesian government's inaction:

That kind of problem is caused by the Indonesian government. They pass the responsibility of training to the agency. They don't provide good training – their concern is only about profit. And we are the ones who need the job… The Indonesian government continues to act the same, but they are being pressured. I really hope there will be no more cases like mine. They really need to take responsibility and not just be after profit. They exploit those of us who are poor. [43]

Erwiana's employer, however, more than "let her down". Law abused her and intimidated her; meanwhile Erwiana was too isolated from Indonesian helpers' community to seek advice or help. Erwiana's employer probably believed that the scale of justice is tilted in favour of the employers in Hong Kong rather than the foreign domestic workers, so she recklessly showed her sadistic side to Erwiana. Or she simply believed that as long as she's sneaky enough and kept her offence behind closed doors, no one would find out about it. But what made Law believe like that? Aside from Hong Kong's laws, such as the live-in rule and the two-week rule, systematic discrimination may also have strengthened Law's errant belief. However, there was something else that made Law believe that she could flout the law with impunity.

Erwiana was not the first helper abused by Law. In fact, Law Wan-tung abused a number of helpers to different degrees before Erwiana. Apart from Erwiana, another two former helpers of Law also appeared at the hearing, but only Tutik was confirmed as another victim by the court. When working for Law, Tutik wasn't allowed to have any rest days. She was beaten (less severely compared to Erwiana) and her parents' lives were threatened by Law. And she was forbidden to use her own phone. Tutik finally escaped because her family demanded that the agency in Hong Kong intervene after having failed to contact Tutik for a long time.[44] However, all the abuse that Tutik suffered had been kept unknown to the public till Erwiana's case came to light. What saddens me about the cases of Erwiana and Tutik is not only Hong Kong's policy failure to ensure domestic workers' human rights but also the indifference of the witnesses and the agency. When Tutik worked for Law, if there were visitors/friends at Law's flat, Tutik would be locked in a room to clean it, but no one said anything.[45] Law didn't need to face the consequences for abusing Tutik because no one unveiled her evil secret, which encouraged her to continue abusing her next helper to a larger extent. When Erwiana worked for Law, Erwiana once knocked at her neighbour's door at 2.00 am to ask for food because she was starving at that time and couldn't find any of food that she was allowed to eat at Law's apartment.[46] The neighbour didn't say anything nor did anything, except to give her food. Likewise, the agency didn't do anything for Erwiana. On the contrary, it was the agency that placed Erwiana in Law's apartment despite knowing how the former helper, Tutik, was treated by Law. How many else could have and should have helped Erwiana and people like her but ended up doing nothing? We won't know.

Then the opposite case of indifference I experienced in New Zealand occurred to me. One day I was having a "cold war" in public with my partner Alan (we didn't quarrel with each other on the street, but we were in a sulk). He was attempting to hold my hand while I was trying hard to push his hand away. My actions caught a kiwi woman's attention. She came over to ask me whether I needed any help and had a serious look on her face. I said no and expressed my gratitude to her, but she didn't leave us immediately. She stayed around just to confirm that I didn't need any help before leaving, as she seemed to worry that I might feel threatened or feel too scared to tell the truth. I don't know her name yet, but if one day I could meet her again, I want to let her know how grateful I was (even though I didn't need help at that time). I appreciated the fact that she approached me to try to help without asking me about my nationality first. Beyond that, I am pretty sure she would do exactly the same thing again if she met any person desperately in need of help like Erwiana or Tutik.

Law was found guilty of assault in February 2015. She was sentenced to six years in prison, and ordered by the court to pay HK$809,430 in damages to Erwiana and HK$170,000 to Tutik. However, it is not the end of the story. It seems Law doesn't feel guilty at all as she has never apologised to the victims. Worse than that, Law was set free in 2018 serving only about half of her sentence. The deduction of Law's sentence still remains a puzzle, and the compensation to Erwiana and Tutik still hasn't been paid.[47] The injustice may indirectly send employers a wrong message that it is not that bad to abuse domestic workers.

After Erwiana's abuse case was revealed around the world, too little has been done to guarantee the rights of FDWs in Hong Kong and prevent them from being abused. FDWs' working hours still remain unregulated; live-in rule is still non-negotiable (two-week rule eventually becomes negotiable because of COVID-19); and unscrupulous agencies still flourish. Four years after Erwiana's case, a new hotline providing 24-hour services to help and support FDWs was eventually set up in December 2018.[48] I now believe when Alice said "we are too weak", she referred to my second presupposition that they do not have power or influence whatsoever and that weakness is just a result of powerlessness. Yes, Alice is right. They are too weak!

Abuse and Its By-product

Evelyn's story is a bit different from Eva's. She didn't go to Singapore to work. Instead, she had worked in Taiwan for four years. Evelyn told me that the she didn't understand much Mandarin or English when she first arrived in Taiwan. So, the first few months in Taiwan wasn't easy for her in terms of communication. Her employer in Taiwan taught her how to speak both Mandarin and English, and gradually, she used these two languages when she went to the supermarket and communicated with her employer. Evelyn thinks that learning two languages at the same time is a mind-bending task. She said: *"For every word, my madam in Taiwan taught me how to say in Mandarin and then in English. But you know it's too difficult for me. So, I said to her 'Mam, I'm not smart like you. I can't remember so many things at the same time.' But she taught me patiently and told me I can do it. So, I practise and practise. Then, I can speak a little English and Mandarin."* After realising that I could speak Mandarin as well, Evelyn was excited, and we had a conversation in Mandarin for a while.

Evelyn came to Hong Kong because she heard that working as a domestic helper in Hong Kong allows her to have more holidays with a bit more salary. When she worked in Taiwan, she was only allowed to have two rest days a month. Even though she thought her employer in Taiwan was kind to her, she found Hong Kong very tempting when one of her friends told her that helpers in Hong Kong are entitled to 12 statutory holidays a year aside from weekly rest days and annual leave (the statutory holidays must be paid as long as an employee has been working for at least 3 months under a continuous contract[49]).

Evelyn's working experience in Taiwan and language ability soon interested a Mandarin-speaking family from mainland China, and she got a job offer from them after an online interview. However, Evelyn wasn't entitled to the statutory holidays as she had expected when she was working for her first female employer in Hong Kong. Besides this, there were some other unexpected things waiting for her. For Evelyn, she found that she had many employers at the same time as she had to work for everyone in that family, and everyone liked to boss her around, except the child. So, in this informal interview, Evelyn pluralised her employer. And I will respect Evelyn's narrative.

When I asked Evelyn how she was treated by her first employers in Hong Kong, she always emphasised that it was only her personal experience as she didn't want to mislead me into thinking that all the employers in Hong Kong are bad. Evelyn often put it, *"It's for me only lah."* Apart from cleaning and cooking, Evelyn had to serve a young couple and take care of a child as well as an elderly couple. Her workload could be heavy indeed. But apart from that, she had to deal with some exhausting and unnecessary tasks now and then, because her first employers were those who hated to see a helper relax in front of them and who happened to be experts on inventing new types of housework. Evelyn was asked to wake up at 5.30 every morning and then work to a tight schedule till 11.00 in the evening. Sometimes, she was woken up in the midnight because the child or the elderly couple needed her. Although she wasn't provided with leftovers, malnutrition was a common problem that she had to face. On public holidays, she needed to work as well, which was very different from what she had imagined before coming to Hong Kong.

Even so, Evelyn still attempted to work until the end of her contract as she thought that changing her employer would be too troublesome and expensive.

It was verbal abuse coupled with social isolation, however, that finally made her break that compromise. When Evelyn made a mistake or wasn't good enough to meet her former employers' expectations, she got verbally abused and humiliated. Perhaps they didn't think about it carefully. Perhaps they just thought scolding their helper could be a useful way to prevent her from dissatisfying them. But meanwhile, they should've also realised that they were causing harm to Evelyn, a human like them. The demeaning language used by them was directed at Evelyn's ethnic background, social status, gender, job position, religion, intelligence, and her educational background. Of course, it didn't make things better. On the contrary, Evelyn thought she was stupid, incompetent, and less respectable because what her former employers said to her made her believe that. And we probably all know that a lack of confidence is highly likely to adversely affect an individual's job performance. Evelyn didn't manage to be a perfect helper as her employers had expected, and her failure to be a perfect helper put her into a vicious circle. She felt so stressed and tired that she still made mistakes, and as a result, she couldn't escape from her former employers' verbal abuse. Evelyn told me that she thought she would never be happy again.

As for Evelyn's public holiday deprivation, from her point of view, the main reason was not that her first employers wanted to exploit her to a greater extent, but the fact that they disliked Evelyn socialising with other Indonesian helpers. Nevertheless, it was an additional de facto benefit for her first employers as they didn't even pay her extra for working on public holidays. Evelyn told me, *"My first employers are not happy if I go out on public holidays. They're afraid I'm going to learn bad things from other helpers. They say they want to protect me, I trusted them first, but then I know it's not true."*

"She can't go out on Sunday. She had no friends at that time," added Eva.

I looked at Evelyn and asked her, "If you can't go out on Sunday, what did you do? Did your first employers ask you to work on Sunday?"

"At first, I had holiday on Sunday. But when I go home, they look very angry and ask me so many questions," said Evelyn. To make me get a better picture of the attitudes of her first employers, Evelyn imitated their tone and used her index finger to point at me (it's a very common but rude gesture to see in an ethnic Chinese community when one is scolding others): *"Who did you meet? What did you talk about with them? Did they teach you any bad things? Did you do bad things together?"*

Evelyn is gifted at acting. Through her actions, the past scene is reconstructed. I did feel the pressure and tension as if I were a new helper in Hong Kong and my employers were not happy about my freedom of mobility because they suspected that my new friends would have a bad impact on me. After having joined the community of Indonesian helpers for a few Sundays, Evelyn was not allowed to have a rest day on Sunday anymore. She was permitted to have any day as her weekly rest day, except for Sunday. In doing so, Evelyn's first employers in Hong Kong believed that Evelyn would be effectively isolated and eventually lose contact with those "potentially bad friends". I can't help thinking: what kind of bad impacts were Evelyn's first employers worrying about? Their definitions of "bad" must be very different from mine.

For me, "bad" means "morally unacceptable/wrong" when it collocates with "people" or "influences on people". But for Evelyn's first employer, "bad" may mean "not beneficial" or the antonym of "obedient". "Evelyn's bad friends" (I'm not sure whether they existed) were probably seen as people who could have possibly told Evelyn how to say "no" to them; and "bad impacts" from her "bad" friends could have referred to what Evelyn may have found out from them about her rights, and thereby this may have led to her disobeying her "masters". Alternatively, "bad impacts" for her former employers could also have meant the unwanted consequences they might have needed to face if their helper found out that she could actually take legal action to protect her labour rights as a migrant worker. And they perhaps also knew really well that Evelyn was most likely to meet those "bad people" in the helpers' gatherings on Sundays and public holidays. Therefore, cutting Evelyn's possible contact with any potential "bad" helpers became a rational choice for her employers back then.

I suppose social isolation doesn't necessarily result from abuse, but if these two elements work together, they will put migrant domestic workers in a more slave-like situation and make it more difficult for FDWs to escape. It is fair to say that social isolation facilitates different kinds of abuse by minimising the victims' possible exposure to aid. For FDWs, the loss of social contact means the loss of freely exchanging information with community members, and it also means that a victim of abuse is more unlikely to get advice or help from those domestic workers who are experienced at defending their rights. As an inevitable result of social isolation, the power of the abusive and exploitative employers will increase, and they will make use of the vulnerability of the isolated helpers to maximise their abuse and exploitation.

It should be noted that the regulations pertaining to the employment of domestic workers per se are difficult to implement, as well as the fact that employment law for FDWs is discriminatory and full of loopholes. In addition to this, the lax governmental regulation of agencies in both Hong Kong and the domestic workers' home countries is questionable. Many of the agencies not only force some desperate migrant domestic workers into more debt, but also facilitate possible abuse and isolation through monopolising or withholding information. As Erwiana mentioned in her interview, some agencies do not provide good pre-service training because they only train helpers to be obedient without equally mentioning their rights. Under this circumstance, FDWs are more likely to be vulnerable to exploitation and isolation. Some deny the helpers' access to need-to-know information about their looming risks when serving certain employers. In Erwiana's case, Erwiana's agency was more like an accomplice of the perpetrator Law. Erwiana was placed to her notorious employer's apartment without any information or warning about Law's abusive record, while the agency knew exactly what happened to Law's former helper. The number of cases of abuse could be largely reduced if all agencies were willing to provide more information about each employer's character as that would allow helpers to consider whether or not to accept a position. Many would argue that it would be impossible in practise as agencies are merely profit-oriented, and doing this would not benefit them at all. However, let us not forget that currently, demand for domestic workers exceeds supply in Hong Kong, and thus economically speaking, it is certainly feasible.

Evelyn paid a large amount of money to an agency in Hong Kong. She also got pre-service training before her placement. This training mainly focussed on improving her job skills (including how to speak Cantonese and how to cook Hong Kong food), learning about the culture of Hong Kong families, how to fit into the new environment, and how to obey her employers. The agency taught Evelyn everything about her duties and how to perform them; however, it taught her nothing about her labour rights. Fortunately, Evelyn was not a new helper. She didn't believe her former employers when they told her: "Here in Hong Kong, we don't always do as we're told by the law. Many helpers need to work on public holidays without extra pay, and so do many Hong Kong people. It's very common here." It is an easy pattern used by the unscrupulous employers to manipulate their newly arrived helpers who have limited knowledge of their rights: If the intent of employers is to exploit their helpers to the maximum extent, all they need to do to achieve this is just to normalise the breach of FDWs' employment regulations or normalise the helpers' unfair treatment in Hong Kong.

Evelyn's experience in Taiwan made her realise that migrant workers in a society with the rule of law can manage to defend their labour rights. Though in many cases, migrant workers in Taiwan choose to tolerate unfair treatment as long as they can. When Evelyn arrived in Hong Kong, she could see that it was also a society with the rule of law. As such, she believed that if she were in a situation where she could no longer tolerate working ridiculously long hours, the verbal abuse and social isolation, she could do something. Nevertheless, her former employers kept telling Evelyn that she should feel grateful about them because they were already better than most employers here, and she would have a much worse employer if she changed employers.

Fortunately, Evelyn didn't believe that her former employers were better than most employers in Hong Kong. After several months of tolerating forced labour and mental stress, she found it hard to go on working for them. So, she went to her agency to ask for help. At first when she told the agency how she had been abused and isolated, she was told to try harder to accommodate her new working environment. Evelyn tried very hard for another few weeks, but she failed as we may have expected. She went to her agency again and expressed her wish to have a new employer. However, Evelyn's agency was still reluctant to place her with a new employer. *"I was crying, I remember. I told the agency I can't bear it anymore. But I was so lucky. I met my current employer that day. She came to the agency and said she want to hire a helper who's already in Hong Kong. And she likes me. She saw I cried, and she know I am not happy to work for my former boss, so she asked the agency if it's OK to hire me,"* recounted Evelyn.

Now, Evelyn's current employer doesn't abuse her verbally. She can enjoy statutory holidays as she had previously wished, and she can meet with the Indonesian helpers' community every Sunday if there is no ban of public gatherings due to the coronavirus pandemic. She has made lots of friends in Victoria Park. If there is a demonstration in Victoria Park, all the helpers who often gather in Victoria Park will make room for protesters. It's like a tacit agreement between those helpers and people from Hong Kong's mainstream society.

Yet Evelyn still needs to work long hours. Currently, she works from 6.00 to 22.00 every day albeit with a few more breaks in the daytime than before. On Sunday, Evelyn needs to get up at 6.30 to prepare breakfast for her employer's family and do the dishes after returning to her employer's apartment. Even so, Evelyn told me that she's happier than before. *"It's OK lah. The family is better to me than my last employers,"* said Evelyn, *"but... my employers in Taiwan are nicer. In Taiwan, I worked less hours a day. When I knew helpers can have more holidays in Hong Kong, I was so excited. But I forgot to ask my friend how many hours she works in Hong Kong every day haha..."*

The Teenage Bride

During the conversation with Evelyn, there was another Indonesian helper who came to join us. She's happy to be called Annisa. After Eva and Evelyn introduced me to her, Annisa soon built trust with me. I gave Annisa a can of iced coffee after saying hello to her, and then shared some cookies with all of them. Annisa was surprised and moved. She said "thank you" with gratitude sparkling in her eyes, as if she hadn't received such kindness from a stranger for a long time.

I told Eva, Evelyn and Annisa that I'd been to Indonesia before. They were excited and asked me which specific place I had gone to. I said Bali. They were a bit disappointed. In fact, it wasn't the first time I had found Indonesian helpers express a tinge of disappointment when I mentioned Bali as the only place I've been to in Indonesia. The more I mention this, the more I realise how self-centred and ignorant I am. All the Indonesian helpers looked less excited after hearing I had travelled to a place which they can't afford to go to at all. They expected to talk about something familiar with a stranger who claimed to have gone to Indonesia, but it turned out that we didn't have any shared experiences of Indonesia.

"Bali is too expensive! It's for foreigners and rich Indonesians to go. I can never go there!" exclaimed Annisa. Eva and Evelyn nodded. The funny thing is that Bali, as one of the most popular tourist destinations in this world, is well-known for its cheap food and accommodation. If we search online for comments about Bali, we'll find that so many foreign tourists are surprised by Bali's affordable prices (I must admit that I'm one of them). However, on the other hand, these Indonesian helpers don't find Bali cheap at all. To them, Bali is a distant island in their homeland and doesn't have any connection with them in the slightest. How ironic!

Annisa got married at 17. As I had found out from Alice, early marriage is prevalent, especially in underdeveloped rural areas of Indonesia. I didn't feel shocked this time. I felt sorry and sad, but not shocked. Annisa told me that she is from a poverty-stricken family. She couldn't complete secondary school because her family couldn't afford it, the same old story. One day, a strange man came to visit her home with some betrothal gifts and asked her parents to arrange a marriage for him, and then this man became Annisa's husband. Getting married is just so surprisingly easy for a powerless young woman growing up in a poor family in Indonesia.

According to UNICEF (2019), Indonesia has the eighth highest rate of early marriages in the world, with one in nine girls married before their 18th birthday, and 1% married before the age of 15 (1,459,000 in total). In 2019, the Indonesian government eventually amended the Marriage Law of 1974 raising the minimum age at which women can marry to 19 years old. Before that, Indonesian girls could get married legally at the age of 16 with parental permission.[50] I think by "parental permission", it means "parental request" in most cases. In some remote rural areas, it was rather common that Indonesian girls younger than 16 years old were "permitted" to marry if their parents requested it. Technically speaking, early marriage or child marriage is unlikely to be ended by solely relying on the law, as it is also determined by customs, economic factors, gender inequality, and parental attitudes. Nevertheless, there is hope for Indonesian girls now.

To many disadvantaged families in Indonesia, marrying off a young daughter to an adult man with some income is a good idea to ease the family's financial burden, and at the same time to honour the family. Although Indonesian citizens are required to finish 12 years of compulsory education (including 6 years of primary education and 6 years of secondary education), many citizens do not complete secondary education, especially those from underdeveloped areas. According to the OECD in 2019, approximately 26% of people aged between 25 and 64 years old have attained upper secondary education in Indonesia.[51] Amongst the people who do not attend or complete high school, the fate of many girls is similar to Annisa's: they are forced to marry early if their families are not able to afford their tuition fees. Early marriage is not only seen as a good way to help both the bride-to-be and the family escape poverty, but it is also a way to transfer the responsibility of protecting their daughter's honour to the husband (so the parents don't have to worry that their daughter might lose her virginity improperly and disgrace the family). In extreme cases, early marriage is even seen as the only way for the family to survive. However, we all know how sad it is and how it will influence the unlucky girls' futures. The parents who decide to make their daughters drop out of school and get married at a young age may not realise that most teenage brides can't really escape from poverty or improve their future prospects. The majority of them, on the contrary, are more likely to get trapped in a vicious cycle of poverty and pass on poverty to their next generation.

The thing is, early marriage hasn't secured Annisa's future as her parents had expected. In fact, poverty has never left, following Annisa quietly from her original family to her new family. Initially, Annisa's husband was the primary breadwinner, while Annisa played the traditional role of wife, mother, daughter-in-law, and caregiver in her nuclear family for many years. Her husband's income could feed the family, but only for food. They thought that was okay, because that was how most residents in that village lived. Nevertheless, when their second child was ready to attend primary school, the couple realised that if their family income didn't increase, they wouldn't be able to afford to send their children to middle school. I guess they also worried about their children's future betrothal gifts or dowry (I don't know the gender of Annisa's children) like many other parents living in a traditional village.

Annisa realised that she had to work, bringing in some income for the family. However, Annisa's dilemma was that there were not so many job opportunities for women in that village, and her lack of education excluded her from getting a well-paid job in the urban areas of Indonesia. Then the story developed as we could have guessed—Annisa chose to be a domestic worker overseas. She heard that the salary of a migrant domestic worker could raise the living standards of a family immensely. She also heard that many Indonesian women who had worked hard overseas for less than 10 years could go back home and afford a new house, pay their children's tuition fees, and save money for their children's future marriages. It sounded irresistible to Annisa, except that she had to be parted from her children and her husband.

Before coming to Hong Kong, Annisa had worked in Taiwan as a caregiver for three years. She had learned how to speak Mandarin and English in Taiwan, like Evelyn. Her main duty was to take care of an elderly woman who had Parkinson's disease (she was the mum of Annisa's employer), which was so different from being a domestic helper. Annisa didn't need to cook for the family or clean the house or serve her employer, because her employer worried so much that her mum would be in possible danger if Annisa was away for too long. *"My boss didn't allow me to cook, she said if I cook then nobody look after her mum. She only allow me to buy take-away. I miss Indonesian food so much at that time, but I can't cook for myself,"* said Annisa.

"Can you cook on your holidays?" I asked.

"I have no holidays, for 3 year. My boss say I can't have holiday because the grandma (her employer's mum) always need a person to look after. This job is so different from a helper. If my job is a helper, I can have holiday every two weeks. But my job is to take care of a very ill and old woman. I do this because I like old people. I understand the grandma always need me, but I'm really tired sometimes and I need a rest. The grandma can't walk. She can't eat by herself. She can't go to toilet by herself. I have to help her do all these things. My life in Taiwan was between hospital and my employer's home. I know Taiwan has many beautiful places. But I didn't have opportunity to travel to other places," recounted Annisa.

"If that's the case, I guess you didn't make it to visit your families during the three years. You must have missed them very much," I said.

"Yes. I miss my family very much. I feel so lonely at that time. You know, I didn't have chance to make friends with other Indonesian

workers in Taiwan. It's a very hard time for me. But I can't go back to see my family and friends. My boss say if I go back to visit my family in Indonesia, she will fire me. And if her mum is dead because I didn't look after the grandma well, she will sue me and send me to jail. So, I had to be very careful. I don't want to go to jail."

I understand that looking after elderly people with problems with their motor skills or with special needs is more difficult and challenging than working as a helper. I also understand that in many cases, it is hard to ensure that a caregiver is given holidays at the correct time. But it doesn't mean that it is reasonable to deprive them of their holidays and wellbeing. Perhaps Annisa's employer in Taiwan should have hired a part-time caregiver so that Annisa could have had rest days and annual leave, and it wouldn't have cost her a fortune. Annisa's story made me think about the situations of full-time caregivers, unpaid housewives and struggling single parents who need to take care of people with problems with their motor skills or nervous system. How many of them have regular holidays and how many of them get enough support from their society or welfare system? Maybe we should place some hope in future artificial intelligence to free us from onerous, repetitive, and tedious tasks. I'm not saying that caregivers should disappear or the job should be replaced. No. I mean caregiving should be optimised. If caregivers can have more time to relax through the use of affordable high-tech products to assist them, they can have less stress from their job and focus more on the emotional needs of the people they care for. Moreover, with the growing aging population, in the near future human society will need more caregivers for the elderly. I hope there will be technology to ensure the wellbeing of both the elderly and their caregivers.

When Annisa completed her contract in the third year, she found she couldn't continue doing her job because her body and mind were sending her a clear message, and that was she should have a long break and go back home to stay with her family. *"In that year, I was much slimmer than now. I always feel I don't have enough energy. It's not because of the food. I think it's because I need holiday. In the first year, my children always asked me 'Mum, when will you come back? We miss you'. I told them next year. And the next year they still don't see me…I'm afraid my children will think I'm a liar. Actually, I should work one more year in Taiwan, because my new contract is for 2 years. But I can't. I have to have holiday and I have to go home,"* said Annisa with a guilty face.

"Oh! Don't mention this! You make me want to go home now," Evelyn said to Annisa. It seems they have already heard each other's story, but it still had an effect on Evelyn while she was listening to Annisa's story again. Before this conversation started, Eva had gone to her tent to sleep as she told me she felt tired and wanted to have a nap. It was around 11.30 am, Annisa felt a little peckish. She asked me if it was okay to have a "smelly lunch" in front of me. I said, "absolutely OK", but I was curious about what Annisa meant by "smelly lunch". When Annisa took out her lunch box and opened it, it caught my attention. It turned out that the "smelly lunch" she had referred to was just lunch that smelled spicy. Annisa seemed to be a little embarrassed because of my curiosity. *"Sorry. It's Indonesian food,"* she mumbled, lowering her head, *"too many chillies! It doesn't smell good."* As a spicy food lover, spicy food means tasty food to me. How could it be smelly? What I did was sit a bit closer to Annisa showing my deep interest in her lunch, and I asked her to tell me what ingredients she had used. Then we started to talk about different kinds of chillies and Indonesian food for a while.

Why did Annisa feel sorry about her food? I asked myself. I used to eat spicy food in front of different people from different places. I never felt sorry about my food. My Kiwi colleagues always felt interested in my lunch box, and because they were interested, I brought more interesting food to my office to satisfy their curiosity, which made me excited sometimes. Some of my colleagues were also spicy food lovers, and they occasionally came to ask me if they could try a bit of my interesting food. Their facial expressions made me feel that I was kind of cool and I was proud of it. In return, I shared the same passion for fine wine and beer as they did. I was happy to be associated with "exotic" things in New Zealand, or let's say I was very happy to be different there. People around me, including Gary, Kate, my previous colleagues (some of them grew up in NZ, and some others were from different corners of this planet), and the researchers I worked for all made me believe that I should accept and embrace my differences from other people. I think it was their positive attitudes that made me confident to show my differences in a foreign society.

Annisa's "sorry" about her Indonesian food sounded like a habitual reaction, just like my habitual reaction for not feeling sorry about my food that had a different smell. Her assumption that I would mind the smell of her food is like a stereotype against another stereotype. I'm not sure whether Annisa's employer minds the smell while she's cooking Indonesian food for her Sunday gatherings, but I reckon some employers would. When those employers who mind the smell pass on the information to their community, it is very likely to create the stereotype that Indonesian helpers' food doesn't smell good. Some may simply not like the smell of spicy food, especially when someone is cooking inside their home, whereas some people's dislike can stem from many complicated factors. Gradually, the in-group's stereotype about the out-group, as a piece of information, will eventually be known by the out-group. Then, the minority group will react accordingly. The reaction of some Indonesian helpers, however, is to presume that most Hong Kong people don't like the smell of their food, and thereby say "sorry" about it.

"Chinese here don't like the smell of our food. My last boss wasn't happy if I cook Indonesian food at home. Eva's boss doesn't like the smell too," Evelyn told me. I feel sorry that Evelyn thinks so. She knows that I'm not a Hongkonger, but she also knows that I look like them, so she assumes that I am more like them, and so I probably won't like the smell of Indonesian food. I know that spicy food has its certain group of fans in Hong Kong, and that many Hong Kong people love to respect diversity and try different cultural elements. The pity is that many helpers may not have had the opportunity to discover this.

After leaving Taiwan, Annisa spent several months with her family in Indonesia. Her husband's income still wasn't enough to pay for both children's educational expenses, so she left home again to work as a domestic helper in Hong Kong. Before COVID-19, her husband's monthly salary was around HK$ 1,500 (194 USD), but due to the coronavirus pandemic, his income is now less than before. Because of the virus, Annisa also fears losing her job more than ever. Evelyn, whose husband runs a small shop in Indonesia, said that she has a similar concern.

"I should go back to Indonesia next month. But because of this virus, I can't go back. If I have to go back now, I think I'm going to lose my job because I may get the virus on my way back home. My boss then will say to me 'don't come back lah'," Evelyn said with a laugh.

"I cancel my trip back to Indonesia too," Annisa continued the conversation.

Now, it is Annisa's second year in Hong Kong. She is working for her second employer. Annisa told me that her work schedule was not that different to working for other employers. However, she didn't complete her first contract. The elderly woman she was taking care of was a Cantonese speaker, but Annisa only could understand Mandarin and English back then, which made both of them frustrated. *"The grandma always got angry about me because I can't understand what she said. It's very hard for me too. So, after a few months, I suggested my boss to change another helper who can understand Cantonese. And she agreed,"* Annisa continued, *"then I found my current employer. She don't mind I can't speak Cantonese. She say English it's OK."*

Compared with many other newcomers in Hong Kong, Annisa thinks she's quite lucky. Her current employer allows her to enjoy all her rest days and holidays. In addition to this, she also has a private room and sufficient food. From Monday to Friday, Annisa starts work at 6.00 preparing breakfast for her employer's family and finishes her work at around 21.30-22.00. On weekends, Annisa has to get up after 7.30 because the young couple who pay her prefer to sleep in and don't want to be woken up by any noise. Annisa looked very satisfied with her current job, though she paid her agency a lot in the first year. Now, Annisa can send over HK$3,000 to her family every month, and in the meantime, she has time to make friends. I suppose if Annisa knew the English proverb, she would say "Every cloud has a silver lining". But for me, the silver lining just doesn't seem silver enough.

Siti's Dark Cloud

Alice wasn't there yet when I left Victoria Park before 2.00 pm. But I was too hungry to wait for Alice at that time. So, I found a restaurant, had lunch, and then took a bus to go back home. I arrived at my flat before 4.00 pm, and I thought: why don't I just go and say hello to my Indonesian friends nearby?

I went to the place where I could find them. This time, I saw Siti again. Emma and Susie were also there, but I didn't see Indah and Anna. Perhaps they were relaxing somewhere else (let's hope so). I bought some iced coffee to share with them and with some other helpers I didn't know. Everyone was so pleased, especially Siti. *"Last time you're here, I'm working. They told me you come to see us again and bring so many snacks. I feel so sad I wasn't here. It's really good to see you again. I feel so happy,"* said Siti.

"It's really good to see you too, Siti," I replied.

There's one more bottle of coffee left. Siti asked me if it's OK for her to take it. I nodded, and she was ecstatic about having two bottles of coffee. Siti told me she has to send HK$ 4,000 (her monthly salary is HK$ 4,630) to her family in Indonesia every month, so she doesn't have much money to enjoy herself. I noticed that Siti's mobile phone has a cracked screen. With so little money left every month, she won't be able to buy a second-hand phone for a long time. I asked Siti how she survived with around 600 HKD per month. Siti said, *"I only buy cheap food. It's OK."*

When everyone else started to enjoy their coffee, Siti preferred to keep hers. She looked at the coffee and said, *"Now I got two coffee. I can drink one tomorrow morning. It will be a beautiful morning. Thank you!"* But Siti's excitement didn't last long, because a helper coming to say hi to Susie and Emma took one of the bottles of coffee on the ground. The uninvited guest thought nobody wanted it, so she took the coffee away and thanked me for the coffee. Siti looked at me and shook her head, pinning all her hopes on me, but I let her down. I didn't know what to do at that moment. I thought it would be rude to ask that helper to give the coffee back to Siti, so I didn't do anything. I felt so guilty that I had ruined Siti's wonderful morning that day as I hadn't guarded her coffee. Then Siti grabbed the only bottle of coffee left on the concrete floor, staring at it as if it was so precious to her.

To ease the atmosphere and avert Siti's attention, I began to tell Siti and other helpers what I had done and who I had met in the last two weeks. When I mentioned Alice, I told them how I was shocked by Alice's experience in Singapore: Alice only got SGD$ 20 as her monthly salary in 2003, but she should've got SGD$220 every month, and her work permit, passport and contract were all taken away by her employer. Siti was silent for a little while, but then told me about her experience in Singapore:

> She's more lucky than me. I got SGD$10 salary every month from…2001 to 2003. In my contract, my salary is SGD$230, but my boss don't follow it. They also take my passport and contract away. They don't give me holiday! No holiday! And I don't have enough food. My boss only provided me dinner. I need to buy breakfast and lunch by myself. But my money is not enough. You see, I don't know the place at first, so I can only buy some bread or biscuits in supermarket. I found some cheap Indonesian food when I know the place later. So, I can change my food. I can't send money to my family at that time. They need money, but I don't have money for them. It's not enough for me to buy food! Also…our government is not useful. The Philippine government is better. Our government don't protect us…

This time, it was my turn to fall silent. I eventually understood why Siti behaved like she did. It was indeed a dreadful nightmare. To be honest, I didn't know how to comfort Siti at that moment. I must be a bad friend. Fortunately, Susie saved us from sad feelings. She made jokes about herself to cheer everyone up. But while I was laughing at Susie's jokes, I didn't literally forget about Siti's experience, I think I never will. After telling jokes, Susie updated her information. In fact, in 2007, the first year Susie started to work in Singapore, she only received SGD$20 every month (her contract showed that she should have received $235). Her employer said that he paid too much money to the agency and on the security bond, and thus Susie had to share the "responsibility". I'm not sure whether Anna and Indah encountered something like this when they worked in Singapore, as they didn't mention it to me. But I can't draw a conclusion now and say that "they didn't mention it to me, so they should've got fair salary and enough food in Singapore". After all, Siti and Susie's cases helped me understand that I am still a newcomer in their world.

I decided to find out more about Siti's first employer in Hong Kong, as I remember Siti only mentioned that her former employer was not good to her but not in detail. I figured out the meaning of "not good" this time. To Siti, "not good" meant she was forced to work for more than 16 hours a day and was frequently verbally abused (sometimes she got physically abused). As for her food, "not good" meant that she wasn't provided with enough food. Siti gesticulated the amount of food she had. Her usual lunch and dinner included three to four pieces of vegetables, a half palm-sized piece of meat, and some rice. And they were all leftovers. The sad thing is, she didn't get luckier when she worked for her second and third employers. Siti added, *"The first three are all no good. Not enough sleeping, not enough food. Sometimes I work until 12 o'clock at night and get up at 5 o'clock to work. This one is the best! I only need to work till 10 o'clock at night. And if I work on Sunday, my boss give me HK$250. My boss now is really nice."* How easily satisfied Siti is!

When I was ready to say goodbye to them, Siti finally decided to drink the coffee. She told me that it was the best coffee she ever had after taking the first sip.

Dear Siti, I should've guarded your coffee.

PART THREE: BEYOND DOMESTIC WORK

Solidarity is not the same as support. To experience solidarity, we must have a community of interests, shared beliefs and goals around which to unite, to build Sisterhood. Support can be occasional. It can be given and just as easily withdrawn. Solidarity requires sustained, ongoing commitment.

bell hooks

7. The Third Wave

On 13 July, due to the third wave of the coronavirus outbreak, the Hong Kong government announced a range of tougher social distancing measures. Restrictions including public gathering ban (from 50 people to 4), dine-in ban (from 6.00 pm to 5.00 am), and the closure of sports and entertainment businesses all took effect from 15 July. My field work and informal interviews had to halt because of the new restrictions. After 29 July, social distancing rules became more stringent. The number of people allowed in public gatherings had been tightened from four to two and wearing a face mask at all times had been made compulsory in both indoor and outdoor settings. After a full dine-in ban had been effective for only one day, the HK government revoked it on 30 July and allowed breakfast as well as lunch dine-in services again.

During these days, many domestic helpers had been kept indoors on Sundays. Some had been forced to work; and some had chosen to work voluntarily. With more of their employers working from home, helpers' workloads, as you may have guessed, all had increased again. I knew that I wouldn't be able to join those helpers' gatherings for a long while. And I also knew that for many helpers, this period would be a tough one.

It was only till 28 August that restrictions got loosened, because the confirmed cases had been lowered. Dine-in services started to be extended from 6.00 pm to 9.00 pm; some businesses like sports centres, movie theatres, and beauty salons were allowed to be reopened. Wearing masks was still mandatory but people exercising outdoors could be exempted. Yet the ban of group gatherings in public still remained.

I've been keeping contact with Alice and Lucille through WhatsApp amid the third wave. For the first and second waves of coronavirus outbreak, Alice's employers were not as scared as this time. During the semi-lockdown, Alice could go to market every day, and she could enjoy her rest days outdoors. The third wave is different. Alice was only allowed to go to market every three to four days, and her female employer made a list of the things she wanted

Alice to buy. Alice said, *"Only this time, Madam is so worried, unlike the previous waves. Madam says you can stay at home, if you want to work, I'll pay for you overtime. But if you wish only to stay at home, it doesn't matter."* Like some of her friends, Alice chose to work on their rest days for extra money, whilst some of her other friends chose to take their days off as usual. As for the unlucky ones, we all know what would happen to them.

Lucille still took her days off every week, but she and her employer tried to quarantine at home because they thought the third wave is too scary. Like the previous semi-lockdown, Lucille's workload didn't increase that much, yet life is still hard. Some of Lucille's friends found it really tough as their workload became heavier again and they couldn't meet friends during that time. Lucille told me that some of her friends are willing to talk to me for my "research" after having heard of me from her, but giving the current situation, we have to wait for the day when their employers allow them to go out.

On Sunday, 30 August, I went to the place where helpers usually relax near my flat. There were approximately one-fourth of the helpers sitting in the same old place following social distance guidelines. I saw Siti and Indah and a few familiar faces. It's the first weekend that Siti and Indah were allowed to enjoy their rest days outdoors since the third wave of coronavirus outbreak. Both of them had worked six Sundays with overtime pay, thinking that they're much luckier than some other helpers. Though Indah went back to her employer's apartment to prepare for cooking at around 16.30.

8. Joy and Sorrow

Sunday, 23 August 2020   Temperature: 31°C   Humidity: 66%

"Your joy is your sorrow unmasked."— Kahlil Gibran[52]

Due to the third wave of the coronavirus pandemic, I haven't left Tai Po for six weeks. I still go to market every day, albeit with more prudence. Disinfection, social isolation and nostalgia can be the three keywords to describe my life during this period. With confirmed cases of COVID-19 having declined lately, I decided to have a tour with my partner in Central, a district of Hong Kong island, the CBD of Hong Kong and also the most popular gathering area for Filipino domestic workers on Sunday.

It took us more than one hour from Tai Po to Central. After having lunch with my partner, I planned to go to Statue Square (a public square in Central) to try my luck to find some Filipino domestic workers to talk to, while my partner said he would walk around and explore some new streets.

I found some Filipino women chatting near the restaurant I dined in. So, I approached them to say hi and made sure that they were the people I wanted to talk to. It is a tranquil, shady courtyard built for the residents who live nearby. To be frank, as an open space for domestic workers to sit and relax, it looks so much better than the space I found in Tai Po or in Victoria Park. I suppose it is very likely to outshine public squares in Central as well. The reason is simple: it has two benches for these helpers to sit. Surely, it is more comfortable to sit on a bench rather than a concrete floor (there are some benches in Victoria Park and public squares in Central, but they're not enough for so many helpers).

The first two people I talked with are Julie and A' Ching who have been working in Hong Kong for 10 years and 8 years respectively and who were willing to share their experience as domestic workers in Hong Kong. Due to the social distancing rule, they were all wearing face masks and they didn't sit close to each other. Julie's current work schedule is from 7.00 to 21.00-21.30, a typical one for an experienced helper here; while A' Ching needs to work from 7.00 to

23.00. Both of them must stand a lot every day. *"Especially now because of the COVID-19, my boss works from home, and everyone is at home. I need to cook more, clean more and stand more. In the past, when my employer went to office, I can have a short break when I finished my task. Now, it's impossible. I can't sit in front of my boss. That's weird, you know. And my boss thinks she pays me to work not to sit. I think she has more pressure now, and I need to be more careful. I don't want to lose my job. So basically, I always stand,"* said Julie.

"Do you have any breaks, Julie?" I asked.

"Yes. I have. When I have meals, I have break, and I can sit on the chair in the kitchen. I think my meal breaks are less than one hour in total," responded Julie. "But I have enough sleep and food. I'm lucky compared to many helpers here."

"In your opinion, Julie, how many helpers in Hong Kong are treated unfairly?

"Hmm, I'm not quite sure because I don't know all the people. But I think 60-70% of helpers here are treated unfairly."

A' Ching has a similar situation during the coronavirus outbreak, but she needs to stand for a longer time. When I asked A' Ching why she must work so long every day, she said, *"It's not because of work actually. It's just because my employer and her family members like to sleep late. They don't want me to sleep earlier than them. So, I have to wait them to get ready to sleep, and then I can sleep."*

Our topic soon attracted the attention of another two Filipino helpers who were sitting on the other bench. Then they joined our conversation and contributed more ideas. The two newly joined individuals are Helena and Joe. When Joe introduced herself, Julie told me with a subtle facial expression, *"I don't know whether we should call him or her."* Joe said to me, *"I'm OK with both "he" and "she", but I prefer you to call me Joe."* Before meeting Joe, my partner Alan asked me whether I've found any gender diverse people amongst the migrant domestic workers; and if yes, what their situations are, and how they deal with their gender identities in Hong Kong. I remember I did see a few domestic workers who looked a bit shy and who seemed to be happy to be included into the LGBT+ group. And I asked myself: as a member of a marginalised group, would the gender diverse people be excluded by other migrant domestic workers? Would they become even more disadvantaged or marginalised in Hong Kong? I have been eager to know the answer, but I haven't found a proper chance to interview them privately. It's hard to do it in group interviews or in individual interviews with people around, and even if it is a private interview, it is hard to talk about too personal topics when I first meet them.

Joe is not shy, maybe she/he would love to share her/his feelings and experience as a gender diverse helper in Hong Kong someday. But now I can be at least sure that Joe isn't excluded or marginalised by her/his friends who are from different age groups. Helena is under 30 years old, the youngest among them; Julia and A' Ching said they became grandmas several years ago. They are all open-minded to this changing world and they all appear to accept Joe and like Joe so much (since Joe actually prefers to be called "he", hereafter I will refer to Joe as "he").

Like Julie, Joe has been working in Hong Kong for 10 years, and he has so many opinions and stories to share as a domestic worker here. Joe has got a bachelor's degree in commerce. After graduating from university, he launched his small business of sugarcane farming and then invested in rice farming in the Philippines. Doing business can be profitable sometimes, but it is risky for Joe. Gradually, Joe felt bored with his business and was tired of begging the buyers to pay off their debt owed to him. He decided to explore something new—to become a domestic worker in Hong Kong.

After Joe knew that I'm interested in domestic helpers' lives in Hong Kong and that I showed my empathy with them, Joe became very talkative and straightforward. He always made everyone laugh, and he's good at it. It's the second Sunday that these four helpers are allowed to have their rest days outdoors. When I asked Joe how he felt amid the third wave of the coronavirus pandemic, he began his stand-up comedy, *"You know what? Other people around the world are maybe suffering from nationwide pandemic, but most helpers here are suffering from their employers!"* His audience laughed, and he continued, *"Imagine you have to see your boss every day. Even though he or she is a good boss, you will feel something wrong, right? Which normal person wants to see their boss every day? Don't mention so many employers are bad bosses. But maybe many employers here think they're suffering from us too! They want to see their friends, not us. Who knows hahah!"*

"How about your employer, Joe? Is she or he a good boss to you?" I asked.

"My current boss is good. But he doesn't talk with me often. You can imagine you work for your boss in the same office. You see him every day, but he seldom talks to you. But... saying nothing is better than saying something I don't want to listen," replied Joe.

"So, what is something you don't want to listen to?"

"For example, my first employer, a local Chinese woman. She always said that I'm stupid. Do you know the hostage incident in the Philippines?"

"Yes, I know it." (In 2010, a hostage incident took place in Manila, the capital city of the Philippines. A former national police officer thought he was unfairly dismissed. To gain public attention and to revenge, he hijacked a tour bus on which there were 20 tourists and a tour guide from Hong Kong. After a failing negotiation between the official negotiators and the perpetrator, he became agitated especially after he saw his brother was arrested on live TV. Then he started to shoot hostages, which caused eight fatalities of the hostages.)

"Good, you're knowledgeable. So, I don't need to explain the background information to you. OK, when the incident happened, that's my first year in Hong Kong. I understand my boss felt really sad for the Hong Kong tourists who were shot dead in the Philippines. I feel very sorry for them too. It's a tragedy. But I didn't kill them, I didn't let it happen. And I'm not the silly government in the Philippines. But my first boss blamed me for the hostage incident. She said I'm stupid and abnormal. After the hostage incident, she often verbally abused me. But you see, the logic is ridiculous! One

person made a mistake, and then people blame the whole group from that country? That isn't right!"

Joe's mention of his first employer seemed to resonate among his friends. They all tried to say something. Julie started first, *"My first boss is not good either. She asked me to get up at 5.oo o'clock and sleep late every day. And my boss only gave me a little food. The plates were sometimes almost empty. I think I was treated like a slave not a helper."* A' Ching added, *"Me too! I didn't have enough sleep when I was working for my first employer. My boss only provided me with a dinner every day. I need to buy breakfast and lunch by myself."* Helena didn't have food issues at the time she was working for her first employer in Hong Kong, but she was verbally abused a lot. *"My first employer is not good also. She...speaks...a lot,"* mumbled Helena.

"Helena meant her first employer verbally abused her!" Joe explained loudly.

I looked at Helena, and she nodded. After a while, she added, *"I got up at 6.00 in the morning, and sometimes went to bed at 1.00 o'clock...because I need to take care of three children, and...so many other things to do."*

"What?" I think it's the first time for Helena's friends to hear about this. They were as shocked as me. Joe said to Helena, *"Hey! When talking about the first employer, I thought I was the champion working the longest hours every day. I worked for 18 hours a day at that time. Now, you're the champion hah!"*

Helena has worked in Hong Kong for 5 years. She is recognised as the luckiest person amongst them now despite her past miserable experience. Her current major job responsibility is to take care of a Popo (it means "grandmother" in Cantonese) who is the mother of her employer, cook for her employer and the Popo, and clean the apartment. She doesn't have a tight schedule. She works from 6.00 to 20.00. And unlike Julie and A' Ching who must stand a lot every day, Helena can sit in sofa and have a short break as long as she wants. Her employer trusts her, and knows that Helena will perform her duties after having a break.

Joe's working schedule is similar to Julie. He works from 7.00 to 21.00, but in a more relaxing way. Joe's main responsibility is to take care of a boy, his boss's child. Joe told me, *"If my boy doesn't need to go to school* (one of his job duties is to send the boy to school), *I can get up at 8.00-9.00 and enjoy my morning tea. Oh, cooking is simple for me too! Usually, I only need to cook for my boy and myself. Sometimes, my boss joins dinner with us, then I cook for him as well."* Joe's boss isn't a perfectionist in terms of housework, which makes his work way easier than many other helpers here.

Julie and A' Ching share their rooms with the children they take care of, whereas Joe and Helena have their real private rooms in Sheung Wan which is well-known for its high real estate price. After sharing the basic information about his private room, Joe told me more details about the place he is living in, *"In my boss's apartment, there're four rooms. He has a room, my boy has a room, I have a room, also my boss's ex-wife has a room. She sometimes comes here to see her son. She also has the right to stay here. In fact, I don't have to listen to her order because she's not in my contract. But every time she's here, she likes to ask me to do so many things. She even installed a camera device in the living room to watch me and check his son. But how come? Perhaps she forgot she is the person who often shouted at her son, not me!"*

"There was a camera device in my boss's place before too!" exclaimed Julie.

"How did you feel, Julie?" I asked.

"Me? I felt uncomfortable. I had to change my clothes in the bathroom because part of my room was seen by the camera also. My boss installed it for two years, and then she thought she can trust me, so no more camera device after that. But I don't like it. It's weird when you know someone is watching you at home," responded Julie.

"For me, it's different. I enjoy it! I feel like I'm a celebrity. It's like I've got a fan, and my fan is so interested in my private life. I forgive her hahah," Joe said ironically. He stopped a while and continued, *"We helpers don't have equal human rights here. Lots of*

discrimination here! But I'm so lucky to meet a friend like you today." Julie added, *"Yes! You'll be always welcome here."*

All these four people came to Hong Kong for different reasons. Julie and A' Ching wanted to support their daughters to continue their studies till they complete their university education. Helena has 6 siblings, and she is the oldest among them. As a big sister of her siblings, she thought it is kind of her responsibility to provide a better life for them. Joe wanted to build a big house for his mum and himself, and if he had worked in the Philippines, it's unlikely he would realise his dream.

In order to become a domestic helper in Hong Kong, they had to pay an extortionate agency fee in the Philippines first. When Julie, Joe and A' Ching came to Hong Kong, regulation on helpers' agencies was so lax in both Hong Kong and their home countries. They paid HK$12,000-13,000 to their agencies eight to ten years ago, Helena paid less than HK$10,000 five years ago. *"Now, the agencies are much better than before because the Philippine government and Hong Kong government are stricter to illegal agencies than before. But the agency fee is still a lot for many helpers. My friend paid her Philippine agency around 8,000 HKD two years ago. But I think it depends on agencies. There're still many bad agencies everywhere,"* told Julie.

I believe Julie is right. Lucille said something similar to me before. Fourteen years ago, Lucille's agency fee was HK$24,000; then, it dropped significantly four years later and it's under HK$10,000 now. Yes, it is getting better, in an ironic way! Joe was the only person among them who didn't borrow money from anyone or any place, which made him feel less stressed compared to many helpers who were in debt. He paid his agency using his own savings. He said, *"I was so lucky, because I made some money from my small business!"* Helena and Julie were not that lucky. It took them more than six months to pay off their debt, and meanwhile, they were facing problems like overwork and insufficient rest and food. A' Ching wasn't that lucky either. She borrowed money from a friend, and her annual loan interest rate was 10%. Even so, it's much better than borrowing money from loan sharks which can turn the loan into bottomless-pit debt.

The differences of policies regarding employment agencies between Hong Kong and domestic workers' home countries have left room for loopholes, becoming a hotbed of underhanded dealings and crimes. Although according to Employment Agency Regulations in Hong Kong, agencies are only allowed to charge no more than 10% of helpers' first-month salary as the commission.[53] In practice, many unscrupulous agencies collude with loan sharks to overcharge helpers using different pretexts (based on Mission for Migrant Workers' service report 2019, 80% of domestic workers have reported they are overcharged by their agencies). And it is still common in those helpers' home countries where the employment agencies are permitted to charge more money than Hong Kong. In Indonesia, according to a decree dated in 2008, the maximum placement fee can be charged is Rp. 15,550,000, which is approximately equivalent to HK$8,100 now. By contrast, as stated by the Philippine Overseas Employment Administration in 2006, it is not allowed to charge any placement fee to those domestic workers bound for Hong Kong.[54] Yet charging training fees and medical checks to those potential helpers is legal. Some Philippine agencies charge the desperate job seekers a considerable amount of training fee to maximise their profit.

If we recollect how much Lucille paid to her agency in 2006, then we'll find the training fee could be up to 150, 000 pesos (HK$24,000 now). Under the Philippine Republic Act No. 10022, which took effect in 2010, the Philippine government became a bit less tolerant to unlawful agencies,[55] but A' Ching, who came to Hong Kong in 2012, still paid HK$12,000 to her agency in the Philippines. These laws haven't been strictly enforced to protect the migrant domestic workers no matter in Hong Kong or in their home countries. I was thinking whether it is because they are migrants, who are not ordinary residents in the host society, nor are they seen as visible citizens in their home countries. It seems they fall into a grey area in which governments from both sides are not so motivated to take real actions for them. Nonetheless, the domestic workers I met are generally optimistic about their lives. They said, "It's getting so much better now!"

A' Ching, Julie and Joe all realised their dreams—A' Ching and Julie's salary in Hong Kong supported their daughters to complete their tertiary education. Part of their savings were used as the dowry of their daughters, and the rest is for their retirement. Their daughters are mothers now. They plan to work for another few years in Hong Kong saving more money, and then go back to their home to enjoy their family life. Joe has his own house now. He shared some pictures of his house with me. And one of them has both his mother and his house, that must be Joe's favourite.

Helena is still saving money for her siblings' education. She hasn't had time to think for herself yet. She hasn't completed her bachelor's degree in technology information because IT is not her real interest. *"I want to be a nurse, but it's too late now. All I think now is that my siblings must choose what they like. I hope they won't be like me,"* said Helena.

Before I left, A' Ching was trying to tell me what degree her daughter got from university, *"She got Bachelor of Social Science in Psychology."* A' Ching remembers every single word on her daughter's degree certificate. This loving mother must have read it so many times.

(Joe's new house in the Philippines)

Values Education

Having got Joe's phone number, we then had some online conversations in the following days. Joe shared more of his opinions and experience.

Joe's first employer, as mentioned earlier, was the one who made Joe work for 18 hours a day and who also blamed Joe for the hostage incident in the Philippines. Joe didn't mention the food issue the first time we met, but he told me through WhatsApp that he often needed to provide food for himself when he was working for the first employer. And when he was feeling both hungry and sleepy late at night, he used to choose sleep over food as he was too exhausted. Joe believes almost 80% of helpers suffer from a similar situation if they are newcomers. When I asked Joe why so many helpers need to work so long hours, Joe replied, *"Their employers think they pay their helpers money and they look themselves on the higher positions, so they treat their helpers like slaves. Helpers are not slaves. Some employers' lifestyle is very busy and unhealthy. I think they just want to make their helpers busier than them. For example, my first boss worked in a bank. She always worked for more than 10 hours a day. Perhaps she thought it would be fairer if I worked 18 hours a day hahah."*

The first employer of Joe is included in the category mentioned above. From Joe's point of view, whether a helper is fairly treated in her workplace is highly dependent on whether the employer shows a tendency of discrimination which is not unidimensional but intersectional and multidimensional. Once individuals reveal discrimination against a group of people, it is very likely for them to discriminate against some other groups on the basis of different factors. For instance, there is usually an overlap between sexists and racists who are possibly inclined to discriminate other people based on social class or origins as well.

Joe told me a friend's story before he continued talking about his first employer, *"I have a friend, her boss was an elderly woman with a dog and a cat. The boss is a horrible person, like an alien. She's abusive to my friend and to her pets too. In her eyes, her helper and her pets are all inferior to her. Once she carried her cat and threw it to my friend when she was pissed off. Of course, the nature of the cat will try to hold something, right? The nails of the cat are very sharp, so the cat accidentally scratched my friend's face. My friend asked her boss why she did that. Her boss said it's because she's very happy to do that. Then my friend decided to break her contract."*

"But breaking the contract may make your friend pay to the agency again, right? I heard that if a helper wants to break the contract and find another employer, even though she's abused, she may need to pay to the agency again."

"That's right! My friend paid her replacement fee to her agency, but she had no choice. She can bear no more," responded Joe.

I think Joe's friend is relatively lucky compared to the pets of the abusive employer. At least, Joe's friend managed to escape, but the cat and the dog can't. It appears that both domestic workers' and animal welfare need to be improved in Hong Kong. I don't know who's the next unlucky domestic worker, but I wish the helper and the pets would be both safe and healthy. I wish abusing humans and animals would become intolerable on this planet one day.

According to Joe's observation and experience, his first employer used to discriminate him and other people. Joe believes that he wasn't seen as an equal human being, otherwise he wouldn't be forced to overwork and be verbally abused. *"Perhaps my first boss is an alien just like the woman who threw the cat to my friend. She has no feelings about other human beings."* said Joe. *"Once my boss and I were waiting for a lift. Suddenly she told me 'Back off Joe! Wait for the next lift!', and I asked her why. She told me 'Don't join them, because they're mainlanders (mainland Chinese).' Then I had lots of question marks in my mind. What? Same face same eyes, what's the problem to take the same lift with mainlanders to her? Then I was staring at my boss. She asked me why I looked at her like that. I said what I said to you. I think she treats mainlanders like they're in a lower position than her. And I don't like that. Even they're all ethnic Chinese, she still sees them as inferior, what about us?"*

Joe continued, *"How can a person hate someone or something without any direct experience? The mainlanders in the lift didn't do anything to her. They were just speaking Mandarin. That's the same logic for her to blame me and other Filipinos for the hostage incident. That's funny and ridiculous. Maybe you will criticise me, I don't care as I have the right to express my opinions."*

"I won't criticise you about this, Joe. And I think what you said is indeed cognitive bias and discrimination," I replied.

"Well, I know that every society has good people and bad people. I also know that not every employer in Hong Kong is like my first boss full of discrimination. But there're many people like my first boss still. Sometimes in metro, if you touch them accidentally, they will stare at you same as you're a criminal even you say 'sorry' or 'excuse me'. But if they did that to us, some of them didn't say sorry or they just pretend that they're superior. I don't mean all Hong Kong people are like that. But that's my experience sometimes. Me and my friends all met some people like that."

It reminded me of something I was told by my partner Alan. There was a protest in Edinburgh Place (another public square in Central) in December last year, and Alan was walking by. Because it was on Sunday, there were many Filipino domestic workers gathering there as well. Soon, they made room for those protesters, leaving the centre of Edinburgh Place for the protesters. Alan told me some domestic workers were having a beauty contest while the protesters were calling out their demands. When the crowd was chanting "five demands, no one less", many Filipino helpers imitated the crowd raising their hands to signify the number of five. Alan thought he hadn't seen such a scene on the media before, so he decided to stay there for longer to observe more and know more about this city. Recollecting the scenes we saw from media reports about the protests in Hong Kong, migrant domestic workers were seldom on camera. I remember a domestic helper expressed her opinion in favour of protesters, and as a result, she was deported by the Hong Kong government. Local people who were pro-protesters were discussing this, they were touched by that domestic helper and some other people who support them from different groups.

However, in many cases, we won't see these marginalised people on camera. They are not even supporting roles in the videos on local issues.

The media reports from different platforms didn't show those helpers' faces that day. No one would know that many of them once raised their hands to try to include themselves in that rally. On top of that, Alan witnessed something that resonates with what Joe said. With more protesters joining the rally, some standing in the rally had to move backwards to make more room for new participants. A few protesters accidentally stepped on a mat where some Filipino domestic helpers were sitting on. *"They glimpsed at the Filipino women and then kept moving backward, but they didn't say sorry. Then a Filipino woman said to them 'at least you could say please,"* described Alan. *"I was so disappointed at them. They should've apologised to those women."*

I told this to Joe. He asked me, *"If this is not discrimination, then what is it?"* I didn't know what to say. I felt sad, disappointed and puzzled. My experience in Hong Kong is: if someone accidentally touched me, they'll say sorry to me immediately. Most people in my daily life are polite and seem nice. Maybe it's because I look like the local people? I've never experienced what the domestic workers have to experience here. I've got the privilege that I didn't even notice. I'm not saying that all the helpers in Hong Kong are doomed to be discriminated. I know that there are local people who respect domestic helpers and treat them as equal human beings and try to change other people's attitudes towards them. I also know that there are organisations and individuals in Hong Kong working really hard to improve the situation for migrant domestic workers. But discrimination still exists to a large extent in this society, and I don't think people from mainstream society are eligible to deny the helpers' feelings and experience. Those who try to deny this might not discriminate the domestic workers by themselves, but in terms of discrimination, let's apply this theory: If we want to know whether there is discrimination in our society, we should go and ask the feelings of the marginalised members rather than the non-marginalised members.

For Joe, the conscious and unconscious discrimination in this society is linked with a lack of values education:

I think values education is not enough here. Education in HK is more about mathematical solving, grades and some practical things. Some students committed suicide, because they were not happy. People care too much about the standard education qualifications and academic performance, but they care too little about their children's happiness. They think sending their children to famous universities and they will become happy. Maybe they think making a lot of money will bring happiness too. So, they send their kids to learn this and that to meet the standard. But that's not the key point of education. Being educated is not measured by which famous university you graduate from. Education should teach children to respect others and care about others. Education should teach them to be happy without hurting others. Human equality should be taught more, but you can't feel human equality here, even anywhere else. We need to learn more about humanitarian ideology but less money ideology.

Due to poverty, Joe couldn't enjoy the best educational resources in his hometown where he grew up. Based on his descriptions, he wasn't sent to a good school. He was always too naughty, and his parents thought he must have had learning difficulties. But I'm happy for Joe that he doesn't have problems in learning at all. In fact, he captured the quintessence of education—he has learned to be sensible and empathetic, and he knows how to gain happiness and bring happiness to others.

After expressing his opinions about education, Joe also shared how he views the social movement in Hong Kong last year:

I lived in Blecher before, a place close to HKU (the University of Hong Kong). I saw many protestors there. I support them to fight for the rights they should have. I respect the rally and I think there's no problem using the barricade because we all have the rights to express our opinions especially when governments don't listen to us. But I don't really understand damaging buildings or burning MTR stations. I think throwing bricks to the buildings or damaging properties doesn't belong to this issue anymore. Buildings have no feelings, they can't fight. Collateral damage is not a part of fighting for your rights anymore. And I don't understand why police here like using tear gas so much. How about helpers who want to go home on Sunday night? They have to smell tear gas! How about the kids passing by?

Joe's comment about the 2019 anti-extradition bill movement in Hong Kong makes me ruminate on an alternative form of political camp that hasn't drawn enough attention from the mass media yet. Having learned a lesson from Umbrella Movement, protesters and their supporters in Hong Kong reached an agreement for the recent social movement, which is not to dissociate themselves from anyone who is a yellow ribbon (a member of pro-democracy camp). This technique promotes solidarity with pro-democracy individuals to the largest degree in spite of their different political spectrum, but it may silence different voices from the same group and discourage the deep reflection on collective behaviour.

If Joe made a comment criticising the behaviour of some radical protesters on any mainstream social media, he would possibly be labelled as either a blue ribbon (a member of pro-government camp) or a yellow ribbon who broke the rule of "no dissociation". I've seen similar things happening to some yellow ribbons through online platforms. Their disagreement or criticism was regarded as a betrayal of their group, and as a result of betrayal, they may be cyberbullied. Same things should have happened in the pro-government camp as well. Gradually, more people in the same camp may choose to be silent if they have different opinions with the majority. As Professor Clifton Emery states, "Silencing internal dissent with bullying is a form of coercive solidarity. The consequence of this coercion is that people with the greatest tolerance of violence rise to become the most influential in the cause."[56]

Yet Joe's criticism doesn't belong to the "internal dissent" in the pro-democracy camp or pro-establishment camp, as he isn't included in any local groups—he isn't even a Hongkonger. He doesn't need to worry that his loyalty to a certain group will be questioned like many yellow ribbons or blue ribbons do. As a forever non-ordinary resident, he isn't expected to have loyalty to Hong Kong at all. His ideas about civic disobedience are not heard by the two political camps, nor do his ideas matter to mainstream society.

But there is a voice different from what we heard before, a voice from a marginalised group in which people's opinions matter as well. And there are a number of domestic workers like Joe—the widely perceived dichotomy between the yellow ribbons and blue ribbons can't be applied to them anymore. They could be beyond colours.

9. Ventriloquism

Sunday, 30 August 2020

I didn't go to the domestic workers' gathering this Sunday. At night, Alice sent me a link from the HKSAR government and asked me *"what do you think about this"*. The link is about the universal community test programme in Hong Kong. Having read news intently, I was informed earlier that the HKSAR government planned to run a free COVID-19 testing for one week starting on 1 September 2020 and it will be extended for one more week if necessary.[57] All residents with a Hong Kong ID card are invited to take a free COVID-19 test, and the non-permanent residents like migrant domestic workers are included.

Since the HK government announced this plan, it has aroused a storm of controversy online. For multitudes of Hong Kong netizens, it is not a merely universal community test program, but a political matter. Due to a lack of trust in the HK government, most yellow ribbons (people who support universal suffrage) are against the universal COVID-19 test. Their concern is that it is probably a hoax of the local government colluding with the central government in Beijing. They worry that the HK government may make use of this free COVID-19 test to collect the DNA of the activists and send their DNA as data to the Chinese central government. In this case, taking the test means a potential danger to them. When Hong Kong's Chief Executive Carrie Lam explained on camera that the citizens' DNA will not be sent to mainland China, it just became more suspicious to the opposition parties and their supporters. By contrast, blue ribbons, as the people who are pro-establishment, tend to approve of this universal test. Some of them even suggested this free COVID-19 test should be compulsory rather than voluntary. People from different sides condemn one another for whatever reasons as long as they think you are not one of them. Anything on the Internet could be attacked; we all know this.

Even within the same camp, there are lots of disagreement as well (it took me some time to figure out why). Among the yellow ribbons, traditional pan-democratic parties have become less favourable in recent years due to the rise of localism in Hong Kong. Despite their common ground on universal suffrage and anti-establishment, netizens quite often see negative comments from the localist camp on pan-democratic camp. Pan-democratic parties are thought to be too soft and made too many concessions to the Chinese central government, whereas the localist camp is believed to represent more of young people's interests. The younger generation in Hong Kong is very disappointed about the government's inaction and pan-democratic parties' reluctance to take radical measures, therefore, most young yellow ribbons joined in the localist camp which not only agrees to use radical approaches to make a social change, but also tends to strengthen their identity as Hongkongers and claim more priorities for local people.

The members of the blue ribbons range from social elites to underprivileged individuals. Their political spectrum doesn't seem as complicated as the yellow ribbons, yet their motivational factors and reasons to choose this side can be various. Some may be simply too patriotic to differentiate the country and the government; some may just want to maintain the order; some may be influenced by their business or job positions; some may be in favour of power and authority; some may just want to hop on the bandwagon if their friends do (bandwagon effect may have a place among yellow ribbons as well).

Hong Kong citizens with different political leanings have got involved in online arguments and quarrels. Because of the social distancing restrictions, they can't have protests like before. Social media then become their battlefield. Our domestic workers, the non-ordinary residents of this society, are naturally dragged into the conflict of ordinary residents.

I clicked the link sent by Alice and browsed the government's webpage. It introduces the aims, the targets, and the process of the universal community testing programme. It looks fine. But as I mentioned earlier, it is not a simple universal COVID-19 testing, it has political overtones now. Alice's employer sent the link to her and asked Alice to register online and have a test. Apparently, Alice didn't want to take this test. But she was not sure about her employer's overtone, so she shared a screenshot of their conversation with me. She asked me, *"I don't think she forced me to do it, don't you think so?"*

"You're right, Alice. I don't think she forced you to do that," I replied.

"I don't understand this at all. Sir works for the government, and he has already done it. Madam will go and ask me to do it also. But some of my friends told me their employers don't agree with this and don't want them to have a test. And some say the results can be wrong," Alice continued.

I explained to Alice the political reasons behind this and told her that she should make her own decision. But it seemed she was under pressure at that moment. I could feel it. Being against employers' wills or preferences is not the top choice for domestic workers here. In many cases, employers don't have to give the exact order when they're in an unequal employer-employee relationship, all they need to do is to express their preferences, then helpers are very likely to follow the implicit instructions from their employers. The helpers whose employers are yellow ribbons are very likely to be told not to take the universal test, while those whose employers are blue ribbons may be persuaded to go to take a test. To test or not to test, that becomes a question for domestic workers unless their employers are neutral or apolitical.

"What do your friends think about the universal testing? Do they want to be tested?" I asked Alice.

"Some of their boss ask them to go. Some of the boss reject this testing, so my friends don't go also. I know now it's because of politics. I think some of my friends realised this too. But mostly, we can't decide things if it's about politics," replied Alice.

I know that Alice's employer wouldn't push her to take the test, as Alice always says her employer is very nice to her. But to be better accepted by the "blue" family she is working for, Alice decided to please her employer and take the test. As for her friends whose employers are yellow ribbons, they followed their employers' decision as well, even though they don't have to worry their DNA would be sent to mainland China and face the fear that they might be arrested because of this. Migrant domestic workers may or may not want to take the universal community test for different reasons, but we wouldn't know which decision is on behalf of the domestic workers themselves. It's like ventriloquism in which the voices and the opinions of the domestic workers are simply those of their employers.

While chatting with Alice online, I started to introspect on the way I used to view this world. I used to think political opinions are essential. I may have spent a long period immersing myself in a certain political camp that I believed in and excluded those having different opinions from mine without notice. I might have been silent for a while when the group members on my side demonise and stigmatise the individuals in another political camp. But after moving to Hong Kong and getting to know these migrant domestic workers, political opinions no longer matter that much to me. They're still important to me, and I'll still put lots of question marks in my head if someone says they support dictatorship. But they're not as important as in the past.

Now, I think having empathy is probably the most crucial thing, way more crucial than having the "right" political opinions. I think empathetic individuals have less likelihood to treat others cruelly and unfairly so long as they don't want to be abused, discriminated, dwarfed and patronised. Whereas having "right" political opinions is rather shaky. Supporters from different sides could all think they are absolutely right. And even if they choose the right side according to universal values, it doesn't mean that they won't make other people suffer. A blue ribbon can treat a helper well (like Alice's employer), and a yellow ribbon can be a racist (I saw racist and misogynistic comments online, contributed by both blue ribbons and yellow ribbons). Choosing the side of pro-democracy doesn't necessarily translate into a morally good person who values human equality and fairness. After all, in democratic societies, a citizen can advocate democracy and racism/sexism/classism simultaneously; and a liberal might have harassed women.

Hence, I want to care less about which political camp people choose, but care more about how they treat ethnic minorities and marginalised people. Perhaps this is a better indicator for us to know whether a person is empathetic and morally good enough. Among those who have hired helpers, both yellow ribbons and blue ribbons could treat their helpers unfairly or see their helpers as inferior to them. They can all claim that they support justice based on their own definitions, but maybe behind closed doors, some of them just don't care about the justice of the domestic workers.

I shared these thoughts with Alice. She texted me with a zipped-lip emoji at the end of her sentence, "We can count how many bosses treat us as a worker not a slave. I think for many people here, justice is for Hong Kong people only, not for the whole Hong Kong."

Perhaps we should have a universal justice test.

10. The Activists

Sunday, 06 September 2020 Temperature: 31°C Humidity: 68%

Here I am, in Central again. After arriving at Statue Square, I saw so many domestic helpers sitting there. I was astonished by the scene I saw—there are a bunch of luxury shops in the pedestrian square, while groups of domestic workers were sitting there in a non-luxurious way surrounded by those fancy shops, forming a stark contrast. Chanel looks like the border between the "ordinary" and "non-ordinary" worlds in this square. To the left of Chanel, as we can see from the photo below, some banners were hung there demanding labour rights and fair treatment for domestic workers. Ordinary residents in Hong Kong usually prefer not to walk in this square on Sunday, and if they do, they prefer to walk in the left world, because there's no one sitting in the middle of the road there. And if there are helpers found to the left of Chanel, they'll sit on the roadside, trying to be more invisible. While to the right of Chanel, it appears to be the particular base for the migrant domestic workers to relax and campaign on Sunday.

Before coming to Central, Alan advised me to find an illustrator among domestic workers, as he reckons it would be better for readers to picture how those migrant domestic workers live and work in Hong Kong if there is an insider perspective. Of course, no one will know better than a domestic worker about their living and working conditions. I believe I kind of know them better now after having got along with them for months. But I still can't imagine exactly how small or how big a helper's room is, nor can I imagine what is like to live in a kitchen. I can't picture the household chores that keep them busy till late night, and if I can, I won't understand why. I believe we do need to view this world through their eyes more—to see what they see and to hear what they hear—then we can better understand what they experience. I love Alan's idea, and my aim today is to search for the illustrator.

CHANEL
Stop Victim Blaming
and Singling out
Migrant Domestic Workers
VOLUNTARY
NOT MANDATORY
Amend Duterte's PhilHealth Law!
SUPPORT MAKABAYAN BLOC'S
HOUSE BILL NO. 6698

CHANEL
Van Cleef & Arpels

(Numerous Filipino domestic workers are sitting under the footbridge, in the middle of the road)

I went to the right side of Chanel and randomly asked a domestic worker if she knows anyone who is good at painting or drawing. She pointed at a small group and told me to ask them. After saying "thank you" to this nice stranger, I moved on to start a new journey. The first two people I talked with are Magi and Lia. Behind them, there are some banners hung by different organisations. I told them my purpose to be here. They said that they happen to have such a friend who is gifted at painting. But their friend Liza wasn't there at that moment, so Magi and Lia asked me to wait there for some time, and we started to chat with each other.

To my surprise, they are the members of a Filipino union and a community organisation. Knowing that I'm writing a book about migrant domestic workers in Hong Kong, something apparently sprang to Lia's mind. She asked me, *"May I know what the title is? If we're mentioned in the title, I hope you will use domestic workers instead of helpers."*

"The Non-ordinary Residents. And I did intend to use 'domestic workers' rather than 'helpers' if there is a subtitle," I replied. "May I know why you prefer to be called as a domestic worker, Lia?"

"Because we hope to be treated as workers. That's one of our campaigns. Locals like calling us 'helpers', but in fact we're more than helpers. 'Helpers' sound like we just help them do housework occasionally. And many people here treat us like slaves or inferior servants, because they don't think we're normal workers. But in fact, we are workers!"

I used both "helpers" and "domestic workers" during my informal interviews, I didn't realise it could be a big difference for them. For me, every human being should not be treated as a slave or inferior to others regardless of their race, job positions, gender, national origins, names, income, age, etc. Even though they are called "helpers", it doesn't change the fact that they are decent workers, and a different name shouldn't be used as an excuse to treat them worse. Yet, to respect Lia, I used "domestic workers" instead of "helpers" later on in our conversations.

Lia told me that the organisations here not only campaign for the rights of domestic workers, but also campaign for the political issues in the Philippines. She is the person introducing me to the leaders of other organisations here (she will also help me find different people to talk to in the future). She asked, *"Novia, before continuing our conversation, could I ask you to meet some leaders in other organisations here? We work closely with each other."* I agreed. And soon, I felt like I was part of the community. After hearing some people singing "Happy Birthday" to a domestic worker, I also joined the group in singing that song. Lia pointed at the woman and said, *"It's her birthday today."* Compared to the outside world, building rapport is much easier here. If you sing "Happy Birthday" to a domestic worker, then you'll be one of them, you'll get a piece of birthday cake, and you'll be looked after well.

Someone came to ask me if I wanted to try their coconut sticky rice, and someone asked me if I wanted some drinks. Someone thoughtfully found a piece of cardboard for me to sit on, thinking that this way I wouldn't have to sit on the concrete floor directly. But I don't mind sitting on the concrete floor now. After having done fieldwork for a few months, I started to generate a sense of alienation from fancy stuff. Those fancy shopping malls, the fancy items in the showcase, the fancy clothes, the fancy restaurants...I feel they're too alien to the world I have always stayed in, or the world of the migrant domestic workers. I feel I don't have connections with the fancy stuff anymore. There are even some moments when I wandered in some fancy neighbourhoods with my partner, I had a strange impulse to sit on the concrete floor. I thought: OK, I'm feeling a bit tired, why not sit on the concrete floor? I guess that's a sign to show that I fit in my new community very well.

Being a mother of a 7-year-old daughter and a domestic worker in Hong Kong with 3-year experience, Lia's other role is the general secretary in a community organisation called Mission Movers HK. Unlike any other domestic workers that I've talked with till now, Lia didn't apply for her first job through any agency. She got the job and applied for the visa all by herself. As Lia said, the good side of not relying on an agency is to save money and avoid debt, but the bad side is: she had no idea how a domestic worker is expected to do things in Hong Kong. No one trained her on how to be a "Hong Kong" domestic worker. She was a teacher in the Philippines before coming to Hong Kong. After finishing her work, she became a caregiver at home and she did housework. In her mind, a full-time domestic worker just meant spending more time on housework, no other issues. And ideally, it should be like that. But when live-in rule is compulsory, when employers have too many unrealistic expectations, when this job is belittled, when there is discrimination inside and outside of the workplace, it becomes something else, something beyond Lia's imagination in the past.

Lia's first job in Hong Kong was to work for an expat family. She heard that expats usually treat domestic workers better. But it seems she still can't break the curse of "the first employers". *"At the beginning, it's my problem. You know, I didn't get training before. I understand. But then my first employer's husband became more and more angry with me. He always shouted at me and verbally abused me. It's very stressful, and the work schedule was very tight too. So, I terminated my contract after one year and seven months,"* Lia said. Now she is working for her second employer, another expat. *"I want to try again. And I think it's not that difficult to talk about rights with my current employer."* Magi agreed and added, "Yes! If you negotiate with the expat families, mostly they'll understand better about the rights you're talking about. But if you negotiate with locals, they will probably argue with you and still ask you to do this and do that. It could be very difficult to explain your rights to them sometimes. That's the big difference."

Working from 6.00 am, Lia finishes her work at 21.00 if everything is smooth, and if not, then she needs to work till 22.00. When I asked Lia whether she has lunch break or dinner break, she laughed, *"Yes, if the baby is sleeping. Otherwise, I need to take care of her while having meals. Many mothers need to do this if they don't have nannies to help them."* But Lia's job is more than being a nanny. She takes care of the baby, she cleans, she cooks, and she goes to the market to buy necessities. In fact, Lia's expat employer doesn't actually make her life easier. Apart from a lack of break time, she needs to work on Sunday evenings sometimes. For example, she was occasionally asked to wash baby clothes after arriving at her employer's flat on her rest days. Although Lia doesn't need to suffer from abuse or insufficient food, overwork and a lack of break are still big issues for Lia. I wonder if it is the job of being a mother too difficult per se.

Without hiring a domestic worker, Lia's employer is going to face similar issues to find a balance between looking after the baby and looking after herself. She probably would need to take care of the baby while having meals. I'm sure that I've seen so many scenes like this in my life. Her workload could be less if she decides on how the housework is done for her own family. Yet it is a fact that a mother with a new-born baby usually doesn't have enough rest, especially when domestic work and poverty coexist. As stated in Hong Kong Poverty Situation Report 2018, about one-fifth of Hong Kong population is under poverty line.[58] The elderly, the single-parent families, and the jobless are the most vulnerable groups. Women living in poverty usually need to be a breadwinner and a domestic worker at the same time, and they are more likely to face the same situation as the migrant domestic workers do—they all suffer from overwork, insufficient rest, and a lack of mental wellbeing, possibly with less respect from the society too. After all, housework has been downplayed and portrayed as only "trifles"; and in a meritocratic society where neoliberalism is pervasive, poverty only suggests a big failure to social Darwinists— "You don't work hard".

Magi, who had been working in Hong Kong since 2001, is the former chairperson of Filipino Migrant Domestic Workers' Unions (FMDWU). She joined this union in 2005. Before coming to Hong Kong, she had worked in Taiwan for a few years. Magi compared her working experience in Hong Kong and Taiwan and concluded:

> Working in Hong Kong has more holidays than Taiwan, but working in Taiwan has more break time every day. I felt less pressure when I was a child caregiver in Taiwan, and my workload was less heavy too. Also, my first employer in Taiwan was nicer to me than my first employer in Hong Kong. My average working hours in Taiwan were 9 to 10 hours a day, but here…I haven't experienced it yet. My first employer in Hong Kong is a typical first employer, but my first employer in Taiwan, at least she cared more about my feelings. I can sit in front of her, you know. I was very lucky in Taiwan. My employer allowed me to enjoy half a rest day every week, but many other domestic workers usually had one or two rest days a month in that time. Both places have discrimination against domestic workers, I can't say which one is generally better because I haven't been in Taiwan for so long time. But for my own experience, I remember discrimination in Taiwan is not as strong as in Hong Kong. I feel discrimination in Hong Kong is getting worse…It's really difficult for us.

After working for so many years in Hong Kong, I thought Magi may have been lucky for a long while. But that's not true. She still has to deal with the problem of overwork. Magi has been working for her new employer for 6 months. Finding a new employer during the COVID-19 pandemic is not an easy task. As a former chairperson in a union, she's familiar with all the terms of her labour rights. Even though her daily work schedule is from 7.00 to 23.30-24.00, and she definitely knows such long working hours can't be right, the pity is that there isn't so much she can do. Magi said helplessly:

As a union leader, I'm experienced about observing people. I actually know which employer is going to be demanding or fussy to us. But sometimes we don't have choices. During my job interview, I knew that it'd be a really stressful job compared to my last one, but I needed a job so much. I know it sounds very ironic to so many people. I'm a union leader, and I helped so many workers here before. But I can't help myself now. Of course, I hope I can get more rights and more time to relax, but I need to survive more. That is also a similar situation for so many domestic workers here during COVID-19. If we complain too much, we may lose our jobs. And we don't want to lose our jobs in this situation. We don't have many bargaining chips in hand. It is very difficult to find a job during COVID-19 even though we're in Hong Kong. Before COVID-19, if we terminate our contracts prematurely, we must leave Hong Kong to apply for a new job and then wait for the contract processing and visa processing in the Philippines. That's a lot of time to wait. Also, we may need to pay to the agency again, which is a lot of money to most of us. Now, some said that the Hong Kong government is more lenient with us, because the two-week rule becomes a temporary four-week rule during the COVID-19. But there're lots of uncertainties. Four weeks are still not safe for us. What if we can't find a new employer and get our new visa within four weeks? Living in Hong Kong without a job is too expensive for us. And if we go back home, it's hard for us to come back to Hong Kong to work. Finding a job in the Philippines is even more difficult now, unemployment rate is rising perhaps till next year. I think...I have no choice but to complete my two-year contract for my current employer.

Every Sunday, Magi needs to prepare breakfast for the elderly couple she's looking after and then come to Central to enjoy her rest day, joining campaigns and helping other domestic workers. After she arrives at her employer's place on Sunday evenings, she needs to wash dishes and clean the kitchen. Her employer is the son of this elderly couple. He doesn't want to wash dishes and clean the kitchen for sure, while the elderly couple are too old to clean up their apartment. So, it's still all Magi's work on her only one rest day in a week. As for the rest days of the week, Magi's workload is unsurprisingly heavy. *"The grandpa is 90 years old, and the grandma is 84 years old with dementia. I need to look after them very carefully. Basically, I have no real lunch break or dinner break. Maybe sometimes I have 10-15 minutes to have lunch or dinner? Then I have to work. Or sometimes, I work while eating. Taking care of children is more demanding, but taking care of elderly people is more stressful. I work 17 hours a day. For me, it's like I need to stand by for 24 hours. The grandpa and grandma sometimes may need me as well while I was sleeping,"* told Magi.

I was trying to ask Magi and Lia more information about their organisations and how they help other domestic workers here especially during COVID-19. But they told me that they were going to have an online meeting with some domestic workers who need help. *"We can't meet them in person, because their employers still don't allow them to go out to have holidays. What we can do is to help them online, and if anyone needs food or shelters, usually we transfer the case to Mission for Migrant Workers (an NGO based in Hong Kong to help and support domestic workers). Many organisations among us work with MFMW, and MFMW keep the files of the aided workers,"* said Lia.

Liza hadn't turned up when Magi and Lia were leaving. They promised that they would introduce me to her. To keep contact, Magi and Lia told me their phone number and said I can text them if I have any questions. After they left, I continued to wander in Statue Square. A banner with "Junk Terror Law" hung at the roadside got my attention, and I decided to interview the person who hung this. Two minutes later, I found this person by asking the woman sitting close to the banner.

The woman who hung the banner to oppose the Philippine terror law is called Amy. She is the chairperson of ACFIL (Association of Concerned Filipinos in Hong Kong) and also a domestic worker in Hong Kong with over seven years of experience. Amy looked very comfortable with the recorded interview. She told me it was not the first time for her to be interviewed. There were some international students coming here to interview her. *"I hope more and more people can come here to talk to us and know our stories. Especially for unions, if no one wants to talk to us, then how can we deliver our message? I hope more people know what's we are fighting for. That's the whole point,"* she said. To make sure I'd sit comfortably, Amy asked her friend to give a tiny folding seat for me. I was treated like an honoured guest there.

Amy is a friend of Magi and Lia. As Lia said to me earlier, different organisations here do work closely, and they unite as one to help all Filipino domestic workers in Hong Kong. ACFIL is under UNIFIL-HK (The United Filipinos in Hong Kong), and like the organisations/trade unions where Magi and Lia belong to, it also works with MFMW. As a leader of a union, Amy is experienced in helping other domestic workers who are unreasonably dismissed, underpaid, and abused. She shared with me on the common problems faced by domestic workers in Hong Kong and how her organisation helps them:

Lots of domestic workers approached us to seek help. Some have the problem with the employers; some have the problem with the working place; some have the problem with long working hours; some even have no place to stay…You know our situation in Hong Kong. We have to live with our employers, then we're prone to abuse. Some are forced to work while they're sick; some sleep in the cupboard of the kitchen; some live on the top of the washing machine; some don't have enough food; some are physically and verbally abused; some are harassed… Then we must try to approach their employers, and if it doesn't work, we contact MFMW to ask them to aid, because they have more resources. During this process, I've learned a lot about what our rights are and how to fight our rights too. And it's important for every one of us to know this. Domestic helpers are part of economy in Hong Kong. We know this, and the government also knows this. We contribute a lot, why can't we fight for our own rights? When some employers don't follow the rules or the contract, we must do something to protect our rights!

She continued, *"Also sharing rooms could be a problem. There's a case I got last time. The helper was asked to sleep with her employer's kid, but the employer's kid is already a male adult. According to the law, helpers can't share a room with the opposite sex except he's a child. So, it's against the law. The helper complained about her employer, and then her employer dismissed her. That is the worst thing for a helper during COVID-19. Another problem is curfew. Most employers in Hong Kong set a curfew for their helpers on every holiday. So, the helpers must rush to go back home on their holidays. Usually, helpers need to go back before 9 o'clock."*

"But I read the employment law for domestic workers, it says a rest day or a holiday should be no less than 24 hours. If they have curfews, that means they may be asked to work on their holidays after returning to their workplace," I responded.

"Yes, it's supposed to be a whole day. But the reality is not like that. And then you'll be on call after returning home. Sometimes even it's your rest time, the employer may knock at your door and ask you to do this and do that. We're engaging with other domestic helpers to assist them to know their rights and we provide them with some free workshops. I told them to keep writing diaries, so they will have reference about what happened to them. Usually, if you keep silent, you'll probably be abused more. But if you know your rights and know how to negotiate with your employer, you'll have better chance."

Curfew is something new for me. I believe many difficulties faced by domestic workers are still awaiting to be uncovered. Amy's comments about agencies are consistent with what I found before. She believes many agencies just want to gain profits and don't care about helpers' rights or difficulties. Based on the information provided by Amy, ethical agencies in Hong Kong only charge 10% of the helper's first-month salary as replacement fee, but unethical agencies here could charge a helper from HK$4,000 to 6,000 as replacement fee, which is against the Employment Agency Regulations in Hong Kong. Even if a helper is abused by her/his employer and has evidence, mostly the replacement fee can't be waived. And if employers want to change their workers after one year, they need to pay their agencies 6,000 to 10,000 HKD as a replacement fee. Both employers and domestic workers can be overcharged by agencies and even cheated by their agencies. The misinformation provided by unethical agencies often becomes a trigger for employers' unrealistic expectations and employees' misunderstanding, which only makes the relationship between employers and their domestic workers go sour. By the same token, the high agency fee paid by the employers might shift the blame to their helpers, and if it happens, that will be a disaster for the helpers.

Amid the COVID-19, everything just becomes worse. There have been more domestic workers approaching Filipino unions or local NGOs to seek help recently. Amy recounted worriedly:

> During COVID-19, we have more workload, and more of us are having mental issues because of the current difficult situation. Many helpers aren't allowed to go out to have holidays. Due to the employers' financial pressure and other kinds of pressure, some helpers are verbally abused more frequently now. Before, if we got sick, some of us would still continue working. But now, if helpers get sick, some of us may lose our jobs. Also, if the employers lost their jobs or had financial problems, their helpers lost jobs too. The good thing is, Hong Kong Immigration Department started to consider our situation in March, simply because there're too many helpers dismissed after the outbreak of COVID-19. If a helper is dismissed by her employer, temporally she has one month to stay in Hong Kong to find a new employer and renew her visa. Before, if we're terminated prematurely, usually we had to go back to the Philippines to find a new employer and apply for the visa because of the two-week rule. But the thing is, it's so difficult to find a job during the pandemic. Even we can have one month to stay here looking for a job, we helpers are very careful not to lose our jobs.

Amy has been working in Hong Kong for seven years. Like every domestic worker I talked with, she had a bitter experience. And like most domestic workers, she didn't know her rights the first time she left home to work in a foreign society. Her first job was to work for a family immigrating from mainland China. Her female employer is a well-educated independent woman, but apparently, degrees don't necessarily generate kindness. Amy was asked to work from 6.00 in the morning to midnight. By "midnight", I mean that she sometimes worked till 2.00 am. The family preferred to sleep late. Amy had to wait for everyone to take a shower and then handwashed the clothes of the child she was taking care of, because that's the rule set by her first employer. And another rule was that Amy, as an inferior maid in the eyes of her employer, was not allowed to use the washing machine for her own clothes. She needed to wash them by hand. In order to do this, she had to sacrifice her own time for sleeping as washing her own clothes wasn't counted as "working" by her first employer. Amy estimated there are around 10% of domestic workers who are not allowed to use the washing machines for their own clothes. I can't find other words to explain this but "discrimination".

Overwork and discrimination were just part of the story. Amy recollected, *"I knew nothing at that time, because that's the first time for me to be abroad. I didn't know my rights, so I just accepted the abuse, physically, emotionally…My employer sometimes verbally abused me, but it's the grandma maltreated me. She blamed me for all the things, she beat me, she poured boiled water on my hands…"*

I think I almost yelled out while hearing the keyword "boiled water". Amy looked calm while talking about her past bitter experience. She had heard so many similar stories after joining the union, realising that almost every domestic worker was meant to be unlucky at least once in their work history. When race, outsider identity, and poverty intertwine, good luck becomes rare to those migrant domestic workers.

After one year and one month, Amy couldn't bear it anymore. She decided to terminate the contract by instinct. Her second employer is also from mainland China, but fortunately, with absolutely different attitudes towards Amy. *"My second employer is very good to me. At first, she didn't really follow the contract. But after I talked with her, I started to have a fairer timetable. If her kids didn't need to go to school, I only needed to work from 8.00-9.00 am to 8.00-9.00 pm with enough break. I think she is very open-minded. Both of my first and second employers have similar background. They're all from mainland China, and they all went to the UK to study. But they're different. I think it doesn't matter where you come from. It depends on people's minds. It is how they think that matters. If a person is open-minded, then it's easier for us to discuss with them about our rights. I have worked for the family for 6 years, but they relocated to Singapore last month. So, I have to find a new employer. Tomorrow will be my one month to work for my new employer. She's a French. My main responsibility is to take care of her two kids.*

Sometimes my boss and her husband make a joke and say they just hope their children are still alive when they return home. Now, I work from 7.30 am to 8.00 pm with lots of break time. I think my current boss and her husband are very good to me," told Amy.

Having heard so many stories of domestic workers here, I am dying to know whether the abusive and exploitative employers have similar characteristic patterns, or whether we can know they will probably be abusive employers in advance. So, I asked Amy, "As a union leader who has helped a lot of domestic workers, have you found anything in common among the abusive and exploitative employers?"

"Ah, I know this after being a union member for a few years! Usually when you are engaging with the potential employer for the interview, you'll identify whether he/she is an exploitative employer or not. For example, if the employer already has a very LONG (Amy stressed this word) list of all requirements and duties, to ask you to do this and you have to do that...blah, blah, blah... Usually this kind of employers are perfectionist employers, and you need to be very careful especially when you need to live with your employer," Amy responded.

I asked Amy how she thinks of the social movement in Hong Kong last year. She answered me without hesitation, *"I support it! The protesters were fighting for democracy and freedom, their basic rights! They're activists, and I'm an activist too. Actually, I joined the protest, with my second employer. We took care of each other in the protest. But after the national security law was approved, she and her husband don't think Hong Kong is safe for them anymore. So, they took their kids to immigrate. In the Philippines, there are many activists too. Recently, because of the anti-terror law, many people have been arrested for what they did or said without any warrants. Our government just want to silence us. My best friend... she was killed last week... She was an activist. She's so young... I'm really sad. I think if I'm in the Philippines, I'll be in the same situation. My parents all know that I'm an activist. They worry about me of course, but they also respect my choice. Now, I'm in Hong Kong, I can still be an activist to say no to my government."*

My final question to Amy is about her self-perceptions. Apart from perceiving herself as an activist, she also identifies her as an open-minded person who cares about fairness. At night, I texted to Magi and Lia to ask them how they identify themselves. Lia replied first, *"I'm an activist, a mother of a 7-year-old daughter, a former teacher, and a Filipino. I love my country and I hope it will be a better place. That's why I become a political activist."*

Magi replied to me after tidying up the kitchen (at 10.45 pm). Her answer is, *"I'm a unionist who promotes humanity and discourages discrimination in all forms. I'm also an activist, a mother, and a friend to all workers."*

11. Liza

Saturday, 12 September 2020

As Lia promised, she introduced me to Liza, the artist. After telling Liza my concepts about the illustrations, she expressed her preference to discuss the details when we meet in person. Then, I met Liza on a Saturday evening (she has a very kind and understanding employer). Recommended by Liza's friends, the tea house we met is a very quiet place. Only a couple of guests were sitting there on a Saturday night due to the pandemic, and I recognised Liza easily based on her description of her dress.

Liza has been to different places to work as a domestic helper. She went to Singapore; she went to the UK; now she's in Hong Kong. She has multiple identities as well. She is an independent woman, an activist, a single mother of a 6-year-old daughter, a full-time domestic worker, an artist, and the chairperson of Filipino Migrant Workers' Union (FMWU). During our conversation, Liza received a couple of phone calls from the leaders of other Filipino organisations. She would tell me something about her friends and her friends' organisations after hanging up the phone. When I asked Liza why there are so many different organisations and unions in Filipino community here. She thought about it for a while and then responded, *"Unions focus on workers' rights. While organisations...some focus on LGBT rights, some focus on women rights, some on culture, some on environment... But we all work together. Different unions work with one another, and organisations work with unions. In terms of the issue of women, we're all women. Workers? We're all workers. And many of us support LGBT groups and care about the environment too. So basically, it depends on which organisation or union you want to be in."*

I was amazed by their sisterhood and civil rights consciousness. Yet it's not a coincidence. They grew up in a gender-equal society in which women are familiar with fighting for equal rights. Many of them started to join protests when they were university students or even high school students. As one of the first countries organising a women suffrage movement, gender equality in the Philippines continues to stand out today. According to the Global Gender Gap Index in 2019, the Philippines ranked 8th on the basis of economic participation and opportunity, educational attainment, health and survival, and political empowerment. Despite the fact that the Philippines' gender gap dropped to 16th in 2020 amongst 153 countries, it still remains as the top gender-equal country in Asia.[59] A great number of Filipino domestic workers are accustomed to rights and gender equality, and many of them have gained relevant knowledge and practice in their own society. What will these well-educated women do if their rights in another society are infringed? They'll fight. More than that, they'll unite, for they realise that no matter what their top agenda is, above all, they are outlanders in this society.

Liza is one of the well-educated women among them. She holds a Bachelor's degree in Fine Arts, and she's been exposed to feminist theories and LGBT groups since university. The themes of her paintings mainly relate to those helpless and powerless people, revealing her sympathy and empathy for the underprivileged. For me, the most impressive painting of hers is about a disabled, homeless man. I can feel his pain because Liza managed to paint his pain. While for Liza, it's not only because she's better at feeling for other people, but because it's part of her pain too.

By Liza

The first place Liza went to work is Singapore. When she was mentioning Singapore, I was a bit nervous. I was hoping that Liza was treated and paid fairly there. But after my glimpse at Liza, I knew that my hope was going to collapse. As recounted by Liza, it's a type of human trafficking. According to Anti-slavery (an international human rights organization), "human trafficking is the process of trapping people through the use of violence, deception or coercion and exploiting them for financial or personal gain. People can be trafficked and exploited in many forms, including being forced into sexual exploitation, labour, begging, crime (such as growing cannabis or dealing drugs), domestic servitude, marriage or organ removal."[60]

Liza recounted, *"I put my CV online. It attracted a British couple in Singapore. They seemed really nice, and they offered me good salary. But when I asked them to find a Filipino agency to help dealing with visa processing, they rejected me. They said they don't want to pay unnecessary fees because our government is corrupted. I said 'OK, but how would you do that?' At that time, I didn't have any experience to go abroad... I was too young. So, I just trusted them. They suggested me to go to Singapore as a tourist first and then they'll help me get work permit in Singapore. Then, I went to the airport. But I was questioned by the immigration officer, because he said: 'You don't look like a tourist. You don't show your money.' The first try failed like this."*

"What happened then?"

She continued, *"Then I told the couple. They said it's OK and asked me to go to Manila as they hired an agency to help me. I felt they really wanted to hire me, so I continue trusting them. I went to the agency as they suggested, and the woman in the agency gave me those documents I didn't understand at all. It's like a Singaporean stranger suddenly became my boyfriend, and the woman in the agency asked me to stop asking her questions but just follow her instructions and submit those documents to the immigration office. I was really confused. The woman told me the Singaporean stranger already knew me through my pictures and what I needed to do is to wait. I entered Singapore as a tourist this time, pretending that I have a boyfriend there. But I was trapped in there, wating for "the signal" of the agency in Singapore. I was so scared. I didn't know what to do, but somehow, I followed their instructions... Then I was sent to the employers' house and started to work before getting my work permit."*

I was getting increasingly nervous while hearing Liza's narrative. I'm glad Liza is still alive, and in the meantime, I wish I could take a time machine to travel back then, telling Liza, "Don't listen to this couple! Don't go there!" I wish I could do the same thing to other vulnerable people too. However, there is no time machine. Nobody can change the past, thus Liza's story still continued in the past.

It was 2011 by the time Liza was trapped in Singapore. In the first eight months, before Liza managed to seek help from a local NGO, Liza believed she had been in hell. Her passport and contract were all confiscated by the couple. Specifically, Liza didn't even have a chance to see her contract. After getting her work permit after a few months, they took her work permit away too. She was forced to work for that family from 4 o'clock every morning till 11.00 in the evening, and only after 11.00 she could be allowed to have her dinner. For these two years, Liza had been working with no holidays. What's worse is that she had received no salary for the first eight months. Her employer only gave her SGD$25 a month as her food allowance. However, SGD$25 was not enough to buy food for the whole month in Singapore in 2011. Fortunately, there was an Indonesian woman working in the same house that helped her a lot. *"The Indonesian lady is a housekeeper, and I am the nanny and cleaner. She stole some food from the family for me. It's funny, isn't it? I was working, and I should be provided with food. But my employers didn't provide any food with me, and I didn't have enough money to buy food. So, I needed another domestic worker to steal food for me,"* told Liza.

"How many meals did you have a day, Liza?" I asked.

"How many meals? Oh...just one... I didn't have time for three meals. I needed to take care of 3 toddlers...their food, their clothes...everything... and I needed to clean the four-floored house. I begged the couple and said, 'Please, let me go.' But they said no way. They said to me, 'You owe us 80,000 pesos (around 1,653 USD), and you need to pay that.' They told me they paid 80,000 pesos to the immigration office in Manila. I didn't know this..." Liza added, *"I really wanted to escape, and they probably knew that. So, they always threatened me they'd take me to the police station if I escaped or I told anyone I was abused. They said they'd tell the police how I cheated the immigration office in Singapore. I was...22 years old at that time...I was really scared...But then, after eight months working without salary, I found a non-government organisation, a humanitarian organisation in Singapore. They helped a little. They wrote a letter to my employers and said if they don't pay me my salary, they will take further action. I think my employers were shocked and a bit scared. After receiving the letter from NGO, they said they would give me salary, starting from that month. But they still didn't pay me my salary in the first eight months. They just started to pay me SGD$500 in the nineth month. That's it! But my timetable didn't change, it's still a type of slave schedule. And I was verbally abused as well. They always cursed me, 'Stupid! Stupid fucking woman!', something like that..."*

By Liza

(This picture shows how Liza felt in her room after working for 19 hours. Besides, she told me that many helpers' rooms do not have proper ventilation.)

Liza heard how some helpers were abused by people from different origins before, but she couldn't predict that she would be abused and enslaved by an apparently civilised British couple with decent jobs, and that she would go through human trafficking in a developed society. She still doesn't really understand why this ever happened in this modern world. She isn't sure which word or words she could use to summarise why people can become so evil behind closed doors. She thought about racism. She almost said that word. But what she had been through in Singapore is more than racism. She was inhumanly treated there; her human dignity was denied. Liza told me that once she was having high fever with body temperature reaching 40°C, her female employer gave her a painkiller and said to her, "Take it! Then go back to work!" Liza tried to protest it, *"What if I couldn't get recovered soon? What if I really need a rest?"* But the reply that Liza got is cold and ruthless: "You'll be fine! It is your privilege to get a painkiller when you're sick! You should feel appreciated and then go back to work!"

Singapore's employment law against FDWs is discriminatory, yet the authority still attempts to protect FDWs from abuse and ill-treatment. It writes on the official website of MOM (the Ministry of Manpower):

> Employers will face severe penalties if they are convicted of abusing foreign domestic workers (FDWs)... We take allegations of abuse and ill-treatment of an FDW seriously, especially if they concern physical or sexual abuse... Complaints of abuse are investigated by the police. If convicted, employers will face severe penalties under the law. They and their spouses will also be permanently banned from employing another FDW.[61]

But if we review Hayma's case mentioned in a previous chapter, we'll know how desperate they tend to be when domestic workers report forced labour, overwork, verbal abuse, social isolation and salary-related problems to the police. Hayma's situation was similar to Liza in Singapore, but when Hayma went to the police station to seek help, the police said they can't help her because she's not physically abused. What the police did was to call Hayma's employer to pick her up, and as you perhaps have already guessed: Hayma was treated even worse after that. Hence, even MOM tried to use the law to deter employers from abusing their domestic workers, yet selective enforcement kind of encourages unscrupulous employers abusing and enslaving their employees. As it stands, the potentially unscrupulous employers will imitate those who exploit and abuse the domestic workers with impunity. It will turn to a negative form of social imitation.

I shared more details with Liza about the policies against domestic workers in Singapore, Liza seemed to be less puzzled. When she heard that a migrant domestic worker needs to get approval from the Singaporean government if she wants to marry a Singaporean citizen, she shook her head and looked aggrieved. She said, *"I see, we're discriminated by the government, the law, and many of the employers there. And inside of the house, whether we're treated like workers or slaves, it's up to the employers. No one will know… Employers can exploit us as much as they can. The government here (Hong Kong) and there (Singapore) couldn't care less about how many hours we work every day, so they don't regulate our maximum working hours. They give the power to our employers, and we're abused by unsupervised power!"* Liza is right. The discrimination that she had encountered is multi-dimensional, and so is exploitation. In most cases, the employers have too much power over their domestic workers, or the employers let their domestic workers believe so. And because the domestic workers' workplace is also a private living place, it is very difficult to identify the victims. People can hardly know whether the domestic workers are enslaved or not.

After finishing her two-year "contract" in Singapore, Liza went back to the Philippines, feeling so relaxed. In her hometown, she had a baby with a man. Then, she started her unknown journey overseas again. This time, she went to the UK. No human trafficking, no abuse, no salary problems happened to her. She was grateful.

Having worked as a domestic worker in the UK for two years, Liza has gained some different experience from many others here. When she was working in London, she got paid by hour. Her working hours were usually within eight hours. If she was asked to work overtime, she got overtime pay. And because the minimum wage is the same for citizens and non-citizens, Liza could earn more money 7 years ago in London than in Hong Kong now. The same minimum wage with local citizens along with being paid by hour effectively discourages exploitation if the employers obey the employment law.

However, from time to time, modern slavery is still found in this well-developed society that values human rights. At the time Liza was working there, she joined a union, and meanwhile, she was a volunteer in a shelter that cares for vulnerable domestic workers. After seeing and hearing so much from the people she helped, she not only realised that how lucky she was in the UK, but also began to rethink humanity and equality in developed societies.

She said, *"Before going to UK, I really thought the UK is a great place for people to live and work. I watched TV about UK, thinking that the employers there must be nice to their domestic workers. They seem to always smile at others. Plus, all the employees can get paid by hour. I was like 'wow'! But when I was there, I realised that there's a lot of abuse happening there. And I think a lot of people know about it. Fortunately, I can speak English, so I can always help the victims to translate what they wanted to say. I'm not a professional translator, but I really wanted to help. Some abuse is really horrible, even more horrible than what I experienced. And the most vulnerable domestic workers there are those who cannot really speak English. Most abuse cases I know there, the victims are from Indonesia. Their employers brought them to UK or hired them through agencies."*

"What kind of people hire domestic workers? I'm curious," I asked.

"Most of them are from the outside of UK. You know, they've formed the habit to hire a domestic worker to do housework or caregiving for them, so when they move to UK or immigrate to UK, they'd bring their domestic workers to there, or they will hire some new domestic workers from other places to the UK. If the domestic workers don't speak English, they may be forced to sign an invalid contract they have no idea what it is. So, what we always do there is to teach those vulnerable workers basic English. Some of them are very good at speaking different languages, just like many Indonesian domestic workers can speak very good Cantonese in Hong Kong. They can speak Arabic, Hindi... but they're not good at speaking English. We also provide some workshops to let them know their rights as domestic workers in the UK. But then the UK immigration

department changed its policies to domestic workers, and it's getting hard to renew my visa. So, I had to leave the UK and come to Hong Kong."

Liza's experience in the UK let me recall the unfair treatment or ill-treatment those migrant workers have encountered in New Zealand. Sometimes, I read relevant news from social media; sometimes, I heard it from my friends. Like what Liza said, the most vulnerable people are those who don't really speak English. They don't know the local law or their rights there. Their employers intimidated them, and they are scared as Liza was. One of my friends Cathy once found that some Chinese migrant workers who don't speak much English were exploited in a Chinese restaurant. They not only received much lower salary than the minimum wage in NZ, but also were only allowed to have two rest days each month. Then Cathy asked some advice from different people and managed to help those poor migrant workers (she got to know this from her friend who was working as a part-time waitress in the restaurant). She was a university student at that point without so much experience in fighting against injustice in a foreign country, but she did it well. I'm proud of her. Cathy contacted the local city council and the victims got free legal assistance as well as translating service after a few hours. She told me she was surprised that government bureaucracy can actually work efficiently. Jean, another friend of mine, used to work as a part-time court interpreter for Korean people in NZ, she shared some cases with me as well. It turns out that domestic violence and all kinds of abuse happened more frequently to those people who knew limited English. They can be migrant workers and they can be immigrants too. Due to the language barrier, however, the majority of people in the host countries will not find out what's happening to these poor migrants and immigrants, and generally those who speak the same language are the ones most likely to identify the exploitation and violence directed at them.

Liza said that she was shocked when she heard what's happening to some migrant workers in the UK, as she thought that such severe abuse cases would only occur in less developed societies. But the sad truth is that abusing migrants through making use of their vulnerability is still happening in almost every developed society. Apart from the language barrier, the protection of migrants' rights is arguably in the grey area of many societies, because the migrants are not like the citizens who can vote, the governments in the host societies just don't have enough motivation to put the migrant issues on the agenda. In this regard, the difficulties faced by powerless migrants are just the hidden shame of every society, no matter it is developed or non-developed.

What Liza experienced in Singapore and the UK has brought her much reflection. She doesn't really believe the widely-acknowledged sentence in Hong Kong—that "expats treat domestic workers better". Especially after working for the first employer in Hong Kong, Liza believes that statistically, expats may tend to be better to domestic workers, but it still depends. *"As a domestic worker, what you will experience is less related to where your employers come from, but more related to your luck. It's only about luck!"* She said.

Liza's first employer in Hong Kong is an expat of mixed Asian and European ancestry. But her female employer is not as nice as the urban legend describes. What they agreed in the interview was not followed by Liza's first employer in Hong Kong. Liza didn't have enough food or a private room as her employer promised to her. She was only provided with instant noodles as well as eggs, and she was asked to sleep in the living room with a mattress. But the couple she was working for always stayed late watching movies, so she had no choice but to sleep in the kitchen.

"I didn't mind sleeping in the kitchen at all...because I was too tired," said Liza. *"I was forced to work 20 hours a day in that family. Unbelievable, right? I sometimes had to work from 4.00 am to 1.00 am. The couple at that time never gave me a chance to have a rest. When they were having meals, I had to serve them food, staying there and waiting them to call me. After they finished their meals, I was supposed to have mine. But most of the time, they would assign me other tasks after I cleaned the table and washed dishes. Even when I sat down and ate noodles, my female employer always said I didn't do anything. So, she would take all the things out from her wardrobe and let me fold her clothes and organise back. I was not allowed to take any day-off for three months, and my first employer here didn't pay me for asking me to work on holidays. I was so helpless, because my agency was on my employer's side too. The agency staff told me I can only have day-off after three months, that's what they said."*

By Liza

By Liza

"At that time, there was only darkness around me. And that's the time I started to believe, there is inhumanity and inequality… wherever we go…especially when we belong to lower social class. Here, there, what's the difference?" sighed Liza. In December, when the family went on holiday, Liza eventually got a chance to seek help. She met a neighbour, also a domestic worker in Hong Kong, who happened to be a member of FMWU. Liza was rescued by FMWU after working four months for that family, and that's how she joined the union. Ironically, her first employer was supposed to pay her one-month salary before she left, but Liza only got HK$3,000. On top of that, she was asked to pay her first employer HK$700 for the broken washing machine, which wasn't Liza's fault at all.

Now, Liza's employer is a very nice and considerate French woman who totally supports Liza's work in the union. She calls Liza by her name, and feels very uncomfortable to be addressed as "Madam". She thought that's weird and unequal. She preferred Liza to call her by her name. Liza once responded, *"But my agency told us to call our employers as 'Madam' or 'Sir' to show our respect."* Liza's current elegant employer refuted this idea and pointed out, *"Oh, that's nonsense!"* My theory is that if an employer prefers to be called by their name rather than "Madam" or "Sir", usually this employer cares more about equality, and thereby probably treating their domestic workers in a fairer way. Liza agreed.

Before we left the teahouse, Liza shared some new information about the training courses provided by her agency in the Philippines. In order to find a job in Hong Kong, Liza paid 70,000 pesos (approximately 11,000 HKD) as training fees to a Philippine agency. Aside from learning about Hong Kong culture, courtesy, cooking Hong Kong food and performing cleaning duties and caregiver duties, the potential domestic workers need to learn how to use chopsticks as well. *"Using chopsticks is part of the test. If you're a slow learner of using chopsticks, you'll be hungry. They won't give you any food,"* told Liza. In addition to this, getting up early in the morning and enduring hunger are a part of the training as well. When Liza was in the training centre, she was asked to get up at 5.00 o'clock in the morning and eat a little. The potential domestic workers were trained to eat only once a day, because the trainers told them that they would experience something like this when they work in Hong Kong.

For Liza, most agencies do not train the trainees to become domestic workers, but to train them to become a type of modern slaves who are good at enduring unfair treatment and abuse. Liza told me, *"Most trainers will shout at you to pretend that they're your employers. And if you cry—of course, you're going to cry—they will shout at you again and ask you to get used to it because you may experience it in the future. It's like the psychological and emotional training, and if you can't pass it, they will think you're not ready for the job in Hong Kong because you don't know how to deal with pressure."*

However, that military-level pressure training does not have a place in this modern world. I can't accept this kind of training. And I can't figure out why on earth some believe that domestic workers have to be trained to endure hunger and emotional abuse. Yet, I began to understand more about why the newcomers are comparatively unluckier. For most migrant domestic workers here and there, they will not know their rights until they empower themselves. If the training centres do not provide sessions about the labours' rights, they will have to rely on themselves: to join unions and organisations, to campaign, to unite, and to fight for the rights that they deserve!

12. Covid-19, Discrimination and Their Wishes

Sunday, 13 September 2020 Temperature: 31°C Humidity: 70%

As the leaders of a Filipino union and organization in Hong Kong, Lia and Liza accepted my interview again. Yet this time is a bit different, as the interview intends to know the situations of domestic workers from a more holistic perspective. The interview recording is transcribed as below:

1. Now, what are the most difficult things faced by the unions or organisations?

Liza: In this current situation, the COVID-19 situation, the hardest part for us is time. Because we are all domestic workers, and we can only gather on Sunday. Our time on Sunday becomes very limited. Also because of social distancing, it's really hard for us to reach more people to help them or to campaign. What we can do is to do it online. We use ZOOM to have online meetings, but the problem with having online meetings is that some domestic workers are not allowed to use their phones inside of the house on workdays. Most of them are newcomers in Hong Kong, especially those who don't know their rights here. As I said before, most domestic workers are trained to be obedient helpers in the Philippines. Even here, some of us are told not to use our phones before 9.00 or 10.00 pm, because the employers think it might distract them from doing their work. They can only use their phones during the night after they finish all their work. So, most of our campaigns now are held at a strange time at night if it's on our workdays. And that's probably the only time we're all available to use our phones. But the problem is night time is also our family time, you know, to contact our families in the Philippines. Plus, most domestic workers' workload has increased a lot, so they might feel really tired already when they attend meetings at night. Every Sunday, we're very busy too. We need to have online meetings with those domestic workers who need help, and we also need to campaign for our agendas, including agendas in Hong Kong and also in the Philippines just in one day. It's really hard.

Lia: Yes. And discrimination is another difficulty. We feel more employers and other local people tend to believe that we, migrant domestic workers are those who are more likely to carry the virus. But the fact is we are really careful. If we get the virus, we may be fired, and then the government might deport us because we're just migrants here. Some employers didn't allow domestic workers to meet their friends on Sunday, and sometimes if they went out on Sunday for a while, their employers would ask them lots of questions like where they went, who they met… blah blah blah. But the thing is, some employers can meet their friends. If our friends might carry the virus, can't their friends have the equal opportunities to get the virus? That's discrimination! Also, we need to go to the market to buy meat and vegetables all the time, you know how many people you can meet in markets here, right? There's no social distancing in markets. And don't mention it's very easy to be touched there. Going to markets is as risky as we meet our friends on Sunday. I can't see there's a difference. A few weeks ago, my employer went to a bar, so I told her that I need to see my friends on Sunday as well. She agreed though she's a bit reluctant.

Liza: Since February, the government here told domestic workers to stay at home. But does the Hong Kong government have any idea what it means to us? Telling domestic workers to stay at home means to tell us to stay in our workplace. That's not our home. Many of us don't have private rooms, and many of us may be forced to work on Sunday with or without pay. We should be protected by the government as well. Our employers always ask us to go to the market or take the kids to go to outside, it's pointless, right? Does staying at home means only staying at home on Sunday? Or does staying at home for our employers and Hong Kong government means it depends on context? Everyone could be affected. Everyone could carry the virus. So, why only domestic workers? Especially when social distancing restrictions were announced, the blame was put on us. Many people here said we're ignorant and we don't know what's going on…They said if we gather like this, we'll be the biggest problem. But our problem is—we don't have the place to go. Where can we go? Stay at home? That's not our home! That's our workplace. Now, it's not raining. We're lucky. But if it's raining, we'll have to move near the shops under their roofs. But the guard might drive us away.

Me: Can you stay in the shopping malls?

Liza: Yes, but if you stand there, it's just for a few minutes. So, you keep walking, otherwise the guard will drive you away. Many people here think we don't have money for shopping, so if we stand there for too long, it must be something wrong. Even when we go to some shops in shopping malls, once they know we're domestic workers, there's something in the shop assistants' faces. We can see, and we can feel it.

Lia: I remember once my employer took me for shopping. She went to Chanel, and she said she wanted to buy me a sample as a gift for me. I accompanied her to Chanel, and I pointed at a tiny bottle of perfume and asked the shop assistant whether I may try to use it. Then the shop assistant sized me up and said, "Oh that one is more than 200 HKD!" I was very uncomfortable. Even my employer didn't buy this to me, I can still pay it by myself. I can afford it! It's just there's no point for me to use luxuries. I don't need luxuries! But I was pissed off back then, so I replied, "I don't care!" And during the COVID-19, there're not many people going to the shopping malls. So, some shopping malls near our gathering places decided to close some toilets on Sundays, because they know that many domestic workers would use them, and they don't like it.

Liza: Yes, last time I was queueing up to use the bathroom in a shopping mall, but I was refused to enter the bathroom. A lady who looks like Chinese was allowed to enter. I asked the guard why, he said, "She can, you can't!" Then I found a sentence near the entrance of the bathroom "Only for Customers". But how can they tell who is the customer? Then I realised that domestic workers are not the customers. And there is discrimination when we get on the bus. You know, when domestic workers get on the bus, some people are going to go away from us.

Lia: It's OK. Some of us developed a new technique, making use of people's discrimination to deal with the rush hours. Sometimes when it's too crowded in the MTR, we just need to pretend coughing a little bit, then people around us will walk away. So, we can get more space hahah. I thought whether it is because we don't dress up?

Liza: Oh, if you dress up, there may be discrimination too. You know I like art and artistic things. Sometimes I like wearing big earrings, but they're not expensive. My employer's local friend suggested her not to hire me, because she thinks I am unreliable by wearing earrings. She implied that I'm a bad woman. My employer told me this. I'm lucky my employer didn't listen to that local lady. But I've seen so many local women dressing up and wearing earrings, why isn't there a problem? Why only me?

Lia: Yes, there's lots of discrimination against us. But during the COVID-19, the discrimination is getting worse. Last time, I saw a report about domestic workers. I knew it's about us, as there's a picture about us. But I couldn't understand it. It's in Chinese. So, I sent it to a local friend, she's also one of our supporters. I asked her what the report is about and how other people comment about us. She said, "You'd better not to know…it's very bad for you." Not understanding Chinese may be a good thing for us, so we can be happier. But actually, the Hong Kong government should do something, because they have funds. If many local people think we block the road or occupy their space on Sundays, or if they think we may carry the virus, then their government should provide us with some places to stay. But the government doesn't do anything. It just lets local people blame us, which doesn't help solve things.

2. How do Filipino unions and organisations help domestic workers?

Lia: Usually, we can only be active to help them on Sundays because all union committees or the members in Filipino organisations here are all full-time domestic workers. Some domestic workers will come here to talk to us; some will call us to describe their situations; some may ask their friends to talk to us because they may not be allowed to use phones. Also, there is hotline to provide help within 24 hours for the domestic workers who need to be rescued. If there're some who need immediate rescue approaching us, usually we transfer the case to Mission for Migrant Workers who can provide shelters, food or counselling to them. In the past, it was easier. But because of COVID-19, there're more domestic workers who need help from either unions or organisations. And I guess Mission for Migrant Workers don't have enough shelters for all the helpless domestic workers.

Liza: Before COVID-19, we used to provide workshops about domestic workers' rights and wellbeing. Especially for newcomers, they really need this kind of workshops. Aside from that, there're also different kinds of educational opportunities and activities such as computers, art courses...so, domestic workers here can learn some new skills for free, and meanwhile, they can make new friends through that. Since we work with some local organisations, if the workshops require us to be indoors, they can provide space for us. Sometimes, a nearby church offers free space for us as well. So, that's really important for us to collaborate with different organisations here. Before, there're some groups for those who had emotional issues or just want to talk to somebody, so the sad domestic workers can feel that someone cares about them. But because of COVID-19, we can't do it anymore. It's very sad.

3. Do you charge any membership fees from your members?

Liza: Different unions and organisations are a bit different, but nobody charged a lot. Some organisations are free. We ask our members to pay HK$20 as registration fee, and then HK$5 as monthly contribution.

Lia: My organisation? Almost the same!

Liza: But it's very hard to collect monthly contributions during COVID-19. Sometimes we're not allowed to go out, sometimes our members may have other things to do... And it's very hard for those who live in really distant places like Tai Po (Liza looked at me while saying this). So, sometimes our members suddenly come here and pay their unions or organisations the whole year's contribution.

4. Who is responsible for taking care of the money? Do you have specific positions for that?

Lia: We have the secretary committee, but we also have elected auditor or treasurer to ensure financial transparency. All the committees are elected. And our members will know where their contributions are spent.

5. How are your elections like?

Liza: We have to set the convenient time for all the members, and gather all the members. Of course, before that we have to prepare for it. We have elections every two years. And if you can win it again, then you continue being a member of the committee.

Lia: Usually our election lasts around two to three hours. Actually, it's more than an election, it also includes reporting. All the committee members need to report what they've done. Unlike general elections, there's no term limit for any position as long as you can win the election in your union or organisation again. I have a friend who has been a chair person for her union for 10 years.

6. Based on the cases you've dealt with, who are the most evil, the governments, the agencies, or the employers?

Lia: The government of course! I think the Philippine government should be most responsible for this. We're forced to work abroad because of poverty in our country. If the Philippine government is not corrupted and provides us with job opportunities that can feed our families, why should we work as domestic workers abroad? Personally speaking, employers are the least evil compared to the governments and agencies. If both Philippine and Hong Kong governments have made good policies to protect our rights, then many of us won't be abused by our employers. For example, if the Philippine government doesn't protect the agencies, then the agencies in the Philippines won't have guts to charge us so much money. And if the Hong Kong government regulates our maximum working hours, most of us won't have to overwork.

Liza: I totally agree with Lia. Because it's the government that makes policies. The Philippine government doesn't care about our rights, and Hong Kong government doesn't want to care either. If governments make good policies and implement the policies well, then the agencies won't be like this. They won't dare to overcharge us. Agencies are the second worst, because most agencies train us to be tolerate abuse and they often work with those lending companies or loan sharks. As for employers here, some employers are good, but some are evil. As we discussed last night, it is the government that empowers them. So, I think even there are evil employers, they are not as evil as the governments (in the Philippines and Hong Kong) and agencies. But I think among them, the Philippine government is the worst in any sense. If you go to the Philippines, you will feel it. Our government not only makes so many of us suffer from poverty and separate from our families for survival, but it also demands us to pay tax when we work in Hong Kong. It's ridiculous! Most of us are suffering from overwork, homesickness, discrimination etc, and our government tax us for we're suffering.

Lia: True! That's why in Hong Kong, we not only campaign for the rights of domestic workers, but we also campaign the issues in the Philippines…because there're too many issues. Later, we're going to have an online campaign protesting the Philippine government building an unnecessary dam. The politicians only consider their own profits because they're going to earn so much money by this. But it's harmful to our environment, and also it violates the indigenous people's rights of self-determination. Many of us here are activists, and if you're activists in the Philippines, you probably are going to get killed because of the recent Anti-Terror Bill.

7. How many domestic workers here can earn more than minimum wage?

Liza: Not many people actually. Many westerners are willing to give domestic workers more salary, and that's why so many domestic workers here want to work for western employers. And some nice Chinese employers are willing to give domestic workers more salary than minimum wage. It really depends. Also, it depends on the workers' experience and performance. Usually, if you have, let's say 10 year-working experience, you can get much more than the minimum wage, and you should get more annual leave as well.

Lia: I've been only working in Hong Kong for three years, but I am still having minimum wage because I'm still quite new for my employer here. Sometimes, people in the Philippines say, "You're so lucky to work abroad. You can earn a lot!" But many of us are not lucky. In fact, we don't want to leave our family to work in a so far place. Many of us are taking care of other people's babies or children, but we can't take care of our own children back home. That's really sad. As for our salary, if you count how many hours we work per day, or how we are generally treated here, it isn't a lot at all.

8. What is the most possible change that can be made within a short time?

Lia: Discrimination (she stopped for a while and laughed), of course, is very hard to be changed for a long time. Maybe...salary? Because usually our salary rises a bit every year. Hong Kong government often announce our new minimum age at the end of September. We're having campaign for our expected living wage now. We hope our minimum wage can be over HK$5,000.

9. What is the first thing you wish to change, why?

Liza: Oh, there're too many...We wish there's no discrimination. We wish to be treated like workers. And we wish we don't have to leave our children to work... But the first thing we wish to change...hmm, this one (she pointed at this banner)! They're always together: humane accommodation and uninterrupted rest.

Lia: Sometimes when are sleeping, our employers wake us up and ask us to do something, like "Hello, I need water…I need tea…" And sometimes we're having our rest after finishing our work, our employers may call our names and to do something as well. 11 hours uninterrupted rest doesn't mean 11 hours of uninterrupted sleeping. We hope we can have uninterrupted 8 hours for sleeping, 1 hour for having meals, and 2 more uninterrupted hours for rest before sleeping. It's not really demanding, right?

Liza: Yes! Sometimes we work while eating, because some employers don't want us to sit down and have a proper meal. Sometimes we are standing there, and employers come to ask us to eat quickly to do other work. Some of our members even only have 5 minutes for having each meal. So, that's the first thing we hope to change. We really hope that every domestic worker can sit down to have proper meals, and we hope that all of us don't have to eat and work at the same time. For example, some employers ask their domestic workers to eat quickly and do the car washing.

Me: But car washing shouldn't be domestic work, right?

Lia: Yes, but the thing is some employers ask us to do that, and some will include car washing in the contract. They want to save money for that.

Liza: In fact, if employers can give us uninterrupted 11 hours for rest and humane accommodation, then we don't need to campaign. We'll be happy workers. But we have been campaigning this for more than two years, we still don't get anything. It's somewhat frustrating. We want to be treated like workers not maids, not servants, not slaves! I know a domestic worker whose employer wants her to call him "Master", and I was shocked! And you can imagine how this domestic worker is treated by her "Master".

Me: Do you think it will be better if employers call domestic workers by their names?

Lia: I think so. We all have names, and we should be called by names. We're not numbers! In fact, in the Philippines, some people also hire domestic helpers, but it's not like this.

International Solidarity

After the interview, Lia and Liza would join the online campaign for the issue they mentioned earlier. They invited me to observe their campaign, and both of them said they would translate what they were talking about during their meeting. Since I have long been curious about where they have meetings and online campaigns every Sunday, I happily agreed. I imagined that they would have their online meetings in a quiet room, like most of us always do. It turns out that, however, they just led me from the front of the square to the back of the square, which is another open space for domestic workers to gather but with fewer people.

In this area, some other different Filipino organisations were protesting Duterte (the current president of the Philippines)'s regime as well as the anti-terror law approved by him. They were also protesting against building the unnecessary dam which will damage the environment in their home country. Some of the activists shared one laptop, and the rest of them were using their phones to play their roles in the online campaign. To the left side of the banners, a few domestic workers were sleeping on cardboard (through the picture above, you can see a person's hands on the floor). I pointed at them and said to Lia with worries, "They look exhausted." Lia replied to me, *"Please do not blame them sleeping here…they must have worked for too many hours yesterday."* The reason Lia said that is because she once saw a local man filming some domestic workers while they were sleeping on the concrete floor with a mat. Lia asked that man why he was doing that, the man responded to her, *"You should ask them why they sleep on the floor in public space!"*

To show my respect, I didn't take photos of the sleeping workers, as this move might mean something different to Lia now. Yet, the activists there took pictures for me while I was showing support for them. After they finished their campaign, we continued chatting on different topics, ranging from the last social movement in Hong Kong to our opinions about LGBTQ groups. I probed into their attitudes towards the anti-extradition social movement first. They said that they were amazed by the huge number of the people who joined the protests, and they admired how the protesters organised different demonstrations and events without obvious leaders. Then, they hesitated a bit, as they didn't know my opinions about it and they definitely didn't want to irritate their new friend by expressing their political opinions (they thought I was a local resident). But thanks to Donald Trump, our common thing is: we don't like Trump, which makes us more relaxed to talk about our political opinions.

One of the Filipino activists began, *"I understood most parts about the Hong Kong social movement last year till I saw protesters waving the USA flags and Trump's photos while calling on Trump to liberate Hong Kong. Then I was lost...I couldn't understand it anymore. You know the Philippines was colonised by the US before, right? For me, that's not liberation to Hong Kong. They're calling for colonization."*

Another activist added, *"Yes. Trump is not going to liberate Hong Kong. He is the wrong person to be trusted. I don't think he cares about human rights compared to profits. He is a racist and sexist! He is also the person who damages democracy and called the Hong Kong protesters as rioters. Why the protesters here called on his name and trust him? I understand that protesters were helpless and they wanted democracy soon, but asking Trump or the US to liberate them is not democracy. That'll be colonization! They can't protest against dictatorship on the one hand, and support another form of dictatorship on the other."*

Then it's their turn to probe into my attitudes towards LGBTQ groups. But this one is easier after we all came out of the closet politically—that we dislike Trump. After knowing I'm also a supporter of LGBTQ, they were so glad. They told me that there's a migrant pride parade every November, but because of the pandemic, they're not so optimistic about this year's pride parade. Lia said she would introduce me to some LGBTQ members to talk to.

Some domestic workers were singing "Happy Birthday" near us, Liza and Lia took me to join them. They offered me a plate full of food. You can find cakes, fried noodles, coconut sticky rice, and spring rolls in one plate. But I turned them down because I wasn't hungry at that moment. They didn't give up. They offered me juice and fruit salad instead. And it would be very impolite to refuse them again. So, I drank the juice and took the salad, enjoying the food like everyone else did. A domestic worker smiled at me with her thumb up. Lia walked close to her and chatted with her in their language. Then Lia told me in English, *"That woman was saying you're great because you're willing to try our food. She said there're some visitors coming to say hello to them, but they seldom are willing to try our food. She said you don't have discrimination against us. She said 'thank you' to you."*

I didn't know what to say. I felt it might be too easy to be described as "great" by them. If you go and say hello, they'll think you're nice. If you agree to try their food, you'll be a great person. And if you accept their food and care about them, you'll be their good friend. I have never thought that I could be a likable person without paying any effort. That is something I've never experienced before in any other communities. But if we think about it deeply, would it suggest that domestic workers have been indeed marginalised and discriminated for a long time in this society? And their lack of confidence is just a result of social exclusion.

Liza left us because she had something else to do. Lia and I found a place to sit and continue chatting. At that time, I already drank up my water, feeling a bit thirsty for chatting so long. I was trying to find a nearby convenience shop to buy a bottle of water, but Lia said, "Wait, let me ask them (she pointed at the domestic workers we just met) whether they could help." Lia went to talk with them, and she brought a can of coke for me. The domestic worker who gave Lia coke was smiling at me, *"You don't need to pay for it."* Lia then explained to me about their Sunday lifestyle here, *"Some workers are allowed to cook for their own food on Sunday, so many of us give them money, and they bring food to Central every Sunday. Those who want to eat and drink with others will contribute some money to the domestic workers who're responsible for cooking and buying things, then we'll share the food and drinks with small groups for the whole day. It's much cheaper than we dine in restaurants here. And that's why you can always find food and drinks among us, even there's no one having birthday."*

Travelling from Central to Tai Po takes more than one hour. Having considered this, I believed it would be wiser to go to the bathroom first before leaving. The smiling domestic worker offered me detailed directions about how to go to a bathroom in a nearby fancy shopping mall. Yet Lia insisted that she would accompany me, so as to make it easier for me to find the place. At that point, Lia was holding a cup of fruit salad. She didn't finish it. She was eating it while chatting with me as we did in the domestic workers' world with her mask hung under her chin. Nobody wears a mask while eating. But I felt some people heading to the shopping mall were sizing her up. And the same group of people sized me up after staring at Lia, seemingly sending me a strong message through their eyes that they're sulky about the domestic worker beside me (they probably were thinking Lia was my maid) and that they hoped me to scold Lia for not wearing a mask (temporarily) in front of a fancy shopping mall. Lia must have felt it as well, so she stopped enjoying her salad and covered her mouth and nose soon. I was upset back then, as I've seen local people smoking, eating or drinking while walking on the street with their masks hung under their chins, but no one sized them up the same way as those did to Lia. I couldn't help asking Lia, "Did you see...how some people looked at you just now?" Lia smiled and replied, *"Yes, but I get used to it...Hey, no worries! Let's take a selfie here!"*

On my phone, there are some pictures with Lia, Liza and me standing in front of a union's banner. I sent them to Lia and Liza that night. Lia asked me whether she could post them on her Facebook. I agreed without hesitation. Then I saw that selfie and the pictures with three of us on her new post. She writes: Long Live International Solidarity!

13. The Rainbow Flag

Sunday, 20 September 2020 Temperature: 31°C Humidity: 66%

I saw Magi this Sunday. The former union chairperson looked exhausted. She shared more information about her current stressful job and the curfews directed at domestic workers. Magi went back to the Philippines in 2018 because her husband was very ill. She reapplied for a new job in Hong Kong in July 2019 and got her visa in March 2020. Usually, the employment process coupled with visa processing takes about 5-6 months (if a domestic worker applies for a job outside of Hong Kong), which is bad enough. But COVID-19 makes things worse: it turns the whole process to 7-8 months. I think now I understand more about why domestic workers here including Magi are so afraid to lose their jobs. Unemployment doesn't merely mean no income for them in Hong Kong, but it means that they may have remained poor for over a half year in the Philippines if they can't find a new employer and renew their visas in Hong Kong within limited time.

(Lia took this photo for Magi and me.)

Based on the data of the union members, Magi estimates that approximately 70% of domestic workers in Hong Kong have curfews on Sunday nights. Consistent with the information provided by Amy, Magi also said that usually those domestic workers who have curfews must arrive at their "home" (workplace) before 21.00. Magi's employer set a curfew for her as well. Apart from this, some of the rest days and statutory holidays are deprived by her employer from time to time albeit with overtime pay. Magi laughed at herself, *"I'm sorry. My knowledge about rights don't fit into reality. I choose my job over my rights this time. Whether I like it or not, I have to accept it! My only hope now is to have eight hours for sleeping."* Many workers in this world are probably still fighting for eight-hour workday, but ironically, domestic workers are fighting or hoping for eight-hour rest. What a divided world!

Lia and Liza were sitting close to me, and they occasionally joined the conversation between Magi and me. While Magi and I were chatting, a domestic worker came to say hello to Magi and the people sitting around her. That was the time my lesdar started to beep. Lia was excited to see her friend again. After short chitchat, Lia introduced me to her friend, *"Ian, this is Novia, one of our supporters. She's interested to talk with our LGBT group members here."* Then Lia turned back and introduced Ian to me, *"Novia, this is Ian, a member of an LGBT organisation among us."* Ian nodded, pointing at a rainbow flag and said, *"Look! That's my group's flag."* My conversation with Ian began like this, and I found out quickly that Ian preferred to be called "him".

Ian has been working as a domestic helper in Hong Kong for 13 years. His another identity is the chairperson of a migrant LGBT organisation: Filguys Gabriela. The name "Gabriela" is derived from Gabriela Silang, the first female Filipino leader of a liberation movement against Spanish colonial government. Now, GABRIELA which means "General Assembly Binding Women for Reforms, Integrity, Equality, Leadership, and Action", is a grass-root based national alliance of Filipino women. It has so many chapters inside and outside of the Philippines to help empower women through collective awareness and action. Filguys Gabriela is obviously part of the alliance. Apart from Filguys Gabriela, I've seen another organisation having "Gabriela" in its name. It's called Gabriela Hong Kong (it can be seen in above photo), focusing on women's rights as well as domestic workers' rights.

In 2015, Filguys Gabriela along with another Filipino LGBT group organised the first Migrants' Pride March in Hong Kong. Regarding the motivation to hold a Pride March specially for migrant workers, it's very simple: time. Usually, Hong Kong Pride Parade is held on Saturday, but many domestic workers who are the supporters of LGBT couldn't join it as their rest day in a week is on Sunday. Thus, Ian and the leader of another LGBT migrant group decided to hold a Pride Parade when all the pro-LGBT domestic workers are available.

Like Liza said before, the agendas of the organisations and unions among Filipino domestic workers always overlap. As a leader of an LGBT organisation, Ian not only leads his group members to fight for LGBT rights, but also for migrant workers' rights. Filguys Gabriela provides free counselling services and educational workshops to LGBT domestic workers. The topics range from handling homophobia to dealing with discrimination or abuse in the workplace. *"I hope they can accept their identity even after they're back to the Philippines,"* said Ian. There are also workshops particularly empowering newly-arrived migrant domestic workers who are recognised as the most vulnerable individuals among them all. Likewise, the slogans of Migrants' Pride call for justice for both LGBT+ groups and domestic workers.

On top of that, Ian and many members of Filguys Gabriela are activists as well. They work with Gabriela Hong Kong and other organisations to denounce the Anti-Terrorism Act and the worsening human rights situation in the Philippines. Because so many dissidents were disappearing, arrested and extrajudicially killed in the Philippines, the Filipino organisation and union leaders I know in Hong Kong have called for an end to state terrorism against the Philippine activists for weeks. *"Stop the Killings in the Philippines"* showed in the above picture is one of the common slogans used by the Philippine activists here.

(The members of Filguys Gabriela and me)

Before coming to Hong Kong, Ian was already aware of his gender identity and sexual orientation. When he received training in a Philippine agency, he was advised to keep long hair and dress like a real maid. Ian recounted with a laughter, *"I asked the trainers why, then they told me because most employers won't give me a job during the interview if I insisted dressing myself in a too manly way. I thought OK, it's just to please the employers. I can do it for the interview! But what I did later was I just had kept my hairstyle suggested by the agency for the first three months, and then little by little, I cut my hair and be myself!"*

"I think some of my former employers including my first employer didn't know this, because they gave me too feminine clothes that I won't wear. But I think one of my potential employers knew, because

she rejected me and said she didn't want me to have bad influences on her daughter," continued Ian. The current employer of Ian is an expat from the USA. He knew Ian is a member of LGBTQ group and supports Ian for being who he is. Ian doesn't have any curfew now. He has meal break each day. In addition to that, he has a private room downstairs (other rooms are upstairs) and his employer allows Ian's friends to visit him. The best thing for Ian about the current workplace is that he met his girlfriend in the same neighbourhood. Sometimes they can see each other through the window of the houses they work in. And they can meet each other after 9.00 pm and talk a walk near the beach on Sunday morning. Congratulations to Ian!

As a gender-diverse domestic worker in Hong Kong, Ian occasionally feels discrimination when he walks on the street. He demonstrated how some local people look at him while describing it, *"When I go out, some Hongkongers look me up and down, which makes me very uncomfortable. Discrimination against domestic workers is already blatant in Hong Kong, and those who are LGBT members at the same time may need to experience double discrimination."* Nonetheless, Ian has made some local friends who are from the local LGBT+ groups or who are supporters of LGBT. He said there is no discrimination when he stays with them:

My group is one of the first Filipino lesbian organisations in Hong Kong. We have worked with local LGBT organisations for a long time. For example, we join their Hong Kong Pride March, and they join our Migrants' Pride. We support each other. There's no discrimination from them. Sometimes, they invite us to have activities together. A local organisation which supports LGBT groups and migrants invited us to watch two documentaries about lesbian migrant workers in Taiwan next month. I think it'll be great. Local LGBT people are fighting for their equal rights as well. They hope they can get rid of discrimination from straight people, and they also hope one day they can get married legally to those who love regardless of their gender. I think, as the minority group in Hong Kong, they can definitely understand us better and respect us as equal human beings.

I'm glad to hear that LGBT migrants are not discriminated by LGBT Hongkongers. It perhaps shows that for many LGBT individuals, their

LGBT identity is beyond borders. By the same token, LGBT migrants are seldom discriminated by other Filipino domestic workers in Hong Kong. In fact, many non-LGBT organisations here are the supporters of LGBT groups, and they participate in Migrants' Pride March each year. Some may not understand or fully accept LGBT domestic workers, but their shared identities as "migrant domestic workers" and "women" kind of break down the barriers and prejudices between the LGBT and non-LGBT groups. Their solidarity is transcendent.

Ian's family has been supportive of him since he came out of the closet. But not everyone is as lucky as he is. Coming out is not the top choice for most members of LGBTQ community in the Philippines as it is still not accepted by many families there due to traditions or religions. Ian told me that some lesbians were forced to marry men in the Philippines, but they don't love their husbands. They're not themselves. For the LGBT migrant workers, Hong Kong becomes a haven for them to be themselves publicly and love courageously. Ian hopes that many LGBT workers will accept who they are and be confident about their identities no matter when they are in Hong Kong or return to the Philippines.

If COVID-19 is not considered, Ian believes that the general situation of the migrant domestic workers is getting better in Hong Kong compared to the past. *"Firstly, our minimum wage increases by around HK$100 every year. It increases very slowly especially if you compare to the speed of the rising prices in Hong Kong, but anyway, it's increasing!"* Ian laughed. *"The most important thing is: now we don't have to clean the outside windows. When I came to Hong Kong, many domestic workers were required to do the window-cleaning from the outside of the flats. It's very dangerous because most people live in high-rise buildings here. And some domestic workers died because of that. Even when there's a ban of outside window-cleaning in 2016, my employer at that time still asked me to clean the outside window. But at least, there's a law about it. So, I can say no to my former employer."*

I heard something about domestic workers and window-cleaning before, naively assuming that it can't be very common because it's too dangerous, and responsible employers or human beings should be aware of that. But when I came back home searching relevant news and reports about high-rise exterior window cleaning, I realised that it was more than common. As stated by the media reports I read, there were at least three domestic workers who fell to death in 2016 because of cleaning the external windows of their employers' flats. This is not exploitation or abuse I'm afraid. This is the wilful misconduct of neglecting other humans' lives. In September 2016, hundreds of domestic workers marched on Sunday protesting against window cleaning from the outside of the high-rise buildings.[62] In November 2016, the Hong Kong government approved the exterior window-cleaning ban proposed by the Philippines Consulate and announced it would come into force in January 2017.[63]

However, this ban is apparently not enough to guarantee domestic workers' safety. Ian told me that window-cleaning from the outside in the high-rise buildings has not been included in their contracts since the ban was issued. But until now, there are still some employers asking their helpers to clean the windows from the outside. Based on a media report published in January 2020, a Filipino domestic helper called Mier was asked by her female employer to clean the exterior window of the flat on the 19th floor last year.[64] Luckily, she didn't fall from the 19th floor for cleaning the exterior window without any protection measures. But because Mier video recorded herself cleaning the window from the outside and sent the video clip to her husband, this video somehow went viral on social media. Mier then was illegally dismissed by her employer. I'm not sure whether this unlucky domestic worker got her compensation later on.

"Some employers have their own schedule. Like my first employer, I had to clean the windows from the inside and outside every Friday. But after raining, my work became pointless. I understand cleaning windows from the inside. Some employers want to see clearer view from the indoors. That's fine. But I don't really understand cleaning the windows from the outside. To let other people passing by see how clear your window is? I think employers here know how crowded

most buildings are in Hong Kong. Nobody will notice whether your window is clean or not from the outside. It's just too hard to find your apartment. There's no point to risk anyone's life to make your window look clean from the outside, right?" Ian added.

Ian's mention of his first employer made me curious about his work schedule back then. After recalling for seconds, Ian shared with me more information about how his life was when he was a newcomer in Hong Kong. In that time, he got up at 6.00 in the morning and worked until 10.00-11.00 pm. Cleaning the exterior windows was just one of the ridiculous tasks, and usually other issues are concomitant with it. As discussed earlier, asking helpers to clean the exterior windows of the high-rise buildings without any protection measures indicates the employers' indifference to other people's lives for they are willing to risk the domestic workers' lives to satisfy their petty perfectionism towards cleanliness. If the employers don't care too much about other people' lives, how much would they care about other people's rights?

Ian's timetable for the first few years was a typical overworked timetable too, but it's not only that. Ian began, *"You know what? At that time, I was always crying. My first boss was too fussy and demanding. She didn't care how I felt. There's no vacuum cleaner or mop in my boss's flat. So, what I used was a piece of rag. And I wiped the floor like this..."* To make me better understand it, Ian acted how he performed his cleaning duties in front of me. He kneeled on the floor, pretending he was holding a piece of rag, then he wiped the floor with a lot of strength. It's saddening to see that. Ian continued, *"I wanted to buy a mop by myself, but my boss said she preferred me cleaning in that way. Can you imagine that? The flat is about 1,800 square feet, and I had to wipe the floor like that. So, I got pain here and there... And the worst thing is after all the family members finished their dinner, I had to clean the floor again, and my boss would watch me wipe the floor like that for a long time..."* Ian laughed after telling me this. I didn't know if I should have laughed with him. My sense of humour got haywire.

Like many other domestic workers here, Ian had a curfew for each holiday. He must arrive at his workplace by 20.00 and continue working. The family Ian was working for had the third baby in the second year, which means more workload to Ian. What's worse, he was asked to sleep with the new-born baby. His sleeping hours were then largely deprived as he was always woken up by the baby or her employer. In other words, he was on 24-hour standby. Yet Ian wasn't lucky enough to stop wiping floors like that for he couldn't have enough rest. He was literally not a worker. He was forced into servitude.

The growing discrimination against domestic workers during COVID-19 makes Ian disappointed and discontented. He still doesn't figure out why many domestic workers were allowed to go to the crowded market but not allowed to see their friends when the confirmed cases were rising sharply. In addition to discrimination from employers and people from mainstream society, Ian also felt discrimination from Hong Kong police officers. There was a period of time during which wearing masks even in outdoor settings was compulsory, and for those who didn't obey this rule, they'd be fined with HK$2,000. Ian said indignantly, *"During that period, so many police came here on Sunday to frequently check whether we wear masks. But at that time, most workers were not allowed to go out. There were not many domestic workers sitting here. I felt the police thought only domestic workers wouldn't put on masks, like we're the only people who make this pandemic worse. Or they just thought checking us is more likely to help them collect fines!"*

Amidst the third wave of COVID-19, Ian worried so much about those unlucky domestic workers who do not have humane accommodation or humane work schedules. He was there before. He knows how hard it is. Besides, he missed his family and his Sunday friends more than ever. During those Sundays when his most friends were not allowed to go out, Ian realised more and more how indispensable they are to him:

Being away from our families is not easy, especially under this circumstance. But I feel all the supportive organisations and domestic workers are like my own family now. Not seeing them for a couple of weeks makes me feel depressed. Now, I feel better because I can meet them again. They make me stronger to combat all the discrimination and unfairness.

(P.S. There was an LGBT group in Indonesian domestic workers' community before, but after the group leaders, a lesbian couple, received an interview from local media. They had been cyberbullied by Muslim communities in both Hong Kong and Indonesia and blamed for the increasing discrimination against Indonesian domestic workers. Eventually, they had to delete their Facebook page. There is no public LGBT group among Indonesian domestic workers now.)

14. Their Follow-up Stories

Sunday, 27 September 2020 Temperature: 29°C Humidity: 75%

I finally met Alice and her friend this afternoon. Heni, who is a community leader and a part-time columnist writing about the stories of Indonesian domestic workers in Hong Kong, usually sits under a footbridge near Victoria Park on Sunday. In order for me to find them easily, Alice sent me this photo.

Heni's major job responsibility is to take care of an elderly man who lives with his son and daughter-in-law in public housing of around 200 square feet. Heni has a private room nonetheless (she said she loved this family).

Having lived in Hong Kong for more than ten years, Heni's Cantonese is much more fluent than mine. The community she joined is particularly for those Indonesian domestic workers who're from the same hometown as her. Heni told me in Cantonese that some of her community members not only have more workload because of COVID-19, but they also have to deal with late payment. Besides that, having fear of losing jobs in this situation, none of Heni's community members dare to take sick leave or tell their employers that they're unwell. A member of her community passed away in the workplace due to a malignant tumour without timely treatment.

Another member from Heni's community was making a phone call with her family while shopping. She got some shocking news from her family and thereby feeling too anxious to remember paying for the goods when she left the shop. The manager of the shop didn't want to listen to this poor domestic worker's explanations, so he called the police. Now, she is facing the charge of shoplifting. *"It's just HK$180, the goods. You know, when people are too sad or anxious, they might forget things easily. But the manager doesn't believe a domestic worker... My friend is waiting for the Court summons. She can't lose her job. Her family needs money,"* Heni said.

During our conversation, Heni mentioned Erwiana and another Indonesian domestic worker's name: Adelina. Adelina was maltreated to death in Malaysia two years ago.[65] But Adelina's employer, the perpetrator just walked away with impunity. On 22 September, the Court of Appeal in Malaysia upheld the acquittal of Adelina's employer S. Ambika who was charged with murdering her Indonesian domestic worker Adelina.[66] A petition was launched to demand justice for Adeline.

Both Indonesian domestic workers and Filipino domestic workers in Hong Kong demanded justice for Adelina today.

Keadilan Untuk Adelina
#Justice4Adelina
IMWU-HK

Keadilan Untuk Adelina
#Justice4Adelina

Keadilan Untuk Adelina
#Justice4Adelina

Justice for Adelina
Justice
for all Migrant
Workers
We are not slave
IMWU
IMWU Hong Kong and Macau

On the same day in Central, Filguys Gabriela was also fighting for their living wage.

Aside from fighting for their minimum wage, Filguys Gabriela hopes that domestic workers will be included in this society rather than excluded.

Sunday, 04 October 2020   Temperature: 31°C   Humidity: 59%

Liza and Ian invited me to attend film screenings with them. The relevant information can be found in the picture below. Salute the director of the two documentaries and TIWA in Taiwan for caring about migrant workers and supporting the marginalised LGBTQ+ groups.

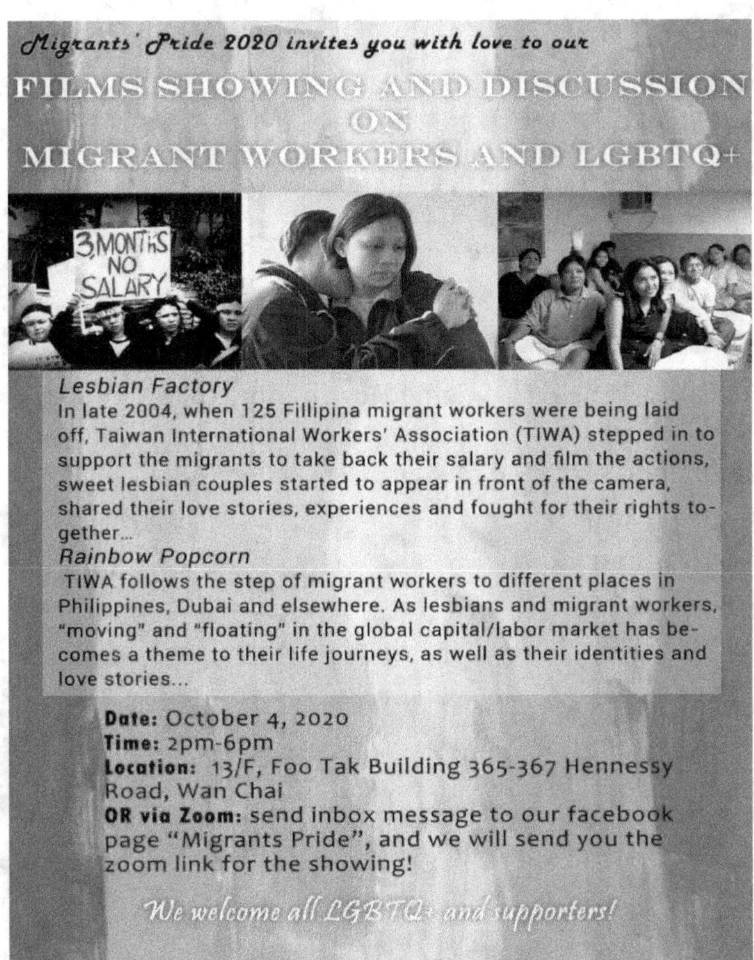

A local organisation named Migrants Solidarity Committee provided the free space. Thanks to this activity, I met some local supporters of LGBTQ and migrant workers.

(Ian was answering questions about LGBT domestic workers.)

After the screenings, Ian told me sadly that the Hong Kong government already announced that there will be no increase in the minimum wage of domestic workers. As for the ordinary residents in Hong Kong, their current minimum wage will freeze at HK$37.5/hour in the coming year.

Monday, 05 October 2020

It is Lia's birthday today. Her birthday wish is: There'll be no more mother in this world having to leave her child to work overseas for survival.

Sunday, 11 October 2020   Temperature: 29°C   Humidity: 55%

An American woman who's an old friend to the Filipino domestic workers came to support their campaign in Statue Square today. She made a speech denouncing human rights violations in the Philippines.

I made some new friends in Statue Square this afternoon. They told me more about what's happening in the Philippines. It's a pity that Magi wasn't there. She was asked to work on her only rest day in a week.

In the picture above, the chair I was sitting on belongs to Amy. She wrote something to me on social media that night, and the last bit, also my favourite bit is: Long live international solidarity!

Sunday, 18 October 2020   Temperature: 27°C   Humidity: 60%

Shiela, the chairperson of Gabriela Hong Kong is going to celebrate her birthday tomorrow, and I was invited to attend her party at lunch time. The picture below shows how domestic workers generally celebrate their birthdays on Sunday. All the dishes in the picture were cooked by Shiela's friends and the members of Gabriela Hong Kong. I brought a birthday cake and a box of polvoron (a type of Philippine shortbread) to join them.

The picture below shows how a Filipino activist celebrates her birthday. Shiela's birthday wishes are: All the political prisoners in the Philippines will be released soon, and there will be justice for all.

After Shiela's birthday party, I went to Victoria Park to meet Alice, as she said that she wanted to give me an Indonesian traditional scarf as a gift. On my way to Victoria Park, I saw an Indonesian domestic worker reading a book alone. She's beautiful.

Because the weather is getting cooler, there are more Indonesian domestic workers bringing their tents to Victoria Park, which should be helpful as well when it's raining. After talking with Alice for a while, she introduced me to the leader of Indonesian Migrant Workers' Union (IMWU): Sring.

Sring is a cultural-diverse person. In her spare time, she loves exploring this city and trying foods from different cultures. During her annual leave, if she saves enough money, she will explore other places of this planet as well. She has learned English by herself, and she's still learning it (I was amazed by her English fluency). For Sring, English is a language full of possibilities, because it allows her to communicate with different people when she goes to different places. Her current employer is a very considerate employer who not only supports Sring for her participation in a trade union, but also sometimes allows Sring to hang out with her friends on weekday afternoons.

The reason for Sring to join a union is similar to other domestic workers: to fight for her own rights and to help her fellow migrant workers. Sring told me when she just arrived in Hong Kong 18 years ago, she was so happy as she thought that she finally could be herself in a freer place. But unsurprisingly, some unhappy things occurred. From 2002 to 2003, Sring had been working for a local rich family. The house is big, and each family member has a fancy private car (there are five adults in that family). One of Sring's duties was to wash their cars. But the rich family didn't pay Sring statutory salary or allow her to enjoy statutory holidays. She was only allowed to have one rest day a month. As for her salary, she only got HK$2,000 per month, whilst the monthly minimum wage back then was HK$ 3,670 (it became HK$3,270 in 2003 because of the economic downturn in Hong Kong).[67] The worst part was that for the first seven months, her salary was all deducted by her agency. She literally had no penny in her pocket.

The second employer of Sring is much nicer to her. Sring drew this picture for me to show how her room looked like when she was working for the second employer. The bed in her room is a typical small double bed (122 x 183 cm) in Hong Kong. She told me that her room was kind of decent compared to many others', because about half of domestic workers don't have a private room, and if they do, usually they'll get a single bed rather than a double bed.

By Sring

In terms of the union Sring leads, IMWU helps Indonesian domestic workers in a similar way that Filipino unions do, and IMWU shares similar issues with the Filipino unions during the coronavirus pandemic. Likewise, "neoliberal" is a frequently used word when both the Indonesian and Filipino union leaders comment on the Hong Kong government's policies against migrant workers. The slight difference is that Sring prefers to organise more activities such as hiking to release the union members' pressure, while Filipino union leaders prefer to organise more campaigns in their free time. Nevertheless, the unions from both Filipino and Indonesian communities support one another.

Sring provided me with some additional information:

- Some employers in Hong Kong take away their domestic workers' documents to prevent their helpers from running away, which is even more common among newly-arrived domestic workers (though it may not be not as common as in Singapore). Some agencies do that too.

- Five members of IMWU reported that they were sexually abused in their workplaces this year. They were encouraged by Sring to report to the police and sue their employers. They're currently living in the shelters provided by Mission for Migrant Workers (I met two of them this Sunday afternoon), waiting to be summoned to appear in court. One of the domestic workers who was sexually abused by her employer lost the case. The reason is that she didn't provide solid evidence, which is discouraging for other victims.

- Some newly-arrived domestic workers had limited food during their 14-day quarantine.

- A member of IMWU hasn't taken any holidays from March till October.

- A member working from 5.00 to 23.00 for six days a week, is asked to cook 5 meals a day and do massage for her "masters".

- Another member who has joined IMWU recently was asked to sleep in the bathroom and work from 6.00 am to 2.00 am. Her employer's favourite thing was to watch her eating noodles within 5 minutes. Once this domestic worker fell asleep in the toilet for being too exhausted, her employer took a photo when she was half-naked and asked her to paste it on her clothes when she went to the market.

- A Nepalese domestic worker who had been underpaid for months (she only got HK$2,800/month) was fired because of being affected by the coronavirus. Her employer didn't buy her medical insurance. Now, she is paying all the unbelievable medical expenses by herself.

Voices from IMWU

As the person who encouraged Erwiana and accompanied her to the police station, Sring updated the information about Erwiana. After returning to Indonesia, Erwiana got a scholarship at Sanata Dharma University and graduated with distinction. Now, she is working at an organisation in Indonesia which aims to improve the welfare of migrant workers overseas. She is also doing research on human trafficking in Indonesia. Erwiana hasn't yet got any compensation from her former abusive employer Law Wan-tung.

I met Tutik after having dinner with my new friends in Victoria Park. Tutik's current employer seems nice to her, and she has been working for the same employer for seven years. But like Erwiana, Tutik hasn't received a single dime from Law.

P.S. Sring was in a band! And she is trying to write a book about herself!

Sunday, 01 November 2020 Temperature: 26°C Humidity: 61%

I was invited to join Filipino domestic workers' a belated Halloween party. Here are a few pictures to show how some members of Filguys Gabriela and Gabriela Hong Kong combined their political demands with the Halloween party.

"NO TO RED
TAGGING
#YES TO
REDLIPSTICKS
JUNK
TERROR LAW
GABRIELA HONGKONG

While there was a politicised Halloween parade organised by Filipino activists, there was also a beauty contest on the other side of Statue Square. It is a yearly regular event among many Filipino domestic workers.

Magi spent lots of time with me this afternoon. I felt she was unhappy, so I asked her why. She told me that her husband had been in hospital for almost a year. The hospital expenses are huge to her. She ended up running out of all her savings, and had to pay off 1 million pesos of debt (almost HK$160,000). Worse than that, her husband passed away last year.

P.S. I met a new friend today.

Sunday, 22 November 2020 Temperature: 26°C Humidity: 66%

Migrants' Pride is an annual march in support of LGBT+ rights and migrant workers' rights in Hong Kong. It is also an occasion for pro-LGBT migrant workers to strengthen solidarity with their supporters irrespective of nationality, ethnicity and class. With the ongoing coronavirus pandemic, I thought there would be no more Migrants' Pride this year, but our dear migrant workers kind of made it happen. Technically speaking, it isn't a parade. It's more like a migrants' pride gathering. Nonetheless, I was incredibly excited when I knew that there would be a substitute under this circumstance, because these migrant workers tried to send a message to the wider community that they hope to be included as members of LGBT+ groups and migrant workers.

It was my first time seeing Filipino Lesbians Organization's banner in Statue Square. I guess the members of this organisation usually congregate in some other places in Central. It just proves that I haven't explored enough about the places domestic workers gather on Sunday.

These domestic workers interpreted the new meaning of COVID, and they hope to act together with locals to fight COVID-19, overwork, vulnerability, inequality, and discrimination. Their interpretation of COVID combined perfectly with their LGBTQ theme.

The participants of Migrants' Pride looked relaxed and happy, though I was told that there were more people joining them in the past (I could imagine this).

This is a photo which shows that people with different ethnic backgrounds come to join in Migrants' Pride.

I didn't take too many photos today, because I was busy talking with my old and new friends. It's a great party for me to meet like-minded people. And I had a couple of decent conversations with different people. Some of them are locals who work in different NGOs and care about marginalised people; some of them come from mainland China, studying politics and gender studies in Hong Kong (they worked in LGBT organisations in mainland China before); some are expats who have engaged with migrant community for a long time. Coincidentally, they all care about human rights and gender equality. My identities as a human and a woman were taken good care of there. Basically, we all agreed how amazing these migrant workers are. As Sophie, one of my new local friends, put it, "These migrant workers don't need anyone to teach them how to fight. Instead, I've learned a lot from them!"

Hong Kong's fourth wave of the coronavirus pandemic has arrived.

PART FOUR: THROUGH THE LENS OF THE DOMINANT GROUP

Each of us is responsible for everything and to every human being.

Simone de Beauvoir

15. The Sexist Elephant in the Room

As mentioned in part one, Hong Kong is a complex combination of both modernisation and tradition. In terms of gender equality, this international metropolis, I regret to say, is greatly impacted by traditional attitudes towards women. In a survey conducted by Women's Commission, women in Hong Kong are generally stereotyped as primary family caregivers. Over half of the respondents (including both men and women) believe that "women should focus more on family than work", and after giving birth, about one third of married women do not return to the workplace due to childcare duties or other family responsibilities. [68] In an article published by Hong Kong Free Press, the women's foundation describes Hong Kong as "a not welcoming city for women, working women or working mothers"[69] It points out that there are only 55% of women joining the labour force in Hong Kong, left behind by Singapore (61.1%)[70] and mainland China (60.45%).[71] In a similar vein, although female university graduates outnumber their male counterparts[72], women, who are severely underrepresented in both the public sector and the private sector in Hong Kong, are not as influential as men in management.[73] Even worse, mothers are treated unfavourably by more than half of the local companies in the hiring process, whereas men with children are favoured by 70% of the companies.[74]

Even though there are Sex Discrimination Ordinance[75] and Family Status Discrimination Ordinance[76] to protect women in Hong Kong from discrimination in the workplace, gender bias and discrimination still prevail. The sad thing is that discrimination against women in the workplace doesn't exist in isolation, it spreads to social life and family life too. For instance, the Small House Policy (SHP) introduced in 1972 to cater for residents in the New Territories (NT) of British Hong Kong is a policy which shows how patriarchy is strengthened in this society. SHP is believed to be a product of explicit sexism, because it regulates that only "male indigenous villagers aged 18 or above descended through the male line from one of the recognized villages in the NT may apply for building a small house for once in their life time."[77] SHP has caused lots of controversy in Hong Kong for it is discriminatory against both female indigenous villagers and non-indigenous Hong Kong citizens. Attributed to the opposition of the interest group in the New Territories, however, it is hard for the HKSAR government to abolish it. Hence, it still remains legal today.[78]

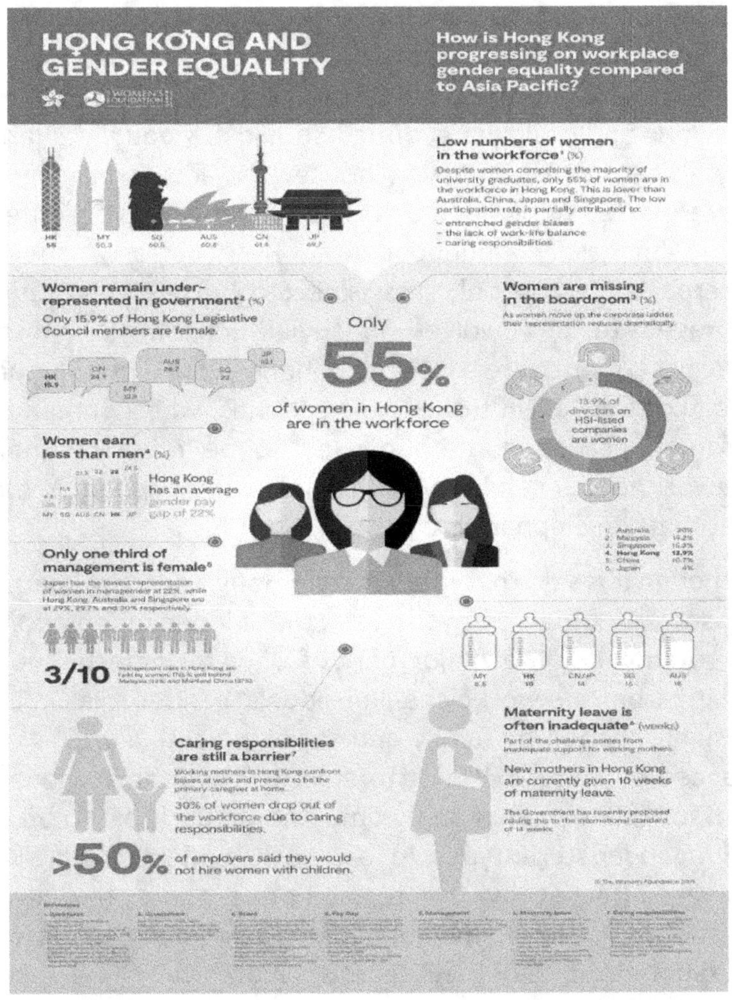

(Source: The Women's Foundation)

For many people in Hong Kong, a woman's failure is more associated with family failure rather than career failure. In a society wherein traditional family values still predominate, a woman who doesn't perform well in the workplace is still safe, but a woman who doesn't take care of her family well is a bad woman. The mainstream opinion in Hong Kong still holds that a well-managed home should be guaranteed by women no matter if they are financially independent or not. And it seems the mainstream opinion is especially unfriendly to the independent married women due to the unrealistic expectations put on them. What I firmly believe is that if women nowadays work outside the home exactly like men, then housework and child care duties should be equally shared in a family. The truth is, however, housework and caregiving are still largely expected to be done by women (it makes no big difference if they're financially independent). By contrast, their male counterparts are not only less expected but also less taught and encouraged to be involved in trivial housework and arduous caregiving. If men share a little bit of housework with their partners, they could show off in front of their friends, while women can't do the same because that's supposed to be done by them. The housework gender gap in Hong Kong is like *the elephant in the room*, except that the elephant is a sexist.

Although it is said that more men in Hong Kong have participated in housework compared to the past, those independent women still need to shoulder the major part of unpaid domestic work after returning from the workplace. Individuals' gender roles in a society are usually shaped by family and social education which is largely influenced by culture. Whilst in a society with an obvious gender gap, unfortunately, men and women are more likely to be brought up with gender stereotypes. In fact, both genders in Hong Kong are seemingly affected by the social norms about the division of domestic work, and many women kind of accept the biased social expectations in spite of their dissatisfaction.

Admittedly, many middle-class women in Hong Kong may have accepted this kind of gender bias. Yet if they have a better choice like numerous men do, they may not prefer to do onerous household chores after finishing their work. Thanks to the existence of domestic workers whose labour force is affordable and even cheap for the middle and upper class, the full-time professional women in this fast-paced city can finally walk away from nasty domestic work by outsourcing it to another group of WOMEN. As for the female domestic workers, on one hand, they become the people who help their employers balance life between work and family, on the other, their prevalence in Hong Kong implies that their female employers give a tacit approval of their traditional social roles and thereby reinforcing the gender stereotyping—that women are just more suitable for dealing with housework and care work.

Technically speaking, the independent women who have employed domestic helpers don't completely walk away from domestic work, as they still need to make family plans and manage their homes. They have the mental workload too. The difference is: with the assistance of domestic workers, their positions inside their homes are better than before. They're more like CEOs at home now. What they need to do is to make decisions and give orders to their staff in the home. Most of the time, they don't have to do the household chores by themselves unless their domestic staff are taking holidays. But essentially, their traditional social role hasn't changed. The majority of them continue to tackle the family-based issues in which their male partners are not really interested. Sadly, they just transfer long-term gender oppression to their female staff at home.

Most employers of the domestic workers whom I talked with are females, particularly females with decent jobs. They are portrayed as "independent women" or "modern women" in the mainstream society of Hong Kong. They take some credit for contributing to local economy, and their virtue of being financially independent is extolled by many feminists. Nothing seems wrong before we take a closer look.

However, if we take a close look, we'll find out that the attitudes of mainstream society towards Hong Kong women are no different from the attitudes of independent Hong Kong women towards migrant domestic workers. In a Cantonese video about how to find a good helper in Hong Kong through CV screening (the video got to the top of search results on YouTube), a female YouTuber who is also an employer of a domestic worker shared six suggestions to those who have the intentions to hire a helper. And one of the suggestions is that *"you'd better not to hire a young mother whose baby is under 3 years old because if her baby is too young and too small, this helper is going to be homesick so much and thus they're not going to focus on doing work and they may resign soon"*.[79] I guess those companies which do not prefer to hire women with childcare responsibilities may have similar reasons. But it's not as ironic as this one—a Hong Kong young mother who is also a member of an oppressed group advised other potential employers not to hire a young migrant mother. After doing a little bit of discourse analysis, I assume what she really intended to mean (her illocutionary act) was: *women with babies do not have the ability to concentrate on their work, because once they have babies, they are too emotional to control themselves.* For me, the most saddening part about this suggestion is that the female YouTuber has accepted this sort of gender stereotyping and internalised it to direct towards other women.

The first time I met Sring in Victoria Park, she told me some sad stories about how Indonesian domestic workers were ill-treated by their employers. After that, she asked me a question: *"These domestic workers are women. Most of their employers are women too. But why women treat other women like that?"*

Yes. Why women treat other women like that? Then, so many conversations with different domestic workers floated in my mind. Lucille's first abusive employer was an air stewardess; Joe's first employer was a manager in a bank; Amy's first employer worked in an insurance company...They're all financially independent and university-educated women. They're supposed to care more about gender equality than others and respect equal rights too. But they didn't. Instead, they have internalised gender discrimination, and they devalue housework as well as caregiving like many of their male counterparts do. The popular logic goes like this: domestic work can't be exhausting because women usually do it; and if women usually do it, it can't be exhausting. But when domestic work is related to migrant women especially those from impoverished areas, the logic becomes somewhat more complicated: domestic work can't be exhausting or valuable because those Southeast Asian women are doing it; and if they're doing it, it can't be exhausting or valuable.

For the domestic workers who I informally interviewed and who have been forced to work over 16 hours a day, their female employers all coincidentally said something that shows their tendency to devalue housework. And because it is usually the female employers who assign the tasks to domestic helpers, it may lead to helpers suffering a lot if the female employers themselves devalue domestic work. Liza's first female employer in Hong Kong, for example, used to think Liza didn't do anything, so she created so many unnecessary but energy-consuming tasks for Liza. For her, sitting down and taking a rest for a while means "not hard-working" or "lazy". After all, domestic work to her is something that doesn't consume time or energy, which makes me suspect whether Liza's first employer in Hong Kong has any experience of doing housework. This misconception about domestic work can be found among many other female employers whose attitudes towards domestic work apparently foster gender inequality.

The devaluation of housework and care work isn't new. It has historical reasons. In the ancient past, women were confined in their homes, performing household chores and taking care of their babies; whereas men were responsible to earn money to feed the family. For a very long period during which sex education and contraception weren't that well-developed, a woman's life was occupied with getting pregnant, giving birth, and taking care of the new-born babies, and then repeating the above process for years. If the average lifespan in the past was considered, women back then were seriously doing endless unpaid housework and care work for almost half of their life time. The ordinary women in the past had no access to education or knowledge. They could not leave their homes travelling or trading to different places like men did. It is therefore likely that many of them had very limited experience too. Then, they took the blame, like the migrant domestic workers do now. Then, there was a belief born out of thin air. Those decent gentlemen full of knowledge and experience believed something that seemed so true centuries ago: the reason why women should perform household chores is that they can't be good at anything else. "It is their rare gift, and they should maintain it," they said (to make it less confusing, here I am only talking about ordinary people in the past, as aristocrats are not typical examples: both men and women with a high social rank or title didn't have to work).

The women in history, our ancestors, began to be stereotyped like this. Their lack of knowledge and experience in male-dominated fields—as the results of gender inequality—became the justification for them to be confined in the home. In the meantime, they had their assigned social roles, which are called traditional social roles nowadays. Even today, the idea of the gender-based division of labour still has a place, and the devaluation of domestic work is just an alternative way to repeat the pattern of "old glory". The thing is, however, domestic work has long been unpaid, and unpaid work hasn't been thought to be valuable in many societies. For those women who have internalised gender discrimination, they may tend to despise historically-devalued domestic work and even the women who are doing it for them.

P.S. Lucille told me that she met her first employer in September, and she was shocked that her former employer still recognised her even she was wearing a face mask. *"My first boss apologised to me. She said, 'I'm sorry, Lucille. I owe you.' Then she took HK$500 from her pocket to me. She looked downhearted that day. You know, she was an air stewardess before, but she lost her job during COVID-19. So, she can't afford hiring a helper now. She has to do all the housework as well as caregiving by herself. She told me that she realised it's a lot of hard work, and she felt guilty to treat me like that before...But I don't know... My feelings were complicated at that moment. I just wish she knew it much earlier. I wish people like her in the past could all realise this and respect us, because our work is actually valuable,"* said Lucille.

16. Internalised Misogyny

This following chapter includes analyses of very offensive language against women, which some readers may find troubling. Reader discretion is advised.

Unfortunately, gender bias is not the only thing internalised by some female employers. Internalised misogyny is another aspect worsening domestic workers' situation in Hong Kong. For me, sexism is a type of discrimination against women on a cognitive level, and misogyny is a more aggressive version of sexism on a behavioural level because it speaks out and acts as hatred and contempt for women. It's more pernicious to the affected women. During the social movement in Hong Kong last year, misogynistic remarks could be found in both political camps.

On different social media, offensive insults and abusive language were especially used to attack women in the opposite camp. Pro-government camp hated protesters, then some blue ribbons (people in the pro-government camp) called female protesters "comfort women", and that they would provide free sex service to male protesters. If female protestors were arrested, a certain number of blue ribbons would judge them based on their physical appearance; and if they were just wearing short pants or skirts, they'd be branded as sluts and whores. Pro-democracy camp hated police, then some yellow ribbons (people in the pro-democracy camp) stigmatised policewomen in the same way. The difference is: policewomen were vilified to satisfy the sexual needs of male senior police officers instead of male protestors. Pretty policewomen in good shape are most likely to be slut-shamed online. There are so many pictures of them with different misogynistic comments on LIHKG (a Reddit-like forum which is popular among protestors and which is criticised for being blatantly racist and sexist by some Reddit users). Apart from policewomen, the Chief Executive Carrie Lam and policemen's wives were slut-shamed as well.

I am not saying that women cannot be criticised. But these remarks are far more than critiques. And everyone should be aware that there is a huge difference between "criticise" and "stigmatise". If blue ribbons are against specific things done by protesters, they should've criticised the actions themselves instead of branding the female protesters as comfort women. By the same token, if yellow ribbons are bothered by the police and the Hong Kong government's attitudes towards protesters, they should've condemned police brutality and the government's specific actions and policies instead of slut-shaming policewomen and the city leader.

However, the reality is extremely disappointing. "Comfort women" isn't only seen in the comments made by the pro-government camp on social media, it was also used to degrade women in the pro-democracy camp, i.e., a policewoman's photo tagged with "comfort woman" received many likes on LIHKG. I wonder whether the users of this phrase know the history of "comfort women". It has a dark history and it is not something that should be made fun of. During the Second World War, thousands of women mainly from South Korea, China and the Philippines were forced into sexual slavery by the Japanese Imperial Army in the occupied territories.[80] What they suffered is unimaginably terrible, and I feel depressed and trembled even reading some of their stories. Using "comfort women" to slut-shame female protester and policewomen is not only a secondary victimisation to the victims, but also shows those netizens' contempt and hatred towards women.

If Hong Kong women are slut-shamed and scorned like that, then with the rising localist sentiment, women with an "outsider" identity especially those who are from a less favourable society are more likely to be demonised and hated. They probably are going to be attacked by a two-headed monster called "xenogyny" (a combination of xenophobia and misogyny). On 1 November, there were seven new confirmed cases of coronavirus in Hong Kong. But one confirmed case grabbed the headlines of the local newspapers in which "prostitute" and "from mainland China" became the keywords. Many comments on these articles are full of contempt and double discrimination against this woman's occupation as well as her place of origin. I could imagine what the comments would be like if it were a migrant domestic worker confirmed to have coronavirus. After reading the comments from these news articles, I searched the keywords "mainland China" and "women" on LIHKG. Then I found that in most comments, the word "women" disappears. Instead, it's replaced by " 鷄 " (gai), which means "whores" in traditional Chinese ("鷄" also means "chicken" in Chinese, but in this context, I'm afraid it doesn't refer to food). As for "mainland China", it is taken place by a derogatory name "Shina" in traditional Chinese. With some background information, perhaps we can understand better about how migrant domestic workers are discriminated and stigmatised in Hong Kong.

Most migrant domestic workers in Hong Kong are women. More than that, in many locals' eyes, they're not only from less favourable societies, but they're in a less favourable social class and doing a less favourable job. Even their skin colour could be less favourable too. The two-headed monster "xenogyny" could become a multi-headed monster in front of them. Middle class-women in Hong Kong as well as so many other local people need domestic workers to liberate them from unwanted housework and care work, and Hong Kong should have given credit to the migrant domestic workers for contributing to its economy. It is fair to say that domestic workers are like the nameless heroines/heroes of this busy city; however, it seems that their contributions to this city are disregarded by those who depend on them. Those migrant women haven't received the respect that they deserve. On the contrary, they need to deal with demonisation and slut-shaming more often than any other women in this society because of their low economic and social status.

Filipino and Indonesian domestic workers are sometimes called "Ban-ban" and "Yan-yan" which carry pejorative connotations in Hong Kong. If we search the keywords "Ban-ban" and "Yan-yan" in traditional Chinese on Google, we'll find some offensive, discriminatory and misogynistic language used against Filipino and Indonesian domestic workers on the first page. Before I translate the top of Google search results, it should be noted that "eat" in Cantonese is occasionally used by men to refer to "get laid" with women, but it shows extreme disrespect and disdain to women. The top one search result is: *the time-tested ways of "eating" Ban-ban and Yan-yan*. The second one is: *...it turns out that ban mui* (similar to ban-ban, it means Filipino domestic workers with a negative connotation) *are easy to "eat"*. Women are not food! As a woman, I was utterly offended by these words. And the third one is: *foreign maids (ban-ban and yan-yan) are suspected to engage in prostitution,* followed by *"Ban-ban and Yan-yan in Hong Kong are miserable" on HKGolden* (another Reddit-like forum in Hong Kong), which at least shows sympathy for domestic workers.

However, more relevant search results on HKGolden are about how to "eat" or how is the experience to "eat" Ban-ban and Yan-yan. One of which could be crowned as the King of Misogyny. The title of the post is: *Seriously speaking, I'd rather eat Ban-ban and Yan-yan now,* suggesting that the man who posted it was actually comparing Filipino and Indonesian domestic workers with someone else. Before clicking it, I made a guess that he was comparing domestic workers with Hong Kong women, and I was proved right later on. After clicking the title of the discussion on HKGolden, I felt like I accidentally strayed into a kingdom of misogyny, and I definitely do not want to visit there again. Nonetheless, let me translate this post:

> Hong Kong women are so annoying. They worship westerners and money. They're not affordable. They have already scared away me and my friends. My friends and I decided not to hook up with Hong Kong girls/women, because we discovered our new continent—Ban-ban and Yan-yan.

> We discovered a dating app, there're loads of Ban-ban and Yan-yan to select: old and young, hot and non-hot... you can select what you like. They're not like Hong Kong women, you don't have to try so hard to invite them out. I can do whatever I want when I'm with Ban-ban and Yan-yan. They're subservient and servile, and they're sex-starved...the most important thing is I don't have to pay. They'll pay for the hotel. I can ask as many as them to get laid. I'm just like a king with so many imperial concubines.

> How can Hong Kong women please you like that? If you must "eat", please eat Ban-ban and Yan-yan. Hong Kong women? Fuck off![81]

What an unbearable post! Women are objectified in both the post and its comments. Hong Kong women are hated because they are not so approachable or just because they do not like these men. Yet Filipino and Indonesian domestic workers are not even seen as individuals but objects or commodities that can be consumed. Did this man in the post and his followers really like Filipino and Indonesian domestic workers? I don't think so. They didn't even show the slightest respect for domestic workers. They used derogatory names to address these women; they stigmatised both Hong Kong females and domestic workers; they bragged about their sexual exploits by probably making up stories; they even made use of some domestic workers' sufferings—who are treated like slaves— to satisfy their pathetic sexual fantasies. However, no one would condemn these men as promiscuous. On the contrary, they tend to be encouraged and accepted by a certain group of men in reality.

All forms of discrimination can be internalised, and when a type of discrimination pervades a society, internalised discrimination tends to be one of the inevitable results. Having been influenced by misogynistic atmosphere on social media and in everyday life, a number of Hong Kong women may be influenced by demeaning language and contemptuous opinions about females. Worse than that, some of them may accept this kind of misogynistic ideology and even apply it into another group of women—migrant domestic workers. Pervasive misogyny among men still hounds these poor domestic workers. But at the same time, domestic workers are plagued by some local women's contempt and stigmatisation.

In a Cantonese video about how to interview a helper, a female YouTuber offered five suggestions. And one of the suggestions is to pay attention to what the helper is wearing during the interview. She said, here I translate:

Usually, the interviews will be arranged on Sunday, and these helpers will hang out with their friends after the interviews. So, you can tell how a helper's private life is like by observing what she's wearing. Some may want to dress up and wear heavy makeup, but my helper during the interview was wearing simple clothes and she proved later that she's a good helper. I don't want to judge people by their appearance, but observing how a helper dresses in an interview can help you predict what she likes to do on her rest days. If a helper dresses too sexy, you'll naturally suspect whether she's going to do other things.[82]

Here, "other things" doesn't mean everyday activities like shopping or going out with friends. Instead, it seems to refer to specific things like "having casual sex" or "part-time sex work" in this context. This YouTuber isn't the only one to connect a domestic worker's dress style with her private life and sexuality. In fact, judging a helper's character based on physical appearance and dress style can be easily found on mainstream social media. Next Magazine, an online Hong Kong magazine, uploaded a series of interviews with employers about how they view a helper doing sex work as a part-time job. Some female employers responded to the interviews and expressed their opinions (negative of course).[81] Almost all the female employers said that they would not hire any young and beautiful helpers, because they believe that "young and beautiful helpers are not reliable". A female employer said in the interview, *"I'm not going to hire young helpers. Even the helpers are newcomers in Hong Kong, as long as they're young enough, they can learn to be bad from their fellow friends."* Reading between the lines, "not reliable" here denotes "sexually provocative", and "bad" refers to "promiscuous". Some of the female employers also expressed their preferences not to see their helpers wearing short pants or putting on make-up inside the home. From the perspective of these female employers, wearing make-up or not dressing conservatively appears to be a generally acknowledged factor contributing to the "not reliable" behaviour of a domestic worker. Women can be sexists and misogynists too.

In the comment section,[83] there are more explicit slut-shaming and misogynistic remarks. I translated some sentences below:

"Indonesian maids and Filipino maids do not have to be young and beautiful enough to seduce your husband. Even they're not young, they will seduce your husband or your husband's dad."

"I had hired some Indonesian maids in Malaysia before. They're all bad! Every one of them! Maids from Cambodia are bad too!"

"Please respect men's will. Only young and gorgeous women can make men energetic!"

"Haha! Some maids are more than 40 years old but they are still sexually provocative. Hire a man to do housework!

"My friend has hired a Filipino maid who wears tank tops and short pants all the time. I guess she often sleeps with her male employer."

"They're all hypocritical!"

"Young and gorgeous women are indeed threats! I've never allowed any women or outsiders to get close to my family."

"Women can make money as long as they open their legs. That's true!"

… …

There is a rare non-misogynistic comment that should be noticed as well: "Let's be fair. We can't blame all the things on helpers."

In a society wherein sexism and misogyny prevail, young and beautiful women are not thought to be trustworthy by many. Men and women hate them for different reasons. But I guess they share the common ground which is a lack of sense of security. For the men who hate young and beautiful women, they doubt these women's fidelity; while for those women who hate young and beautiful females, they regard these attractive women as their biggest competitors over their partners or husbands. For some married women, young and beautiful women are more like potential threats who will steal their husbands and ruin their heterosexual marriages. And a young and beautiful domestic worker who is good at dressing herself up is apparently perceived as a real threat to a female employer, for the simple reason that the domestic worker has more opportunities to get along with the employer's husband than any other women. To avoid this happening, young and attractive domestic workers are largely excluded in the hiring process. They become the most unwelcome and unwanted group among domestic workers due to their beauty and youth. In order to make this kind of social exclusion more supported and accepted by mainstream society, rumours about young domestic workers especially related to their sexuality are spread here and there. Gradually, more and more people tend to associate physically attractive domestic workers with sexually provocative women or sex workers.

Apple Daily and TVB, which have a large audience in Hong Kong, also reported helpers doing sex work as their part-time jobs in Hong Kong, because bad stories of outsiders make news. Most comments are misogynistic too. I am not suggesting that all domestic workers are righteous and kind-hearted, nor am I denying that some of them are in fact doing sex work as their part-time jobs. But should the domestic workers who have bad work performance be deprived of their labour rights? And even though there are some part-time sex workers among them, should they be insulted? No. The tone used by the mainstream media seems to deliver a message to the public that a great number of domestic workers in Hong Kong are promiscuous and doing sex work as their part-time jobs, and thus in many people's minds, domestic workers are somehow related to the words "immoral", "untrustworthy" and even "filthy". Then physically attractive domestic workers are demonised as sluts-to-be; those who are good at dressing up are seen as evil. Every female domestic worker can be suspected. But I wonder whether it is just a kind of pretext for mainstream society to exclude and marginalise foreign domestic workers.

I recollected all the conversations with different domestic workers, and I began to understand more about the meaning implied by both employers and domestic workers. Lucille's first female employer asked Lucille, *"Do you have to change your clothes every day?"* That was 14 years ago, and Lucille was in her early twenties. Changing clothes every day for Lucille was very natural, but for her female employer at that time, it was "not reliable" and "bad". The second time I met Lucille, she was pissed off by how passers-by looked her up and down because she was wearing a short skirt. I think when she said *"I can feel some people don't like it"*, she meant that those passers-by thought she may have a disgraceful part-time job. And when she said, *"My boss's friends sometimes look at me in a weird way if I dress up"*, she implied that her employer's friends thought she's sexually provocative and immoral.

Probably when Evelyn's first female employer in Hong Kong isolated Evelyn from other Indonesian domestic workers who are "potential bad friends" in the eyes of the employer, "bad" not only meant "not obedient", but it also may have suggested something related to sexuality. Additionally, Liza's female employer was advised by her friends not to hire Liza, because Liza wears earrings. Even wearing earrings can be sinful too. How sarcastic! This weird standard is not easy to be found against Hong Kong women in mainstream society nowadays. But for those women who have a high level of internalised misogyny, a helper wearing earrings may suggest that she's a bad woman who might seduce the employer's husband or engage in prostitution on Sunday. Nonetheless, the female employers and their friends who tend to slut-shame domestic workers in this way have double standards applied to themselves: They, the women with higher social status, can dress up and put on make-up without being branded as "bad women" or "not reliable". They won't be slut-shamed by just wearing earrings either.

Rather than viewing female migrant domestic workers as potential competitors or even enemies, how about women in mainstream society change another way to think? Let's think: *would it be more difficult for these powerless female outsiders to live in a society wherein they are degraded and despised?* I believe this way is much better to enhance women's solidarity than think that young and beautiful domestic workers are more likely to be sexually immoral and seductive.

17. Employers' Grievance

I thought about interviewing employers of domestic workers as well, but interviewing employers is far more difficult than interviewing domestic workers. For one thing, employers do not congregate like domestic workers do, thus I can't know where to find them. And it would be awkward if I randomly ask someone that I come across in the street, "Hey, have you hired any domestic workers before?" For another, fluent Cantonese, as an essential element to build rapport with local people, is an entrance ticket to enter in mainstream society and, apparently, I haven't got this ticket yet allowing me to interview local employers. But to be fair, I believe we also need to understand the issues faced by domestic workers from the employers' perspectives.

The employers of those domestic workers, just like their counterparts, have multiple identities as well. And numerous employers are employees in their workplace at the same time. It is worth noting that domestic workers, the non-ordinary residents in Hong Kong, are not the only group whose maximum working hours are not regulated. In fact, there is no standard working hours legislation to ensure any employees' wellbeing and work-life balance in Hong Kong. In a report released by Swiss Bank UBS in 2016, Hong Kong employees work an average of 50.1 hours a week, ahead of other workaholic cities such as Bangkok (42.1), Mexico City (43.5) and Mumbai (43.7).[84]

As one of the freest economies in the world, Hong Kong has been deeply influenced by neoliberalism, and it seems that it isn't ready to get out from its "comfort zone". Instead of putting limits on corporations, the Hong Kong government still adopts a sort of laissez-faire attitudes towards labour issues, which are basically in favour of capital and market. Local unions have fought for standard working hours for years, but they haven't achieved their goals yet. In this regard, with all due respect, Hong Kong is not a friendly city for workers.

Such long working hours lead to many problems. One of which is that Hong Kong people may have become more intolerant to inefficiency and slowness. Multitudes of employees not only have to cope with long working hours but also intense work schedule. Not having enough quality time for themselves and their families is just part of the story, let alone stress and anxiety caused by heavy workload and sky-high living cost. Nevertheless, a great number of Hong Kong people have evolved to utilise their time more effectively than most people in the world. It is a city which is well known for its fast pace. Everything needs to be fast, even the elevators here are faster than many other places. If housework occupies too much time, they'll outsource it to full-time domestic workers. If eating meals occupies too much time during work, they'll eat more quickly. For those who do not hire domestic workers to help with housework, if they think cooking occupies too much time, they'll always buy takeaways. Waiters and waitresses at restaurants don't seem to have enough time to wait for their customers considering what to order in front of them: please make sure you have decided what to order before calling them over.

Arguably, the conflicts between migrant domestic workers and their Hong Kong employers are essentially the conflicts of culture and lifestyle. For many Hong Kong people, fast-paced lifestyle is normalised. No matter they are bosses or employees in their workplace, they may all take a hectic schedule as a given. As a result, they kind of expect other people, such as their domestic workers, to keep pace with them. In contrast, however, those domestic workers from Southeast Asian countries do not have the same expectations for busy work schedule as their Hong Kong employers do. I think it is likely that, except for their pre-service training, most domestic workers hadn't experienced such intense hard work in their real life before coming to Hong Kong. Plus, there is something else, something subtle and tricky. If domestic workers' socio-economic status were considered—which is most likely to happen in reality— many employers would expect domestic workers to work much longer than them. And indeed, unfortunately, over 40% of domestic workers in Hong Kong work more than 16 hours a day, if we still remember the data provided by MFMW. After all, in some employers' words, "It just doesn't make sense for a maid to feel more relaxed than her employer."

Perhaps many agencies realised this, so they designed a series of training courses as a kind of "warm-up" sessions to let those potential domestic workers know and experience Hong Kong culture and lifestyle in advance. For some who received my informal interviews, they thought their pre-service training was indeed cruel, but it was not as cruel as reality. Heni's training schedule was from 5.00 am to 9.30-10.00 pm. But as we may have guessed, her actual work schedule of the first few years in Hong Kong could be only more intense than that. *"The training I received in Indonesia just let me know Hong Kong's work style better, and thus let me have fewer expectations but more preparation for coping with pressure. Indonesians never work like that. I remember the training staff always said to us 'hurry up' 'hurry up'!"* Heni and Sring all told me that they were trained to eat a meal within 15 minutes and take shower within 5 minutes. I was utterly shocked the first time I heard it until I knew something from Lucille's employer, Ms. Peggy.

I met Lucille and her employer Peggy at the end of September. They invited me to have lunch with them, and after that, we went hiking. In fact, I didn't interview Peggy, but she provided some valuable information. While we were eating ice cream, Peggy laughed at herself for eating too fast. *"Haha I know I eat too fast lah and I know it is not good for health. But it's really difficult to change my habit,"* said Peggy with a laughter and a sigh, *"eating fast is very common in Hong Kong. I think many Hong Kong people have stomach problems because of this. Many just finish their meals within 30 minutes and then go back to work. Some eat even faster than me. You know what? They can eat their meals within 10 to 15 minutes. So fast! Hong Kong people are too busy. Not healthy lah."*

If eating fast is somewhat common in Hong Kong and if many local people can actually finish eating their meals in such a short time on weekdays, what will they expect from others especially those who become their employees inside the homes? Some domestic workers that I informally interviewed are given 15 minutes for their meal breaks. Some of them have only 5-10 minutes for each meal, and some even have to eat while working occasionally. I guess a certain number of local employers may feel wronged if anyone criticises them for not giving enough break time to their helpers. After all, some local employers have to manage their busy lives in a similar way. But the problem is not that they only allow their helpers to have short meal breaks because that's what they get used to in their life. The problem is: they don't see there is a problem.

A female employer once complained about her domestic helper on a Facebook group that is usually used by local employers to exchange information. She claimed that her helper always looked sulky and wasn't patient with her son due to her disagreement over her helper's preferable work schedule. The helper was asked to get up at 6.30 in the morning and work till 10.30 pm, but she preferred to finish her work at around 9.00 pm and then have a rest.[85] Some considerate people criticised this employer for asking her helper to work unreasonably long hours, but this employer felt deeply wronged by her accusations. She responded online, *"I don't understand why you guys criticised me...I get up at 6.00 am and work till 11.00 pm. Do you want me to work overtime and take care of my baby simultaneously and then let my helper sleep after 9.00 pm?"* This might be an extreme case, but what this employer said could reflect the mentality of a certain group of employers in Hong Kong. Some suggested that the employer could let her helper take a nap or hire another helper because normally no one would be pleased about working so long hours. Yet this employer turned down these suggestions and replied, *"My helper has 8 hours for rest"*, which implied that she believed her helper has sufficient rest. The employer didn't find any problems with her demands, as she was suffering from long working hours and kind of normalised it. And apparently, she didn't want to empathise with her helper.

On a forum named *baby-kingdom* (a forum for Hong Kong parents, mainly mothers to discuss childcare and early education), a topic on *"How many hours do your helpers get rest per day? And do they help with housework on their days-off?"* was discussed by employers several years ago.[86] The initiator of this topic asked the members of the forum, here I translate:

> May I ask you guys how many hours you allow your foreign helpers to get rest, e.g., when do they get up and go to sleep? On their rest days,

when do your helpers go out and come back? After returning home, will your helpers do occasional bit of housework?

I've never asked my helper to do housework after she returns home on Sunday. At first, she seemed to be willing to clean the floor using a sponge mop and help organise kitchen ware after she's back on Sunday. But later on, my helper told me all her friends don't work on their days-off. She also told me that she doesn't need to do anything on her rest days according to Hong Kong law. She said many of her friends can choose what time to go out/come back freely. My helper also wanted me to treat her like that. Any advice?

The initiator of this discussion received many replies. I translated some below:

"I've never asked my helpers to work on rest days, but my current Indonesian jeh jeh (helper) does a bit of housework voluntarily. Hong Kong law says it's not allowed to ask helpers to work on their rest days, but it doesn't say we can't leave some work for their helpers to do the next day."

"My jeh jeh gets up at 6.30 and goes back to her room by 11.00 pm. But there are 7-8 hours when she's alone in the home. She can't be exhausted. On her holidays, she takes the garbage out after returning home, and she also wash dishes."

"On Sunday, I allow my yan-yan (it means "Indonesian helper" in Cantonese but carries a derogatory connotation) to go out at 9.00 am and come back by 8.00 pm. She helps me do housework voluntarily on her rest days. She'd clean the floor and help my child wash face before going out. After she's back, she would wash dishes."

"My helper sleeps before 10.00 pm. She gets up at 6.00 am to feed my baby and then she can continue sleeping till 8.30-9.00. She has one-hour rest in the afternoon. She must feel so happy and satisfied! On Sunday, she'd feed my baby before hanging out with her friends and she'd wash dishes after coming back."

"My helper sleeps from 11.30 pm to 7.00 am. I'll watch her clean the whole flat, cook, and wash dishes…On Sunday, I don't ask her to work, but I'll leave some work for her to do on Monday."

"My bun-bun (it means "Filipino helper" in Cantonese but with a negative connotation) goes back to her room at 10.30 pm and starts to work at 8.00 am. She's got 9.5 hours for rest! I don't regulate what time she should go out on Sunday, but I demand that she need to be back before 9.00 pm."

"My jeh jeh always helps me during her holidays. She prepares breakfast for my baby before going out, and then cleans the kitchen after coming back on Sunday. Sometimes, me and my husband are too tired, my helper would help us take a shower for our baby, if we asked her to do so. As a return, we sometimes take her out to eat at restaurants."

"My helper is a Filipino. On her holidays, she can decide when to go out, but I made a rule that she has to return home by 8.30 pm. Usually, after she's back, she'd take a shower and go to sleep as soon as possible. She is active at work on her work days, but she refuses to do any work on her rest days. I once tried to ask her to collect the washed clothes because I was busy with tutoring my children, but she ignored my instructions. I had asked her three times; she still didn't walk out of her room to help me. So, finally I did it by myself."

… … (there are many other comments similar to these translated ones)

There are also two comments written in English: 1. "All of my helpers (Bun-bun and Yan-yan), current and ex, do household before and after coming back home. Some even prepare lunch before leaving." 2. "You guys' maids (who voluntarily work on holidays) are so good!"

The initiator of this topic appeared to believe that there is nothing wrong to ask her helper to work occasionally on Sunday. Perhaps she herself sometimes is asked to work overtime without extra pay and thus she doesn't seem to think there is anything wrong with doing the same to her helper. Initiating such discussions is more like an act to find like-minded employers and thereby gaining support for her preferable work schedule of her domestic helper. As for the replies that she had received, she evidently got what she wanted. In addition to this, all the comments and replies to this topic prove that the information I got from domestic workers does not exaggerate at all—that a great many of them actually need to work on their only rest day in a week and that most of them do have curfews.

If we analyse the tone used by these employers, we could gain insight into their general attitudes towards domestic workers' work schedules. If a helper got 11 hours for rest in total (not uninterrupted rest), then her employer thought *"she must feel so happy and satisfied"*. Another helper got 9.5 hours for rest, and her employer believed that it deserved an exclamation mark, suggesting this helper got lots of time to relax. All the domestic workers voluntarily work overtime on their rest days were praised as "good maids", which lets me predict the meanings of "bad maids". On the contrary, a domestic worker, who was reluctant to do any work on her rest days, was apparently complained about by her employer.

Domestic workers may have complaints too. Yet their complaints and emotions are seemingly not understood or approved of by their employers. It is interesting to note that there is an urban myth about domestic workers—that many of them, who refuse to obey their employers' instructions, get impatient with work or make frequent mistakes, are unscrupulous maids who collude with their employment agencies to gain profits (both employers and domestic workers can terminate the contract by giving no less than one month's notice or paying one month's salary in lieu of notice. And if domestic workers are fired without one month's notice, they could get one-month salary as compensation). Lia once told me her opinion about this urban myth:

> Yes. Some of domestic workers may collude with their agencies to get additional financial benefit. But I don't think there're many of them. It's not practical, you know. One-month salary? Usually HK$4,630, right? They probably have to split it, and if it's true, of course the agencies will get more money. I don't see the point why many workers will do this if their employers are good to them, because having a good employer is such a difficult thing. We all know that! So, if we are lucky, most of us will appreciate our chance. In fact, the usual case is that many domestic workers can't bear with the heavy workload or their abusive employers. And if we can't bear with our employers for one more month, we'll have to break the contract, and then we'll pay the cost. Some may wait for their employers to fire them, because being fired is cheaper than terminating contracts prematurely by domestic workers. But if that is the case, the motivation of domestic workers' disobedience is different

from the urban myth: they don't aim to gain additional profits. They just want to find a better employer and be better treated by using a less expensive way.

From employers' perspective, if their helpers suddenly become uncooperative and reluctant to work as hard as their employers expected, it might be seen as intentional misconduct in which their helpers conspire with agencies against them. But from domestic workers' point of view, their unwillingness to work overtime on their rest days or their reluctance to follow their employers' unreasonable instructions may be just a protest for fairer treatment and a more reasonable work schedule. I think a domestic worker doesn't want to be fired when she/he isn't willing to work on their holidays. I tend to believe that they just want to enjoy their holidays.

Hong Kong was seen as an unhappy city prior to the 2019 social movement as well as being socially divided. As one of the top ten unhappiest places in the world for political and economic reasons,[87] there is no doubt that so many Hong Kong people are suffering from great pressure and anxiety. And the social movement along with the COVID-19 pandemic only makes this city even unhappier. Perhaps instead of transferring unhappiness as well as overwork to their domestic workers, those Hong Kong employers who have created unreasonably tight schedules for their domestic workers should realise that it is problematic for themselves to work so long hours, and it is more problematic for them to force domestic workers from outside of Hong Kong to work 16 hours a day. Surely, the system in Hong Kong has failed them. But their failure to fight against exploitation in their workplace should not be normalised, nor should they accept exploitation and apply it to a group of more powerless people.

(P.S. Some employers like claiming "I treat my helper as a family member" to defend themselves, showing how nice they are to their domestic helpers; thus, their helpers' uncooperative behaviour as a sort of protest against overwork and unfair treatment inside the home may sound less reasonable and acceptable for many. However, treating a domestic worker like a family member doesn't mean that a domestic worker has full access to labour rights that they deserve. Domestic workers hope to be treated as workers and gain their workers' rights rather than being treated as so-called family members and taken advantage of by this pretext.)

18. Peer Pressure

Outsourcing housework as well as caregiving is quite common in Hong Kong, because it can bring tangible benefits to those Hong Kong people who suffer from overscheduling. In addition to this, the affordability and attainability of outsourcing domestic work to full-time migrant workers also contribute a lot to its prevalence. Compared to hiring a Hong Kong citizen to do domestic work, Hong Kong people could pay much less to hire a domestic worker from abroad attributed to the Hong Kong government's discriminatory policies on foreign domestic workers' employment. Admittedly, employers need to pay a large amount of money to agencies if they hire FDWs through agencies, and normally agency fees range from HK$7,000 to HK$13,000 (depending on which agency and which country's FDWs employers want to hire), but the economic benefits for hiring an FDW are nevertheless irresistible for many. Using less than HK$5,000 can hire a live-in helper who stands by for 24 hours a day and work for six days a week. Many people would think: why not?

Regarding what people have eligibility to employ an FDW, the Immigration Department in Hong Kong gave specific financial criteria:

> In general, for every helper to be employed, the employer must have a household income of no less than HK$15,000 per month or assets of comparable amount to support the employment of a helper for the whole contractual period.[88]

Apparently, the financial criteria set by the Hong Kong government aims to allow as many as Hong Kong ordinary residents to employ a migrant domestic worker, if they have such an intention. Although the Hong Kong government also requires employers to provide domestic helpers with "suitable accommodation and with reasonable privacy", as I argued before, it is rather difficult to guarantee, especially based on the universal definitions of "suitable accommodation" and "reasonable privacy" (let's not forget the data provided by MFMW: more than half of domestic workers do not have private rooms).

On a Sunday evening, I met Johannie, the Community Relations Officer of MFMW, in Victoria Park. As a person who was born and raised in Hong Kong, Johannie can approach local employers more easily than me. And one of her job duties is to intervene in the conflicts between employers and domestic workers, and help domestic workers gain their rights. Johannie provided some information that suggests we could look at things from a different angle:

I have talked with so many employers. There're some good employers who do treat domestic workers like their families, but usually the ones I talk with are those who have problems with their domestic workers. Some don't care about domestic workers' rights, and some even hate domestic workers. For those who hate domestic workers, to be honest, I don't understand why they have to hire domestic workers. Many of them can't provide humane living conditions for their domestic workers. Even though they meet the financial criteria set by the Hong Kong government, some of them still have financial pressure to hire domestic workers. In this sense, they may think it is all their domestic workers' fault and blame their helpers for occupying their limited space and spending their money. But if that's the case, they shouldn't have hired domestic workers in the first place, right? I asked these employers why they felt they must hire domestic workers when they actually couldn't provide adequate conditions or when it was not that necessary for them to hire domestic helpers. Some of them told me they had lots of pressure, and they couldn't handle it by themselves. And some of them told me they had to hire domestic workers because their friends are all doing this, and they thought that's sort of pressure too.

The prevalence of outsourcing domestic work to full-time migrant workers seems more complicated than I thought. What Johannie said made me recall a conversation with a local friend Mandy. After Mandy enquired about my basic situation. She asked, "Have you hired a helper to cook for you?"

"No, I cook for myself", I replied.

I didn't think too much at that moment, but when I think deeply about it, Mandy's question just suggested how common it is to employ a domestic helper in Hong Kong. And it seems that it is a common question to ask people here too. In fact, Mandy knew that the flat I rent, measuring 300 square feet has only two rooms, and she also knew that I have no children and I have plenty of time to take care of myself, but she still assumed that I may want to hire a domestic worker.

Would this kind of assumption bring peer pressure to some local people? I guess, to some extent, it would. Some may think hiring a helper is a trend that they should adopt. In many cases, I regret to say, it is the social assumptions that make people anxious and cause stress. Here, women are assumed to have to get married and have children; single people are assumed to be bored with themselves; couples are assumed to buy an apartment or a house; children are assumed to have various skills; students with good academic performance are assumed to be successful in the future; and couples with a stable income are assumed to hire domestic helpers. Some may feel stressed even when they hear the questions entailing the assumptions that stem from generalisations, and thereby starting to question themselves: *"What does this question suggest? Does this person want me to do this as well? Should I do this like others? Do I need to fit in?"*

The thing is, however, the more popular outsourcing housework is, the more likely people will jump on the bandwagon. I believe what Johannie said is true. In fact, it is not necessary for some employers to hire any domestic workers to "help" them, but they may have not thought about it carefully and thus may feel pressured if they don't follow the trend. And among the full-time workers who do have the needs to hire domestic helpers to deal with caregiving, some of them may find themselves in a dilemma: *to handle pressure because of being a full-time worker and overwhelmed caregiver at the same time, or to hire a domestic worker and then handle pressure generated by limited disposable household income and space to do so.* Either choice, from my point of view, doesn't enable this group of people to escape from stress. Yet, I wish they could get more support from Hong Kong's social welfare system.

Among the employers who do not have enough space and financial resources to hire domestic workers, but who eventually choose to hire domestic workers because of conformity, their pressure is more likely to be transferred to domestic workers. Some employers do not have enough space to hire a domestic worker. In this situation, a lack of privacy is a shared problem for both the employers and the domestic workers, and everything can be magnified in a cramped space. For employers, they may have a grudge against their helpers due to different lifestyle habits. While for domestic helpers, working in a flat where there is not enough space for another person to stay only means two options: 1. living with the people whom they need to take care of (at least they have rooms); 2. living in inhuman conditions (e.g., living in the kitchen or bathroom). Both of these two options do not seem satisfying.

In Hong Kong, housing expenditure could account for a large percentage of a family's monthly income. And for some who do not have sufficient disposable household income to hire a domestic worker, it is doubtful whether these employers can provide their domestic helpers with proper food and whether domestic workers can get paid on time (I'm not implying that rich people can be exempt from the doubt). Domestic workers, under this circumstance, may be blamed for causing financial trouble for their employers, and they are less likely to be fairly treated. In some extreme cases, domestic workers are even regarded as the enemies of these employers.

Unfortunately, peer pressure not only makes some local people jump on the bandwagon when they consider whether they need to hire a domestic worker, but it pervades employers' everyday life. Based on my observation on different social media, a certain number of employers tend to compare their domestic workers with those of their friends and relatives, for example, which helper cooks better; which helper is more obedient; which helper is more considerate; and which helper is more voluntary to work overtime... If an employer's domestic worker provides good service or cooks nicely, it definitely deserves some posts on social media. A Hong Kong pop singer shared some pictures on Instagram about how his helper cooks nicely for him, then it's on the news. A multitude of local people expressed their admiration. After that, comparing helpers' cooking skills suddenly has become a trend among employers, and many also posted the pictures of what their helpers cooked for them. But what's the story behind it? If domestic workers who are good at cooking and varying the food were praised on social media, would some who fail to do so be complained or blamed by their employers for losing the competition? For those employers who are easily affected by peer pressure, they may generate some unrealistic expectations on their domestic helpers, and it thus further aggravates the situation of domestic workers and sours the employment relationship.

To better understand how employers think and what problems they have, I joined a Facebook group which is particularly for Hong Kong employers to exchange and share information. Thankfully, I found some considerate employers who care about domestic workers' rights and who do not have too many unrealistic expectations of their helpers. There are some employers complaining about how inefficient their domestic workers are/ how incompetent their helpers are/ how morally wrong their helpers are. I am not going to deny their feelings or the problems they are confronted with. Yet, I want to quote what Johannie said to conclude:

> Many employers complain about how bad their helpers are, but I am not there to discuss with the employers whether their helpers are good or not, or whether they are competent or not. All domestic workers should have basic human rights no matter what. That's what I care about. And I hope all employers can realise this too. If domestic workers steal employers' items, then employers can call police. If domestic workers do not meet employers' expectations, the employers can talk with their helpers and perhaps adjust their expectations. If domestic workers' work performance is unacceptable, employers can terminate the contract. But asking domestic workers to work for too long hours or asking them to sleep in the kitchen, or not allowing them to have holidays, or abusing them, or illegally deducting their salary...that is different. Denying domestic helpers' human rights and labour rights shouldn't be allowed, and there should be no excuse for that.

Outsider and Insider Perspectives

*A person will, however, **not** be treated as ordinarily resident in Hong Kong while employed as a domestic helper from outside Hong Kong.*[89]

—The Immigration Department of the Hong Kong Special Administrative Region (HKSAR)

Migrant domestic workers in Hong Kong are a group of individuals who have left their own families to take care of other people's families. They are also a group of people who are marginalised, unfairly treated and even abused by both the system and individuals in Hong Kong. Being regarded as non-ordinary residents by the Hong Kong government, their access to civil rights is inexorably denied. They are excluded from the possibility of gaining Hong Kong permanent residency because they are foreign domestic workers; they are excluded from the Hong Kong statutory minimum wage (HK$37.5/hour) because they are not ordinary Hong Kong residents; they are excluded from equal social opportunities because their rights are not fully protected by the local law; and they are excluded from mainstream society because they have limited social resources.

Collins Dictionary defines "civil rights" as "the rights that people have in a society to equal treatment and equal opportunities, whatever their race, sex, or religion". Yet, the plight faced by those migrant domestic workers in Hong Kong makes me wonder whether we have to become permanent residents or citizens of a certain society before having some basic civil rights there. If we have to, does it mean that it can justify the unequal treatment those non-permanent residents or non-citizens have encountered? No. I don't think it should be justified in any sense. And if citizenship is an essential precondition for individuals in a society to be protected from unequal treatment and unequal opportunities, it seems that we need to question the concept of citizenship. Perhaps conceptualising modern citizenship by only focusing on its legal status is not enough to adjust to this changing globalised context.

In this increasingly interconnected and interdependent world, both global opportunities and challenges have blurred the borders between countries. Migration flows, frequent international trade, technological cooperation and cultural communication all invite us to embrace the differences; whilst some global challenges such as environmental problems, poverty and COVID-19 all call for our collective solutions, which need to be motivated by world citizens' sense of duty. The point is, we cannot call for global citizens' actions in terms of solving global problems on the one hand, but deny their universal human rights because they are non-citizens in a certain society on the other. I understand that some civil rights such as the rights to vote can be granted to only citizens in a society, yet the civil rights which guarantee individuals to be treated as equal human beings ought to be granted to all. Only in this way can "the right to have rights"[90] become an inalienable characteristic of a human condition; and only in this way can a more just, equal, and sustainable society be formed.

In fact, unlike other non-permanent residents in Hong Kong, migrant domestic workers are the only group of people who are excluded from the Hong Kong statutory minimum wage. Apparently, the Hong Kong government is considerate to other non-permanent residents and has managed to protect them to be treated equally under the local minimum wage ordinance. However, among those non-citizens, migrant domestic workers are treated discriminatorily, for the local statutory minimum wage doesn't apply to them and they have their own minimum wage which is HK$4,630 per month. On top of that, they are not as qualified as other temporary residents to apply for permanent residency in Hong Kong because of what they do for a living. Some may argue that based on the compulsory live-in rule, employers have to provide domestic workers with accommodation and food which cost a large amount of money, and it is therefore not suitable to apply the same standard of minimum wage to domestic workers. But I want to ask: why on earth domestic workers have to live with their employers?

If a government makes a policy or a law excluding or marginalising a category of people, it might send a message to dominant group members that it is acceptable for them to marginalise others as their government does. As a result, some members in the dominant group may imitate their government and discriminate against the marginalised group without guilt, simply because they tend to believe that their government acquiesces in such behaviours. Many examples in Hong Kong and Singapore mentioned in previous chapters all prove this to some degree. And because the Singaporean government's policies against migrant domestic workers are even more discriminatory than those in Hong Kong, it seems that domestic workers in Singapore even face more difficulties.

It is worth mentioning that there is no other way to ease migrant domestic workers' difficulties than to empower them. If migrant domestic workers cannot get access to equal rights and fair treatment in the workplace as local residents do—no matter where they are—there will be always a number of them who are more vulnerable to exploitation than any other groups. If the live-in rule is not optional, there will be multitudes of domestic workers susceptible to forced labour and abuse. And if domestic workers are still required to leave Hong Kong within two weeks after they terminate their contracts prematurely, there will be so many domestic workers choosing to tolerate their abusive employers due to their fear of unemployment and uncertainties.

As a temporary resident in Hong Kong, I feel like an outsider in this city most of the time, just like those migrant domestic workers. Hence, it is not difficult for me to feel for them. My outsider identity in Hong Kong always invites me to ask myself: *if I were a migrant domestic worker here, how would I feel? Would I feel desperate in many cases?* I believe I would. But in the meantime, like many domestic workers who care about social justice from local to international levels, I feel like an insider of the global community, wherein I am included rather than excluded.

Likewise, I am both an insider and outsider in the community of migrant domestic workers. Apart from being a temporary resident in Hong Kong, I am, above all, a human and a woman, just like them. I empathise with them as a human being and a woman. The rights that they are fighting for are in fact basic human rights in which there is an overlap between labour rights and women's rights. However, I am not one of them after all. I am not a domestic worker; I am not from a poverty-stricken family; and I have got some privileges that I didn't even notice before I met them. I have more choices, but sadly, they don't. When "choice" is pluralised, it sounds only close to a certain group of people who are not underprivileged, whilst those migrant domestic workers only feel that "choices" sound too remote to them. I have to admit that I don't have exactly the same experience as them, and I probably can't feel the same as them. Thus, I cannot claim to speak for them. They, migrant domestic workers, speak for themselves. I am just a passer-by who happened to see them and has learned so much from them. Beyond that, I am an immature writer who feels honoured to know them and write their stories and opinions down, and who sincerely believes that their voices must be heard.

Sources

1. Statistics on the Number of Foreign Domestic Workers in Hong Kong https://data.gov.hk/en-data/dataset/hk-immd-set4-statistics-fdh/resource/063e1929-107b-47ae-a6ac-b4b1ed460ac3
2. Unemployment and underemployment statistics for Apr - Jun 2020 https://www.censtatd.gov.hk/press_release/pressReleaseDetail.jsp?pressRID=4662&charsetID=1
3. Noam Chomsky: Coronavirus-What is at stake? https://www.youtube.com/watch?v=t-N3In2rLI4&t=649s
4. A Handbook for Employing Foreign Domestic Helpers https://www.fdh.labour.gov.hk/res/pdf/Handy_Guide_FDHs_eng.pdf
5. MFMW Service Report 2019 https://www.migrants.net/index.php/publications/item/92-press-release-mfmw-service-report-2019
6. What is modern slavery? https://www.antislavery.org/slavery-today/modern-slavery/
7. Ronald Weitzer, "Modern Slavery and Human Trafficking", *Great Decisions 2020*,41-52
8. Hannah Arendt, *The Origins of Totalitarianism* (London: Penguin Classics, 2017), 390.
9. Hannah Arendt, *The Origins of Totalitarianism*,389.
10. Statistics on the Number of Foreign Domestic Workers in Hong Kong https://data.gov.hk/en-data/dataset/hk-immd-set4-statistics-fdh/resource/063e1929-107b-47ae-a6ac-b4b1ed460ac3
11. Population By-census 2016 https://www.statistics.gov.hk/pub/B11200982016XXXXB0100.pdf
12. Guidebook for the Employment of Domestic Helpers from Abroad https://www.immd.gov.hk/pdforms/ID(E)969.pdf
13. Issues other than Those Stipulated in the Employment Contract https://www.helperchoice.com/c/domestic-helper/employment-contract-regulations#:~:text=Working%20hours,of%2011%20to%2016%20Ohours.
14. Guidebook for the Employment of Domestic Helpers from Abroad https://www.immd.gov.hk/pdforms/ID(E)969.pdf
15. Submission to the Legislative Council's Panel on Constitutional Affairs on the Third Report by HKSAR under the ICESCR

https://www.legco.gov.hk/yr13-14/chinese/panels/ca/papers/ca0217cb2-850-7-ec.pdf

16. 國際婦女節
2020：疫情下，婦女有話兒https://womencentre.org.hk/Zh/Newsroom/Pressrelease/iwd_2020/

17. John Steinbeck, *Of Mice and Men* (London: Penguin Red Classics, 2006).

18. Eligibility for the Right of Abode in the HKSAR https://www.immd.gov.hk/eng/services/roa/eligible.html

19. Meanings of Right of Abode and Other Terms https://www.immd.gov.hk/eng/services/roa/term.html

20. Hong Kong's Statutory Minimum Wage, 2019 https://www.labour.gov.hk/eng/news/mwo.htm

21. Minimum Allowable Wage and food allowance for foreign domestic helpers to increase https://www.labour.gov.hk/eng/news/press20190927.htm

22. https://geoexpat.com/forum/418/thread213778-2.html

23. Singapore's foreign domestic workers vulnerable to forced labour, report finds https://www.scmp.com/news/asia/southeast-asia/article/2182233/singapores-foreign-domestic-workers-vulnerable-forced

24. Employers' Guide: Foreign Domestic Workers, Ministry of Manpower https://www.mom.gov.sg/passes-and-permits/work-permit-for-foreign-domestic-worker/employers-guide

25. Rest days and well-being for foreign domestic workers, Ministry of Manpower https://www.mom.gov.sg/passes-and-permits/work-permit-for-foreign-domestic-worker/employers-guide/rest-days-and-well-being

26. Maid Home Leave in Singapore https://www.helperchoice.com/c/maid/home-leave

27. How Much Is A Maid's Salary in Singapore https://www.msig.com.sg/lifestyle-library/how-much-maids-salary-singapore

28. As a Work Permit holder, how do I apply for approval to marry a Singaporean or permanent resident? https://www.mom.gov.sg/faq/foreign-worker/as-a-work-permit-holder-how-do-i-apply-for-approval-to-marry-a-singaporean-or-permanent-resident

29. Work Permit Conditions, Ministry of Manpower https://www.mom.gov.sg/passes-and-permits/work-permit-for-foreign-worker/sector-specific-rules/work-permit-conditions

30. $5,000 security bond not forfeited if maids got pregnant, MOM https://www.mom.gov.sg/newsroom/press-replies/2011/5000-security-bond-not-forfeited-if-maids-get-pr

31. Security bond requirements for foreign worker, MOM https://www.mom.gov.sg/passes-and-permits/work-permit-for-foreign-worker/sector-specific-rules/security-bond

32. Rest days and well-being for foreign domestic workers, MOM https://www.mom.gov.sg/passes-and-permits/work-permit-for-foreign-domestic-worker/employers-guide/rest-days-and-well-being

33. Hunger hits as many Indonesians struggle during COVID-19 pandemic https://www.thejakartapost.com/news/2020/04/21/hunger-hits-as-many-indonesians-struggle-during-covid-19-pandemic.html

34. Unemployment and underemployment statistics for Apr - Jun 2020 https://www.censtatd.gov.hk/press_release/pressReleaseDetail.jsp?pressRID=4662&charsetID=1

35. Virginia Woolf, *Three Guineas* (London: Hogarth Press, 1938), 197.

36. Adjustment of minimum allowable wage for foreign domestic helpers, 2006 https://www.info.gov.hk/gia/general/200605/30/P200605300186.htm

37. John Locke, "Of Tyranny", *Two Treaties of Government* (first published in 1689).

38. Domestic Helper Contract Termination https://www.helperchoice.com/c/domestic-helper/termination

39. Practical Guide for Employment of Foreign Domestic Helpers https://www.fdh.labour.gov.hk/res/pdf/FDHguideEnglish.pdf

40. Legal Placement Fee Charged by Domestic Helper Agencies https://www.helperchoice.com/c/domestic-helper/legal-placement-fee

41. Minimum Allowable Wage and food allowance for foreign domestic helpers to increase https://www.info.gov.hk/gia/general/201909/27/P2019092500606p.htm

42. Employer in Hong Kong maid abuse case is sentenced to six years' jail https://www.theguardian.com/world/2015/feb/27/hong-kong-court-sentences-woman-to-6-years-in-prison-for-abusing-indonesian-maid-0

43. Interview: Erwiana Sulistyaningsih
https://www.timeout.com/hong-kong/blog/interview-erwiana-sulistyaningsih-052016

44. 'Kicked, slapped and threatened': two more maids tell court of abuse by Erwiana's employer https://www.scmp.com/news/hong-kong/article/1671460/erwiana-case-two-more-maids-allege-abuse-hands-hong-kong-boss

45. Boss of abused domestic worker Erwiana ordered to pay HK$170k in damages to another ex-employee https://hongkongfp.com/2018/02/27/boss-abused-domestic-worker-erwiana-ordered-pay-hk170k-damages-another-ex-employee/

46. Employer in Hong Kong maid abuse case is sentenced to six years' jail https://www.theguardian.com/world/2015/feb/27/hong-kong-court-sentences-woman-to-6-years-in-prison-for-abusing-indonesian-maid-0

47. 'Salt to the wound': NGOs decry early release of employer jailed for torturing domestic worker Erwiana https://hongkongfp.com/2018/11/22/salt-wound-ngos-decry-early-release-employer-jailed-torturing-domestic-worker-erwiana/

48. Labour sets up 24-hour hotline for FDHs http://hongkongnews.com.hk/news/labour-sets-up-24-hour-hotline-for-fdhs/?fbclid=IwAR3Up4FFYcHbVJjFoklkVF5pLhYo-I8QtZLYak6yBp7RAzVlM6dlcmW5KOM

49. Frequently Asked Questions about the Employment Ordinance, Cap. 57 https://www.labour.gov.hk/eng/faq/cap57f_whole.htm

50. Saying No to Child Marriage in Indonesia https://www.unicef.org/indonesia/stories/saying-no-child-marriage-indonesia

51. Education at a Glance, 2019 https://www.oecd.org/education/education-at-a-glance/EAG2019_CN_IDN.pdf

52. Kahlil Gibran, "On Joy and Sorrow", *The Prophet* (first published in 1923).

53. Employment Agency Regulations https://www.elegislation.gov.hk/hk/cap57A?xpid=ID_1438403483428_002

54. The Law Versus Reality https://helpfordomesticworkers.org/en/get-help/understanding-your-rights/employment-agency-issues/

55. Republic Act No. 10022
https://www.officialgazette.gov.ph/2010/03/10/republic-act-no-10022-s-2010/
56. When both sides of the political spectrum are equally guilty of violence, Hong Kong is in danger https://www.msn.com/en-sg/news/other/when-both-sides-of-the-political-spectrum-are-equally-guilty-of-tolerating-violence-hong-kong-is-in-danger/ar-BB146FRh
57. Universal COVID-19 test plan set https://www.news.gov.hk/eng/2020/08/20200821/20200821_164439_859.html
58. Hong Kong Poverty Situation Report 2018 https://www.statistics.gov.hk/pub/B9XX0005E2018AN18E0100.pdf
59. Philippines Drops to NO. 16 in Gender Gap Report 2020 https://www.rappler.com/nation/philippines-rankings-gender-gap-report-2020
60. What is human trafficking? https://www.antislavery.org/slavery-today/human-trafficking/
61. Abuse and ill-treatment of a domestic worker, MOM https://www.mom.gov.sg/passes-and-permits/work-permit-for-foreign-domestic-worker/employers-guide/abuse-and-ill-treatment
62. Hong Kong maids seek a high-rise window cleaning ban https://www.bbc.com/news/world-asia-37271705
63. Window-cleaning ban for Hong Kong's domestic helpers will not keep them safe, campaigners say https://www.scmp.com/news/hong-kong/education-community/article/2047296/window-cleaning-ban-hong-kongs-domestic-helpers
64. DH says she filmed herself cleaning 19th floor window in case she fell http://www.sunwebhk.com/2020/01/dh-says-she-filmed-herself-cleaning.html
65. 100 Women: Maid dies in Malaysia after being left to "sleep outside with dog" https://www.bbc.com/news/world-asia-43049684?fbclid=IwAR23jhuwKgaEli3xsV-yyRcIoHZpgBAR5LnNW7X257Ir7ArFTg-dlvF5QQg
66. Court confirms acquittal of woman charged with murdering Indonesian Maid https://www.freemalaysiatoday.com/category/nation/2020/09/22/court-affirms-acquittal-of-woman-over-death-of-indonesian-maid/
67. Adjustment of minimum allowable wage for foreign domestic helpers, 2003 https://www.legco.gov.hk/yr02-03/english/panels/mp/papers/mp0328cb2-1515-1e.pdf

68. "What do Women and Men in Hong Kong Think about the Status of Women at Home, Work and in Social Environments?", Women's Commission https://www.women.gov.hk/download/research/WoC_Survey_Finding_Economic_E.pdf

69. https://hongkongfp.com/2019/03/08/intl-womens-day-hong-kong-not-welcoming-city-women-working-women-working-mothers/

70. https://www.singstat.gov.sg/find-data/search-by-theme/economy/labour-employment-wages-and-productivity/latest-data

71. China: Female labour force participation https://www.theglobaleconomy.com/China/Female_labor_force_participation/

72. Women and Men in Hong Kong Key Statistics, 2020 https://www.statistics.gov.hk/pub/B11303032020AN20B0100.pdf

73. Hong Kong and Gender Equality https://twfhk.org/blog/hong-kong-and-gender-equality

74. A Study on Family Status Discrimination in the Workplace in Hong Kong, 2018 https://www.eoc.org.hk/eoc/upload/ResearchReport/20188211629521937156.pdf

75. Sex Discrimination Ordinance https://www.elegislation.gov.hk/hk/cap480

76. Family Status Discrimination Ordinance https://www.elegislation.gov.hk/hk/cap527

77. Background brief on processing of small house applications and review of small house policy https://www.legco.gov.hk/yr05-06/english/panels/plw/papers/plw0228cb1-986-1e.pdf

78. 丁權造成嚴重不公 政府應做政治改革 https://www.hk01.com/%E7%A4%BE%E8%AB%96/268605/01%E5%91%A8%E5%A0%B1%E7%A4%BE%E8%AB%96-%E4%B8%81%E6%AC%8A%E9%80%A0%E6%88%90%E5%9A%B4%E9%87%8D%E4%B8%8D%E5%85%AC-%E6%94%BF%E5%BA%9C%E6%87%89%E4%BD%9C%E6%94%BF%E6%B2%BB%E6%94%B9%E9%9D%A9

79. https://www.youtube.com/watch?v=WemrIUhu8nw&t=204s

80. History of the Comfort Women of World War II https://www.thoughtco.com/world-war-ii-comfort-women-3530682

81. https://forum.hkgolden.com/thread/5122369/page/1

82. https://www.youtube.com/watch?v=f3W-jR-lu8E&t=136s

83. https://www.youtube.com/watch?v=UVDPSFF8veE&t=17s

84. Which country works the longest hours?
https://www.bbc.com/worklife/article/20180504-which-country-works-the-longest-hours

85. https://hd.stheadline.com/consultation18/news-detail.php?y=2018&r=731113

86. https://www.baby-kingdom.com/forum.php?mod=viewthread&tid=7381990

87. Hong Kong One of the Top 10 Least Happiest Places in the World
https://coconuts.co/hongkong/news/hong-kong-one-of-the-top-10-least-happiest-places-in-the-world/#:~:text=Your%20instincts%20are%20solid.,Ouch.

88. Guidebook for the Employment of Domestic Helpers from Abroad
https://www.immd.gov.hk/pdforms/ID(E)969.pdf

89. Meanings of Right of Abode and Other Terms
https://www.immd.gov.hk/eng/services/roa/term.html

90. Hannah Arendt, The Origins of Totalitarianism, 390.